Carlisle In 1745: Authentic Account Of The Occupation Of Carlisle In 1745 By Prince Charles Edward Stuart

John Waugh, George Gill Mounsey

CARLISLE IN 1745.

CARLISLE:
PRINTED BY JAMES STEEL, AT THE JOURNAL OFFICE,
3, ENGLISH STREET.

AUTHENTIC ACCOUNT

of the occupation of

CARLISLE

IN

1745

BY

Prince Charles Edward Stuart.

Engraved by Freeman

Bate's Patent Anaglyptograph

LONDON;
LONGMAN & Co. PATERNOSTER ROW.
CARLISLE;
JAMES STEEL, ENGLISH STREET.

CARLISLE IN 1745.

AUTHENTIC ACCOUNT

OF THE

OCCUPATION OF CARLISLE

IN 1745,

BY

Prince Charles Edward Stuart.

EDITED BY GEORGE GILL MOUNSEY

LONDON: LONGMAN AND CO., PATERNOSTER ROW.
Carlisle:
JAMES STEEL, 3, ENGLISH STREET.
MDCCCXLVI.

PREFACE.

THE Reverend JOHN WAUGH, D.C.L., whose Correspondence and Narrative constitute the most material part of this volume, was the son of JOHN WAUGH, Bishop of Carlisle, from 1723 to 1734. He became a Prebendary of the Cathedral Church of Carlisle in 1727, and Chancellor of the Diocese in 1729. He married ISABELLA, second daughter of THOMAS TULLIE, Dean of Carlisle,—of a family of old standing and large property at Carlisle; one of whom, ISAAC TULLIE, was in the city whilst it was besieged by the Parliamentary forces under Sir THOS. GLENHAM in 1644-5, and kept a diary of the occurrences of that period, which has recently been published.

Dr. WAUGH was then, by virtue of his official appointments, his relationship with the Diocesan Prelate, and his matrimonial connections, in a position of the first consideration and influence in the city and neighbourhood of Carlisle.

His political principles were those of the Whigs. A zealous supporter of the Revolution of 1688, and the Protestant Establishment in Church and State, he regarded the claims of the STUARTS with unmitigated aversion. Moreover he was a man of sound judgment and sagacity; and whilst others equally zealous, but more immersed in the strife of domestic faction, looked carelessly upon the first proceedings of Prince CHARLES EDWARD, he seems to have formed a more correct estimate of the impending danger, and to have been deeply impressed with anxiety to meet and avert it by timely measures of precaution.

Hence Dr. WAUGH was led to arrange a correspondence with JOHN GOLDIE, Esquire, an active and intelligent Magistrate of Dumfries, and others in Scotland; who furnished him from time to time with accurate intelligence of the progress of the insurgents; and he communicated the information thus obtained to his friend Dr. BETTESWORTH, Dean of the Arches, in London; and also, it is believed, to the Duke of NEWCASTLE, then Minister of the Crown. The letters to Dr. BETTESWORTH have been preserved; those to the Duke of NEWCASTLE are not forthcoming. No doubt they were of similar import—very possibly contained more important particulars. If they had met with so much attention on the part of the government as to have induced the despatch of a single regiment to Carlisle, there is little question that the city would have been held for the King, the irruption of the Highlanders into England arrested, and much danger, misery, and confusion prevented.

The narrative of Dr. WAUGH affords many particulars of what passed within the city; and the minutes of the Court Martial which subsequently sat for the trial of Colonel Durand, the Commandant, supply a full and authentic account of the military operations. Some additional facts have been gleaned from other sources; and it is believed that the whole have been wrought together so as to give a clearer and more accurate view of the transactions of that period as regards Carlisle than any that has yet appeared.

For the papers of Dr. Waugh I am indebted to the Reverend Tullie Cornthwaite, the descendant and heir of the family of Tullie. By the kindness of Philip Henry Howard, Esquire, of Corby Castle, I was enabled to obtain an engraving of the medal of Prince Charles Edward, which appears on the title page—a cast of it being in the possession of the family of Mrs. Howard, who also possess other relics, the gift of Cardinal York, the last male representative of the Stuart line, to the late Mrs. Canning, of Foxcote.

This medal was struck by Charles Edward in 1745, on the eve of his daring and romantic enterprise; and indicates a feature in his character which redeems it from much of the obloquy with which it has been loaded. It shows that, though a foreigner by education, he was an Englishman at heart, and understood the basis whereon the glory of England subsisted—her naval power. The navy of England continued during his after life, through weal and woe, to be his "*amor et spes*"; and even when hope must have expired within him, his love survived. Long afterwards, when a naval victory of the English fleet drew from him an expression of pleasure, and provoked a sneering remark in relation to the medal of 1745 from the Prince of CONTI, CHARLES EDWARD replied, "*Je suis l'ami de la flotte d' Angleterre contre tous ses ennemis ; comme je regarderai toujours la gloire d'Angleterre comme la mienne, et sa gloire est dans sa flotte.*"

As time rolls on and change of circumstances gives a new direction to the antipathies of men, we come to form a more correct judgment of the past. The character of CHARLES EDWARD has hitherto taken its colour mainly from the latter years of his life; when blasted hopes, and the bitter retrospect of opportunities lost, and of friends involved in irretrievable ruin, appear to have overpowered his better feelings, and driven him to a careless and sensual course of life. Yet it is impossible to review his earlier career,—the bold conception which aimed at the crown of Britain by a *coup de main*, as it were,—the gallant bearing which won the hearts of all that approached him, and wrought up the Highlanders almost to the realization of his own daring views,—his humanity and constant generosity in success, contrasting so markedly with the cruelty and meanness of his opponents,—and his courage and constancy in defeat and peril—without feeling that the constitution of his mind was of the better order; and that his misfortunes much outweighed his faults.

GEORGE GILL MOUNSEY.

May 15, 1846.

REFERENCES.

'arquis of Tullibardine's approach. 10th November 1745.

'he Prince's approach.

'he Duke of Perth's approach.

'he Trenches opened against the Citadel, Nov.r 13th.

'uke of Cumberland's Batteries on Primrose Bank, Dec.r 28th.

'he City Mill-race cut off by the Duke of Cumberland.

'he march of the Highlanders from Stanwix. 9th Nov.r

y Rockliff, Peatwath &c. coloured blue.

h Knells

CARLISLE CROSS, 1745.

AUTHENTIC ACCOUNT,

&c.

One hundred years have elapsed since the events detailed in the following pages: the actors in them have long since disappeared: those also whose childhood witnessed them, and of whose age it was the delight to recount their early recollections,—forming, as it were, a connecting link between the past and present generations,—have in like manner passed away; and all around is changed. The citizens of 1745, could they arise, could now scarcely recognize their city. They would look in vain for the ancient walls, the gates, the citadel: the very aspect of their own dwellings would be strange. During the last century we have floated rapidly down the stream—the ordinary progress of several has been accomplished in one. Hence we look back upon the events of 1745 as mere matters of general history; and know as little about the proceedings of Charles Edward as about those of Edward the First, nearly five centuries before. The present publication may, therefore, in one sense, possess the charm of novelty. It does not, indeed, contain much that was unknown before; but it embodies much that was forgotten. It pourtrays the city as it was in the days of our forefathers; when, after a long repose and, as regarded its military character, a gradual decay, it suddenly resumed for a time somewhat of its ancient importance as a barrier fortress against Scotland.

The population of Carlisle at that period did not exceed 4,000 persons; almost all within the walls, there being as yet nothing of the suburbs but a few cottages outside the gates. The castle and walls erected in the reign of Henry the First, and the Citadel (now transformed into Courts of Justice,) built by Henry the Eighth, though neglected, were yet standing in their pristine form. A non-resident governor kept the Castle by means of a company of invalided veterans; and the city-gates closing at the sound of the evening gun intimated to the inhabitants that their's was yet a garrison town. But all the warfare they had witnessed was of a bloodless kind; they were much divided in political feeling, and in their electioneering contests not less valiant than their children have since shown themselves. The principal people in the city were the members of the Ecclesiastical body, the Dean and Chapter; and those who composed the Corporation of the City; between whom not the best understanding appears to have subsisted. In short Carlisle, in 1745, in regard to its condition to sustain a siege, differed from the Carlisle of border history when a Dacre or a Scrope lay in it, as widely as it is possible to conceive.

The union of the kingdoms of England and Scotland had in fact removed all reasonable grounds for maintaining it as such. As a frontier town against Scotland its importance was early perceived by William Rufus, who seized on and fortified it—and so long as the two crowns graced different heads, Carlisle remained the key of the western marches of both kingdoms. By it our Edwards projected their most energetic invasions of Scotland; and upon it in return fell many of the severest retaliatory attempts of the Scottish Kings. But all this was past and forgotten in 1745. Invasion of England from the side of Scotland was not looked for, and consequently took all by surprise.

Prince Charles Edward Stuart, eldest son of the Pretender, sailed from the river Loire on the 22nd of June, 1745, on board of a small vessel, accompanied by eight persons—viz., the Marquis of Tullibardine, Sir John Macdonald, a French officer, Mr. Eneas Macdonald, a banker in Paris, Mr. Strickland, Mr. Buchanan, Sir Thomas Sheridan, Mr. O'Sullivan, and Mr. Kelly. On the 23rd of July they reached the island of Erisca, one of the western isles of Scotland, belonging to the Laird of Clanranald; and, on the 25th, landed at Boradale, in Avasaig, from an arm of the sea called Lochnanuagh. At first there appears to have been a misgiving amongst the friends of his cause, and many advised his return. The Prince, however, was resolute. On the 19th of August he set up his standard at Glenfinnan, at the head of Lochshiel, and was immediately joined by Lochiel, Keppoch, and others, with 1,400 men.

At this time the King was abroad; Great Britain was deeply engaged in a Continental war; and consequently at home destitute of its most efficient military forces. On the first news of the insurrection, Sir John Cope was ordered into the Highlands with 1,400 infantry to suppress it. On the 26th of August he was at Garvaimor, and the Highlanders awaited his approach at the strong pass of Coriearag. The general expectation and hope was that he would crush, or at least repel the attempt; but he suddenly turned aside, marched to Inverness, and thus left the road open for their advance. On the 4th of September the Prince made his entrance into Perth; where he was joined by Lord George Murray, brother of the Marquis of Tullibardine, and of the Duke of Athol, whom he appointed Commander-in-chief.

The affair, which in the beginning had been treated with something like ridicule in England, now assumed importance, and at this period Dr. Waugh commences his correspondence. Before the letters are given it may be proper to explain that the Mayor of Carlisle was at that time Mr. Aglionby, the younger, who resided in the country, and had a deputy in Carlisle, Mr. Thomas Pattinson, between whom and Dr. Waugh there was nothing like cordiality. Indeed Pattinson appears in the sequel to have so demeaned himself as to have excited suspicions of his disloyalty; though the motives by which he was really actuated were probably nothing more than self-interest and petty political jealousy. He had acquired great sway in the corporation, so that although Mr. Aglionby, the mayor, quitted office at Michaelmas, 1745, and Mr. Backhouse, resident in Carlisle, was then appointed Mayor, yet Pattinson continued to exercise the authority of the office, the Mayor being a mere cypher. By some expressions in Dr. Waugh's narrative, Pattinson appears to have been, or at all events to have given it out that he was, in correspondence with the Duke of Newcastle—and authorised by his Grace to organize and arm the townsmen, for defence of the city, and to grant commissions to their officers. And this was probably the "*particular share of confidence*" referred to in the address of the Mayor and Corporation to the King in October, 1745. No such correspondence or documents, however, are now extant.

The members of the Corporation were—

HENRY AGLIONBY, Esq., Mayor.

Aldermen.

Messrs. PARKER	Mr. BACKHOUSE
" TATE	Sir JAMES LOWTHER
" HALL	Messrs. GRAHAM
" PATTINSON	" COULTHARD
" AGLIONBY, sen.	Major STANWIX
Lord LONSDALE	

Bayliffs.

Thomas Wilson	Thomas Stordy

Councillors.

Joseph Simpson	Robert Wilson
Samuel Railton	Jos. Coulthard
James Nicholson	John Pears
Thomas Sowerby	Thomas Coulthard
Ed. Blamire	John Richardson
George Railton	George Blamire
Richard Jackson	Thomas Hodgson
William Tate	Robert Knagg
John Brown	Thomas Parker
George Sowerby	George Pattinson
Richard Hodgson	William Nixon

The representatives of the City in Parliament were General Sir Charles Howard, son of the Earl of Carlisle, and John Hylton, Esq. General Howard will be found in the course of the correspondence in military command of the town; and to have been more perplexed and annoyed by the self-interested importunities of his constituents than by the burden of his military duties.

Lord Lonsdale was Lord-Lieutenant of the county; and by the above list of the Corporation would seem to have had strong personal interest in that body: but Henry Earl of Carlisle had as yet the ascendant in the parliamentary influence of the town. Both were of Whig politics: there was no avowed Tory or Jacobite interest. Party contests must therefore have been of a very contracted description in Carlisle—having for their object hardly any thing political; but merely the predominance of the one great man or of the other.

The See of Carlisle was at this period filled by Sir George Fleming, Baronet, of Rydal Hall, in the county of Westmoreland: his advanced age, seventy-eight years, precluded him from any very active exertion. He was then resident at Rose Castle, and though he appears to have quitted it at the first approach of the Highlanders, yet he returned thither shortly afterwards. The Dean of Carlisle was Dr. BOLTON; the Prebendaries, Mr. BIRKET, Dr. WAUGH (the Chancellor), Mr. WILSON, and Mr. HEAD: of these, Mr. BIRKET, Dr. WAUGH, and Mr. WILSON are mentioned as having been in residence.

The office of Governor of the Castle was held by Lieutenant-General FOLIOT, who had not seen it for seven years before. Captain GILPIN, a gentleman of good family and connexions in the neighbourhood of Carlisle, held the command of the two companies of Invalids which formed the garrison; whilst Mr. JOHN STEPHENSON, a native of Penrith, as the Master-Gunner, with three quarter-gunners under him, represented the artillery force.

Such was, in brief, the civil and military condition of Carlisle in August, 1745, when the alarm of a Scottish inroad first came across the imagination of its people.

Let us now proceed with the correspondence of Dr. Waugh:—

"*Dr. Waugh to the Dean of Arches.*

"Good Mr. Dean,—

"As your last letter assured me that if you had any correspondent on the Rine, in Flanders, or Silesia, I should have partaken of the intelligence you should have received from thence, it is but just in me to apprehend that you will claim an account of any intelligence we that are on the Borders of North Britain may at this time receive from thence; at least if you are in any measure alarmed at Westminster, tho' in proportion only to your distance, as much as we have been at Carlisle; indeed, so many strange Storys have been told us of the Force and number of the

Rebels one post (as that they had 1400 French troops with them, an experienced General, plenty of money, Arms and Canon, with 12 sail of ships, &c.) and of their insignificancy another, that we can make no more guess at the truth than those that are 200 miles farther off. I shall not trouble you with any of these accounts, but refer you to the inclosed, which is a copy of a letter I received this morning from a Magistrate, one of the most considerable by his posts on the Scott's Borders, whom I verily believe to be thoroughly well affected to the present Government, and to have as good intelligence as can be had from Edinburgh. Do not understand me, good Mr. Dean, that our apprehensions arise from the force we think can be raised in the Highlands of Scotland : no, we think the attempt so mad if nothing more is intended, that we cannot but fear that to be the case; and if an invasion should be attempted in England before these people are dispersed, or any considerable succours should be sent them; or if, which is most to be apprehended, these Rebels should, by the situation of the country or any accident, gain an advantage over General Cope, (who by this account has not above half the force we have all along been told he had with him,) we have strong reasons to fear all Scotland would soon be in an uproar, and we not in a very pleasant situation; tho' I verily believe the loyalty of the people in this country to the present Government is as great as in any part of the kingdom, and the Scotts are a very different people from what they were in 1715. I hope the King is got safe home before this, and pray heartily that we may soon have better accounts of the situation of affairs both at home and abroad, for we cannot help thinking here that England was never in greater danger, at least in this age, than it is now. All my family join in humble service to you Sir, Mrs. Bettesworth, Miss, and the young Gentleman. If I have any clearer intelligence, or any thing worth your knowledge, you may be assured it shall be communicated to you by, Sir,

"Your most obliged and most

"Obedient humble Servant,

"JOHN WAUGH.

"Carlisle, Sept. 2nd, 1745."

"*The same to the same.*

"Good Mr. Dean,—

"I am sorry to tell you our accounts from Scotland this morning are different from what we had last post. The ships seen in the Frith proved only the London trade, however they hope soon to see the Dutch. The Highlanders are at Perth, it is uncertain when or which way they will march. Some say they were to begin to march on the 5th, and march straight into England by Dumfries-shire ; others say they will try to increase their numbers before they move from Perth. Expresses are gone from Dumfries to Edinbrough and Glasgow for intelligence, so I expect we shall have a better account soon. The Provost of Perth and the Magistrates are escaped to Edinbrough, being desired to proclaim the Pretender. The Duke of Perth, as he is called, it is said has set up a standard, and that 800 have joined it; and that Lord Ogilvie has taken possession of Dundee, and has got his clan together; besides which they are said to be 5000 strong, and have 18 pieces of canon one-pounders ; it is said they behave very civilly, and pay for every thing they take. In their camp it is believed that there is an Insurrection in Wales, and another in Ireland. There are no French officers with the Rebels, all Irish and Scotts, and among them General M'Donald, uncle to the Earl of Antrim. Two of General Cope's Aids de Camp came to Edinburgh last Wednesday night; one of them set out for London, so things may be better known there than here; for as no part of what was brought was published, all we can learn of Sir John is that he and his army got safe to Inverness, and that the Highlanders blame themselves for not attacking him at two passes, but they say he escaped the danger by feints, tho' I have no notion they will ever attack a regular force; how he intends to move backwards is not known, but we much wish he will come up with these people before they get any farther, for there is nothing now before them to keep them out of this country, or when they come here to stop them; but without larger canon, tho' I don't think our town very strong, if we can have any reinforcement to the Garrison, they will hardly meddle with us, as they do not love great guns. I gave you an account of our apprehensions of danger at first, by way of news; and as these differ so frequently, it draws fresh trouble upon you; but I hope, Sir, you will take it as it is meant, to show my readiness on all occasions to approve myself,

"Good Mr. Dean,

"Your most obliged and most obedient humble Servant,

"JOHN WAUGH.

"Carlisle, Sept. 3rd, 1745."

"*The same to the same.*

"Good Mr. Dean,—

"Tho' I make no doubt but from some quarter or other you have accounts of what is done in North Britain at this time, yet I think that my advices are as good as any that come here from Edinburgh, and believe my correspondent a very well affected and intelligent man. I shall, in conformity to my promise in my last, give you a detail of what I have received. No accounts have come lately from General Cope; the last said he was arrived within fourteen miles of Inverness; what he intended by that march is not foreseen, nor the consequences; but by it the Rebels have a clear country before them, and as they are said to have broke and spoiled the roads, he may not so soon get back as could be wished: this put the people of Edinburgh and all this part of Scotland in great fears for the mischief they might do in their country—though, as General Blakeny is said to be at Sterling with Gardener's Dragoons, it was hoped with the assistance of the Hamiltons, and the men he has, they would be stopped there; these Dragoons were luckily left, as they could be of no use in a mountainous country, nor get forage there. The Rebels seem certainly by all accounts (for I have just seen two merchants who are come directly from Glasgow that give the same accounts) to have advanced very fast. The last advice from Edinbrough saies that last Wednesday Lord Nairn at the head of 400 men took peaceable possession of Perth, and that the whole party was expected there that day, that they gathered strength in Perthshire, but are said to be very ill armed. They are in Scotland much easier; and they hope, when General Cope gets back, to be an overmatch for all disaffection can produce, as twelve ships were coming up the Frith with Forces from Holland, as believed. The Rebels we are told whisper that they are not to stay to attack Edinbrough or Sterling, but to pass the Frith, above the last mentioned place where it is fordable, and march directly into England through these Borders, where they give out great numbers are ready to rise in arms; if they fail, this young rash adventurer threatens to make the invitations he has from them publick. If this be his scheme, I have no fears of his coming into Cumberland,—Northumberland I don't know so well; but I am clear, that unless it were a few poor papists, and few we have, he would hardly get a man in the country to join him; and that he has no invitations from hence I most sincerely believe. We are told they spread all sorts of reports to dispirit the Loyal people of Scotland, and magnify their numbers, which has had some success, as General Cope had left the country open to them, by which even the people of Edinbrough were put in great fear. The Dukes of Athol, Montross, and a great many others of distinction, are come there. Lord Rothes' baggage is sent over from his seat in Fife; Lady Stair and several others have lodged their plate in the Castle of Edinburgh. It is said that the Duke of Athol's brother and the party have taken possession of his seats at Blair and Dunkeld; that at the first place they met with good entertainment, the Duke's Chamberlain (as they call Stewards in Scotland) waiting upon them with a list of provisions about the house; that after dinner they played at bowls; and after supper, having drunk a moderate glass, went to bed; and in the morning made the Chamberlain write a letter to his master, whom they styled Lord J. Murray, signifying that his Grace the Duke—meaning the brother—and his company returned him thanks for providing so well for them, and that they only wished he had vouchsafed them his company. This letter the Duke is said to have received at Edinburgh. My correspondent concludes, 'But now that his Majesty is arrived in safety and the Dutch troops come into the Frith, as we have the greatest reason to believe, their designs are in a fair way to be frustrated, and they will be dispirited to purpose in their turn.'

"I am not at all surprised, if you have in London no apprehensions of an Invasion in the South or West of England, that you are under very little or no apprehensions for what is doing in Scotland. Surely if the Pretender trusts to a Rebellion at home only, it is as mad a piece of work as ever was set about, which has made us fear something more; if no such thing was intended, or has miscarried, tho' those among whom this rabble come may be frightened, it certainly can end in nothing but the destruction of the people engaged in it, and will, I hope, afterwards have a good effect, by showing the enemies of his Majesty, and the present happy constitution, that the people of Great Britain will give no encouragement to a Popish Pretender, or the ambitious designs of France.

"I am, good Mr. Dean,

"Your most obliged and obedient Servant,

"JOHN WAUGH.

"Carlisle, Sept. 7th, 1745."

"*The same to the same.*

"Good Mr. Dean,—

"Yesterday's post brought me a paper of which the inclosed is a copy, as that paper was of one sent by the Provost of Glasgow to the Magistrates of Dumfries by a messenger they had sent for intelligence; the messenger they sent at the same time to Edinburgh was not returned when the post came to Dumfries, so that they had no accounts more than what that paper contains, except that they were told in letters by the post that the people of Edinburgh were very busy in repairing their walls, and planting canon on them, being determined to hold out the place. And that the transports were certainly gone from Leith for General Cope, who is blamed much by the people in Scotland for his conduct, which they can in no way account for. We are busy here to see what defence we can make should the rebels come this way, an uneasie situation to the inhabitants, all well affected, and seem harty in their promises of resisting the rebels—pray God grant they may be stopped before they reach us: from, Good Mr. Dean,

"Your most obedient Servant,

"JOHN WAUGH.

"Sept. 11, 1745.

"I am told orders are come for raising all our Militia."

[INCLOSURE.]

"'The news I have just now received from Edinburgh are, that the forces who went from thence to defend the passage of the Forth are lying at Sterling; that there are arriving at that place dayly great numbers of Volunteers, associate companies, and Militia; so that they are already near 500 strong. The report of the Rebels marching from Perth towards Sterling does not appear to be true; on the contrary, it is said they are entrenching themselves; and Lord John Drummond (brother to the Duke of Perth) who came from Dunkirk lately with the Irish Regiments, of which he has for some time commanded one in Flanders, is gone to Aberdeen to bring up Lord Lewis Gordon * (brother to the Duke of Gordon) and his men. If you have any dispatches of moment pray forward them immediately.

"'Am, &c.

"'Tuesday one o'clock, from Scotland.'"

"*Dr. Waugh to* ——.

"Dear Sir,—

"I wrote to you as I hoped before you left London, and to Bess before I left Allonby, but have had no answer; should be glad to know she received it. The people in Scotland are in great consternation on account of these rebels. Sir J. C. by letting them slip by him, and going such a march as from Sterling to Inverness, and then coasting round and not getting back to Edinbrough, having left the Rebels a clear country; we apprehend their marching this way into Lancashire, and are preparing to keep them out of Carlisle;

---

* Third son of the Duke of Gordon; was a Lieutenant in the Navy, but declared for Prince Charles, raised a regiment, defeated the Laird of Macleod near Inverary on the 23rd September, and then marched to Perth.

we are told they have no large guns, but 16 pieces of small canon of one pound. They have no Foreigners with them, but all Scotts and Irish, one General Mc.Donald, uncle to the Earl of Antrim, the chief under the young Pretender; if they come forward and are now 5000 strong, which I doubt is too true, I fear they will be 10,000 before they get here—pray God send they may be stopped where they are; which if the three regiments mentioned in the inclosed get safe in, in time, I hope they will, as there are two regiments of Dragoons at Edinbrough and Sterling, besides the forces with General Cope, which are called 2000. The people of Edinbrough are fortifying their town, and we are told the ships are certainly gone from Leith for General Cope. The inclosed paper was sent me this post from Dumfries, and is a copy of one sent from the Provost of Glasgow to their Magistrates (from one of which I had it) by a messenger sent by them to Glasgow for intelligence. Our people here are all hearty and loyal, and in good spirits; orders are come for raising the Militia, and General Foliot, our Governor, has sent word he will soon be with us, but I trust in God these Rebels will be stopped before they reach us. With hearty service to all at Yately,

"I am, Dear Will,

"Your's faithfully and affectionately,

"JOHN WAUGH.

"Carlisle, Sept. 12, 1745.

"The people of Glasgow, Dumfries, and the trading towns, seem to be well affected, and will it is said be able to make some stand; but the other side of the Borders I doubt bad enough."

[INCLOSURE.]

"'By latest accounts Lord Nairn, Young Lockyle, and 260 Camerons, came into Perth on the 3rd, took possession of the Main Guard, and placed Sentrys; on the 4th, as many more arrived as made 1000, and came into the town; about 12 Mercer of Adie, Young Lockyle, and others proclaimed their King; and their whole army said to be in and about that place—their number uncertain—some of them badly armed and cloathed,—the standard was set up in the North Inch of Perth on Wednesday, and all required to repair to it under pain of Rebellion; their other behaviour as informed is as yet civil, and pay for what they get. Sir John Cope was at Inverness the 1st September and was to come South next day, some say by the coast,—lost not one man in his march, all hearty; two regiments of Dutch and one of English dayly expected. The Highlanders attacked the Barracks of Ruthven, and were repulsed. What is above is pretty certain; it is reported that they had a letter brought to the Camp, of a landing by General Keith at Portsoy with 4000 men, but this is certainly not true; at other times they give out, as is said, that 6000 Spaniards are to land in the West of England; and they to come South by Glasgow, and on to the Borders.

"'From Stirling on Sunday, that the Highlanders are still at Perth, badly armed, their number about 5000. From Edinburgh that Sir John Cope has returned to Aberdeen on Friday, was expected at Montrose on Sunday. That transports were going over to him from Leith, which it is believed he would meet at Dundee. The Dutch troops dayly expected.'"

From Mr. Goldie, of Dumfries, to Dr. Waugh.

"Dear Sir,—

"Our last accounts from Edinbrough represent the Highlanders to be fewer in number than we represented formerly, and that many of them are ill armed. When they made their proclamation at Perth and Dundee, the principal inhabitants kept their houses and shut their doors and windows; and even such of the commonalty as look't on gave no huzzas, but on the contrary look't sour, which chagrined the party not a little. I enclose one of Edinbrough papers, and refer you to that. I am glad to find by your's and other accounts we have from London, that the Government begins to awake.

"Surely their indolence has given the disaffected all the advantages they could wish. But as yet we hear nothing of Lord Lieutenants being named, which at least would put the well affected in motion, and I despair of seeing a proper spirit arise till once the country is gathered together. I flatter myself our Governours are secure of a sufficient force of regular troops to quell not only what is in the North, but any other insurrection may happen in England or invasion there; otherwise their conduct to me is inconceivable. Transports are sailed to fetch about Sir John Cope, I wish we had him at Sterling Bridge.

"That gentleman has laid himself open to raillery; it's said he lock't up the King's troops in a chest, and that now he will not sail till he be certainly informed that he and they are insured against loss from the sea as well as the enemy, tho' after all it must be owned that if he had attacked the Highlanders upon the great hill of Corrigearoch they might have destroyed his men by tumbling stones down upon them there; he by forced marches got through a pass in his way where a small number might have done him infinite damage, and what must infallibly justify him, he had express orders to march to them wherever they were, which was extremely dangerous in such a country.

"The inhabitants of Edinbrough have been greatly divided; some, I hope the greater part, keenly disposed to hold out the city to the last extremity,—while others, who are either lukewarm or worse, ridicule all this, represent the place as untenable, and are for making no opposition, which they say would only exasperate the enemy and expose the town to plunder. However many of the inhabitants have entered into a solemn association to defend the place, &c., and all possible diligence is using to put the same into a good state of defence. In a conference held between the magistrates and ministers on this subject wherein some reflections were made as to the dispositions of some, the Ld. Provost, thinking they were pointed at him, took occasion to make great protestations of his own loyalty, to which one of the clergy answered that nobody would call his Lordship's loyalty in question, but it was undeniable that he was son in law to Sanballat the Horonite. The councill of that city were unanimous in addressing the King; but a dispute arose whether the M. of Tweeddale or D. of Argyle should present the address,—it carryd in favour of the D. Another, and indeed a very extraordinary question happened *Whether the young man should in the address be termed the son of the Popish Pretender, or the Rash Adventurer*,—but they agreed on the last, which is very surprising. Several papers have been wrote to stir up a spirit of loyalty in Edinbrough. I send one of them, and indeed all our clergy are using their utmost efforts for the same purpose every where. The three clergymen mentioned in the newspapers are non-jurors, and remarkably hot and zealous. You see in the newspapers a very curious letter from Galloway; the author is a little fellow the follower of those who have seceded from the Church of Scotland, and teaches the children of their principal support in this country.

"The firing mentioned by him was heard on our coast on Sunday was seennight; but upon the most diligent enquiry, it came from a West India ship belonging to the sugar house at Whitehaven which that day came into port. However from this letter and others it was firmly believed at Edinbrough that an engagement had happened on the coast of Galloway, and it was even given out that General Keith was landed with an army at Wigtown. So easy is it to alarm at such a conjuncture. I had written what is above before the express arrived, and would not detain the messenger we forwarded to your commandant till I finished it; and I expected we should have further accounts from Glasgow but none are yet come, tho' hourly expected; when we have any certain notice, you shall have early advice from,

"Revd. Sir, yours, &c.,

"13th Septr.

"P.S.—We have just now an express from Glascow advising that the rebels were expected there this day, and that they are 5000 strong the last accounts from Dumblain."

"*Mr. Goldie to Dr. Waugh.*

"Revd. Sir,—

"I acknowledge the favour of yours of the 11th and 13th, but I do not know how to express my gratitude for your obliging offer of preserving me and my family. All that I can do is to return you our most hearty thanks for the retreat you offer us. But it was at the desire of some others that I wanted to know whether a few could be admitted into your city; for, as to myself, tho' it would be very improper I should be here if the Highlanders came this way, yet I should think it indecent to be far from my friends in that event; and besides they will not probably make any stay here; and I should wish to have it in my power to return as quickly as possible. For tho' they may pass now unmolested, yet I hope the time is not far distant when those that are well affected may still be of use. It is, indeed, but little I can do, but it shall be with affection.

"I am extremely glad to find such a spirit among you: I hope it will be an effectual means of preserving you. We are uncertain as to the real strength and designs of the Highlanders. Our best accounts say, they have 2,000 fine fellows and desperate, who are well armed; and upwards of 1,000 more, who are very indifferent, and by us termed Waliedragles; but whether with these they will venture into our country, and so to England, we'll soon know. We are told from Edinbrough that the army from Aberdeen, which comes in barrel bulk, might sail on Friday and be there in a day, if the wind be fair, or in a month, if it be blown to Norway. However, the terror of it and of the Dutch, who are dayly expected, will probably keep the young gentleman from looking East, tho' there are many who still think he will march to Edinbrough. I send you the Thursday's paper; but by a letter I had from thence, dated on Friday, I am advised they have no notion their numbers are so trifling as that paper represents them—that an express came in there on Thursday night with advice that that day they had appeared within four miles of Sterling,—and that a detachment had marched up and tryed some of the Fords about four miles above that place. An express arrived here this day, about noon, with a letter dated yesterday, advising that the night before two expresses had arrived there, who brought accounts that the Highlanders had passed the heads of Forth, and were advanced within 12 miles of Glascow; but as we have had no advice of this either from Edinbrough or Glascow, we suspend our belief of it. We are told that the rash adventurer entered Dumblain on horseback, with a bible in his hand, out of which he read aloud the 25th, 26th, and 27th verses of the 21st chap. of Ezek.;* that the D. of Perth had shot three of his tenants who refused to

---

* The verses are as follows:

"25. And thou profane wicked Prince of Israel, whose day is come, when iniquity shall have an end.

"26. Thus saith the Lord God, remove the diadem, and take off the Crown: this shall not be the same; exalt him that is low, and abase him that is high.

"27. I will overturn, overturn, overturn it: and it shall be no more, until he come whose right it is; and I will give it him."

take arms, and that the M. of Tullibardin also shot one of his on the same account; but whether there is any truth in these story's I know not. The contribution raised on Perth was, I believe, only £500; and the reason for taking hostages from thence was to prevent the town's-people from giving any disturbance to the Airly men, who were not come up but behoved to pass that way. It's said there are six or seven gentlemen from Y——e, arrived in the Highland camp with an invitation to march into England, and that it is firmly believed in the camp that the D. of O——d is to land in England, and the E. of Marischall in Scotland, each of them with a great force. I wish Major Farrar joy of his commission, but cannot expect he'll gather laurels with such a command.

"I am, dear Sir,

"Yours, &c.,

"J. G.

15 7ber."

"*The same to the same.*

"Revd. Sir,—

"I send you coppy's of the intelligence we received from Glascow this day. We have just received accounts from Edinbrough, bearing that the Highlanders are betwixt Stirling and Edinbrough, and that they were expected yesterday at Edinbrough, and I am sorry to tell you that I expect any resistance they may meet with there will have but little effect, as the towns-people are miserably divided; and Sir John Cope has not yet made his appearance. Things have a miserably bad aspect in Scotland. Every thing misgives that should give us relief, and every thing succeeds against us. This will come by some private hand, and the gentleman who carries this, the length of Annan hastens me, and I have only time to assure you

"I am yours,

"J. G.

"16th 7ber."

[INCLOSURE.]

"*The Provost of Glascow's first letter to Dumfries.*

"Glascow, 14th Sept., 1745.

"I wrote you yesterday at 4 o'clock, and the gentleman promised me if he did not go to Dumfries he would send it per express from Moffat. We were yesterday very uneasie about our mob, from whom we are in more danger than from the Highlanders' army; and their madness was such there was great fear of their falling upon the Commissioners that were sent to treat with us about our contributions. It's said they were threatened, and a stick thrown at them; but since they went off we have been very quiet, but how long none can say,—for I'le make half a dozen drunk Tradesmen putt us in greater fear by raising our common people than as many express from the enemy would; and it's extremely hard that our manufactory's, from whom we get our wealth, and which is so happy for the country, should so often put us in fear of all we think valuable. Inclosed you have a copy of the letter sent us yesterday, which all disapprove off; and our men of letters have taken it to pieces, and say it's not to be understood; but others think it plain. Nothing will please him but a larger sum of money. As yet our commissioners are not returned, so cannot tell what bargain they have made; but the best will be bad enough. The Highlanders left Leikie-parks yesterday about 11 o'clock, and came to Bannockburn about 3. They did not enter Stirling, but sent for provisions, which were sent to them. The castle fired 4 guns, the number of their standards, and then they proceeded up the water of Bonniё, and to Faulkirk in the evening, tho' their prince was only to be at . So far the contents of an express from the Provost of Stirling. This is also confirmed by many other accounts. I am just now with the magistrates and council, who have got information that they will be in Pentland hills this night.

"'And by our best accounts they will go by Dumfries, which I'le be extremely sorry for. As the bearer had no letter from you, I do not incline to trust him; but have sent another express upon his horse.

"'*Past* 11, *Forenoon.*—Our commissioners are returned without treating with the enemy; they are inconsiderable; and we are all, I believe, going to arms as we can. I am just going out to ye country to reconnoitre them. I am ever yours, &c.

"'I'le send you word before I return, if I can. You see I am in a hurry.'"

"'*To the Magistrates of Glasgow.*

[INCLOSURE 2.]

"'I need not inform you my being come hither, nor of my views in comming; that is already sufficiently known. All those who love their country and the true interest of Britain ought to wish for my success, and to do what they can to promote it. It would be a needless repetition to tell you that all the privileges of your town are included in my declaration; and what I have proposed I will never depart from. I hope this is your way of thinking, and therefore expect your compliance with my demands.

"'A sum of money, besides what is due to the government, not exceeding £15,000 sterling, and whatever arms you can raise in your city is what at present I require: the terms offered you are very reasonable and what I promise to make good. I choice to make these demands, but if not complied with, I shall take other measures, and you must be answerable for the consequences.

"'CHARLES, P.R.

"'Leikie, 12 September, 1745.'

[INCLOSURE, 3.]

"'*The Provost of Glasgow's second letter.*

"'Glasgow, Saturday, 14th Sep., 1745. Past four.

"'I wrote you a long letter since my last pr. Mr. Gilchrist, acquainting you with our present unhappy situation, betwixt our mob and the enemy; but I fear it has not come to your hands. This tells you that about 12 o'clock this day two men from the Highlanders came to town with a letter signed Chas., P.R., demanding of our city £15,000, besides the public money, and what arms can be got, or he would levy it; and that we were answerable for the consequence. We are all mad at the proposal, but what could we do but send out 5 gentlemen to the camp, to make the best terms we can. I shall not add, but wish you and our other friends may never be in our present situation. I am in haste.

"'Yours, &c.,

"'J. C.

"'It's said their number is 5,000 foot, and 700 horse,, and that they intend to make a general rendesvouz in Pentland hills.'

"*The same to the same.*

"Rev. Sir,—

"I hope you have received mine of yesterday, which was to be forwarded from Annan. I am glad to find by yours that the King is in high spirits, long may he continue to be so: but of late I dislike the phrase, because it has been frequently applyed to Sir Jno. Cope and his army; and I am sorry to tell you that I have it from good authority, that those who govern here have in all, even their latest accounts of this Insurrection, represented the whole body as a rascally contemptible mob that would soon be quashed, tho' they have not hitherto done any foolish action, and our people as few that were right. How will it be relished if they shall make themselves masters of Edinbrough. The Duke of Argyle has been confined to his house almost ever since he went up, which has been a great loss, as his advice would have done great service. There is not yet one Lieutenant appointed for Scotland, but Gen. Wentworth is sent down to Harwich to cause five of the Dutch regiments expected to sail directly for Leith without disembarking; but I am afraid before they can arrive they may be more wanted in another place. I wish Ligonier with the ten regiments were safe in Britain, and hope that the ship may still be preserved; but if an invasion be made with a considerable force, which is in the cards, I own I shall have my fears. We are informed from Edinbrough that the Commissioners from Glascow had compounded the sum demanded from that City for £9,000, and that the same was payed; but by an express which came from Hamilton near Glascow on Sunday evening we are informed that those Commissioners were mett in their way to the Highland camp by a townsman of their own, a gentleman of the law, who by sundry arguments dissuaded them from proceeding; and that they went all back to Glascow with him; and this is confirmed by one who left Glascow yesterday morning. The Highlanders quartered about Falkirk, Torwood, and the adjacent places, upon

Saturday night were at Borrowstonness, where they broke up the Custom house, and some of them were at Linlithgow on Sunday morning early; and that the whole were to march to Edinbrough which they expected to reach by sunsett; their number about 5000, but many of them not armed.

"That Gardner's Dragoons, who had been at Stirling, retired towards Edinbrough, and were to be joined by Hamilton's, the Volunteers, &c., who all marched from Edinbrough on Sunday (several of the clergy being among them, under arms,) to Corstorphine about 2 miles west from Edinbrough, where we are told they would give the Highlanders battle; but, I dare say, they can only intend to retard their march to give time to Cope or the Dutch to arrive. And if one or other of these come not speedily, I shall have no hopes from Edinbrough. We were this day refreshed with an account that 1200 Dutch were landed near Dunbar, 20 miles east from Edinbrough, and that sundry ships were seen coming up the Firth, who were supposed to be the transports with Sir John Cope; I pray God either of them may have arrived so as to succour Edinbrough.

"By some unaccountable conduct the subjects on this side of the Forth who are, generally speaking, as loyall as any in Britain, have been restrained from taking arms till it is too late: tho' I am certain a sufficient number of brave men might easily have been gott to have kept the Highlanders in the North, if properly supported by the two regiments of Dragoons, which indeed would not have been left, but that it was foreseen they could neither be of use nor have forage in the Highlands. We have this moment received an express from Glascow, and this comes by the express that goes on to London with letters for the Dukes of Argyle, and Montrose, and Marques of Tweeddale. I send you a copy of the letter sent from Glascow to us, by which you will see we are like to be in a very bad situation; but I cannot believe their numbers are so great as they are represented, tho' much greater than we have been made to believe. We are in great fears for Edinbrough, having no accounts from thence since the Highlanders approached it; but it is confirmed that the Dutch are landed near Dunbar, and that Sir J. Cope was at Dundee on Saturday: you may depend on the best intelligence I can get, but as matters come nearer a crisis our intelligence turns worse, tho' we have sent gentlemen to all quarters from whence we can expect it.

"I am, your's, &c.,

"J. G.

"17th September, 1745."

"*7 at Night*.—P.S,—I forgot to tell the postman to delay sending off the messenger till I had finished my letters, and I hurryed so much that I thought it impossible he could have one ready before I was: however, I was mistaken. There is no truth as to the ravishing or ill usage further than you have heard."

[INCLOSURE,]

"'Glascow, 16th September, ½ hour after five.

"Sir,—

"'When I wrote yesterday, you would have thought we were determined to make a stand at all events; and, in consequence of it, I and many others were sent out, to bring intelligence of the enemy, and to desire the country to come in with what arms they had. I did not return till eleven this day, and then found all over; and I fear it would have been happy if our commissioners had gone forward, for some say they will be displeased at our manner of treating their commissioners, as they call them. As to news, Edinbrough is now the place,—for its too true those that came first over were to be within two miles of it this day by ten o'clock; this makes us long with great impaticnce to know the behaviour of that city where they are well provided for a defence.

"'I can assure you that yesterday night at five of the clock, 2,130 men of the Highland army past the Forth commanded by Lord Nairn, and this morning marched for Linlithgow, where they are to be this night. I am sorry to acquaint you this is not all; the men of Athole, the Grants, many of the Stewarts, &c., are still to pass; by the best accounts above 4,000 men. There has been some desertion among them since they passed the Forth, some say about 200 men. Our post was stopt this day, and the news and many letters taken out. Our provost gives his service, and desires me to put the three inclosed letters under your cover, which must be sent by a flying packet to London, being for his Majesties service.

"I am, &c.,

"'J. C.'"

"*Mr. Goldie to Dr. Waugh.*

"3 in the morning, 18th Sept,

"Rev. Sir,—

"According to your desire, I send the bearer express with the copy of the letter we have just received from two gentlemen we sent out for intelligence towards Edinbrough. My fears with respect to it have been too well grounded. May Almighty God watch over the fate of Britain; I have no time to add further than that I am,

"Dear Sir, yours,

"J. G."

[INCLOSURE.]

"'Crasstrons, four miles from Edinbrough,

"'*Tuesday Morning*, 8 *o'clock*.

"'Sir,—

"'By the best information we can learn upon the road, the Highlanders went into Edinburgh about five this morning; the magistrates were with

them before they went in, and the gates laid open. The two regiments of Dragoons retired to Musselburgh last night. This day they design for Hadington. No accounts of the Dutch or Cope. We are proceeding to Edinbrough to inform ourselves of every circumstance which you shall be informed immediately upon our going into Edinbrough, either by ourselves or by our express.

" 'R. H.
" 'W. M.' "

"*Dr. Waugh to the Dean of the Arches.*

"Carlisle, Sept. 18, and 19, 1745.

"Good Mr. Dean,—

"I have had so much writing and so much business upon my hands for some time passed, that I could not advise you as I wished every post of the accounts we received from Scotland: for indeed we have not been asleep here. Every method that could be contrived for saving this little city, the castle, and stores, has been endeavoured; and we were in hopes from the accounts we received of the strength and arms of the rebels, that with a very little assistance, we should be able to keep them out. General, Officers, Colonels, and Governor, and I know not who, were to come to us; but like General Cope to Edinburgh, I doubt; a more loyal town there is not in the kingdom; a little divided in election interest, but upon the first applying to them to lay all that aside in this time of common danger, all quiet; in which, and the intelligence procured from Scotland, and bringing the people up to a right spirit, I flatter myself I have been of no small use—sure I am I have not wanted inclination or industry. Greatly have we been alarmed for some days past with the expectations of the rebels coming this way; but nobody began to get out of the town, or to secrete effects for fear of giving an alarm. No judgement could be formed from any intelligence whether these rebels would go to Edinburgh, or come our way into England: I should now rather think they will go by Newcastle; this way they can get no strength, in Northumberland and Newcastle they may, for anything I know, and in the latter place their own mob will make dreadful work. What Sir John Cope has been doing, God knows; this is a dreadful stroke, as they will get numbers by it to declare for them, I fear, in Scotland; and what I more apprehend, it will encourage foreign invasions: all this might surely have been prevented. Nothing that I can learn has been done in Scotland—not so much as Lord Lieutenants for their countys named, and there are many loyal people in it. I have had either three or four expresses within this two days—the post, and one came this morning.

I shall send you some letters and copys I have received, which will show you a better state of this affair than I can give you. I thank God I keep up my heart and spirits; but perpetual writing and receiving letters, perpetual meetings of magistrates and people, settling terms, and confusion of intelligence, leaves my head not so clear as I could wish to have it when I write to you on this subject; but I am not quiet 3 minutes together in a morning, either from enquiries or business. All the intelligence yt our commandant has had, that was of any use, he has had by me, which he has acknowledged to the D. of Newcastle. I gave his grace an account of the chief correspondence I had held, and sent him a letter of my friend's, at the commandant's request, last Saturday, together with an association of all the members of our Church and precincts, which I had drawn up and called them together to sign.

"Nothing that we can do in this country will be wanting if the people above will take as much care of us. I hope to hear more before the post goes out, and I have many letters to write; if any thing comes before I send, you shall have it; give us your prayers, good Mr. Dean. God preserve you and yours; my friend in Scotland, who is a very loyal magistrate, has been the only person that never trusted to accounts of defence from Edinbrough. He said they were miserably divided, and I have no doubt this Rash Adventurer has been invited there, or they might have called him a Popish Pretender.

"*Wednesday night*, 5 *o'clock*.—I have just received a letter from the Provost of Dumfries, yt their messengers are not returned; the person that brought it tells me that contributions were demanded from all the towns, and they again talk of coming our way. Their numbers are very great, and General Blakeney thought it impossible to defend the town of Edinbrough. I hope they cannot take the castle, which is the strongest place I have seen, but I have not seen many fortifications. They now talk of the Rebels being 10 or 12,000, and I doubt not where they are will increase.

"*Thursday morning*.—I have sent by a messr. a copy of the express I received yesterday to our Knight of the Shire, and have asked him if he does not think a meeting of all the gentlemen and clergy in this country to concert proper measures for the safety of the Government will be of use, and shall hint it to our Bishop; but I doubt he is so timerous he will propose nothing: however, I now hear from him, or see him every day, and am his dear Chancellor, he is so pleased with my intelligence.

"My Lord Bishop has been with me; I have mentioned this thing to him; he has not resolved, but will wait my answer from Sir J. Lowther, and if he approves it, would have me go to a meeting of the Dep.-Lieuts. to be held next Saturday, at Penrith, 18 miles from hence—if the Rebels do not advance towards us in the meantime. You will observe some of these letters are wrote as from a private friend, some from Magistrates, as such; I wish you may understand this letter wch. I have wrote at 7 or 8 different times. You will preserve these letters to send me back, if I should want them, not otherwise.

"I am, Mr. Dean,

"Your obedient servant,

"J. W."

"*Dr. Waugh to the Bishop of London.*

"My Lord,—

"I take the liberty of sending a letter and packet of intelligence of our knowledge of the affairs in these parts of the world to my friend, the Dean of the Arches, under your lordship's cover; I chose to send it unsealed for your lordship's perusal, if there is any thing mentioned in these letters that may be of service to the government your lordship will make what use you please of them; they come from the magistrates of the neighbouring towns in Scotland, but chiefly from John Goldie, Esq., Sheriff and Steward Deputy, and Commissary of Dumfries. May the Almighty preserve us in these perilous times, and restore peace to these kingdoms; that God may prosper the work of our hands in the defence of his Majesty's person and government, and defend us from the miseries of popery and arbitrary power is, my good lord, the hearty prayer of your lordship's most dutiful and

"Obedient and humble servant,

"JOHN WAUGH.

"Carlisle, Sept. 19th, 1745."

"*Mr. Goldie to Dr. Waugh.*

"21st Sept., 1745.

"Reverend Sir,—

"Our two gent. are returned, and report yt. last night the Highlanders and Sir John Cope's army were within canon shott of one another, near Cockeny, a village near Preston

Pans, where ye. two gent. viewed both camps. That ye. Highlanders were above 7000 in number, all well armed; that Cope had with him 2300 Foot, 700 Dragoons, and about 500 Highlanders—that the two armies canonaded each other the whole night. The gent., as they could not safely reach Sir Jno. Cope's camp, lodged last night at Dalkeith, but got up early in ye. morning to go back towards ye. two armies: and in their way thither met one in livery who called himself Coll. Hamilton's servant, riding on a Dragoon horse, and several Dragoon horses following, some with and some without saddles, and ye. bridles among their feet or broken—that they were informed ye. Dragoon horses would not stand fire, and had immediately fallen into disorder,—that soon after they saw many Dragoons flying, some one way, some another—particularly one considerable party wherein they were told Lord Drumore was took to ye. hills above Dalkeith—that they stopped awhile with some of ye. Dragoons, till a gent. of their acquaintance who had been in Cope's camp over night came galloping up, who informed them that the Foot also were in disorder before he left them, and he believed would be cut to pieces,—that thereupon they returned with him, and made the best of their way home. They further say yt. ye. Adventurer was not engaged, the Highlanders having positively declared they would not fight if he would expose himself. Those are all the particulars we could gather, and, alas! too much.

"I am, Rev. Sir, yours, &c.,

"21 of Septr. "J. G."

"Sir Jno Cope marched early on Thursday morning from Dunbar, where he landed with 3,000 Foot, and 2 regiments of Dragoons. He came to Haddingtown that night. On Friday he reached Tranent, and took possession of ye. ground betwixt that and Cockenie,—the Highlanders marched from Edinbrough and reached Tranent that night. When they came up Sir Jno. waited for them in order of battle, but they declined it and filed off towards the town of Tranent. Sir Jno. threw a good many small shells into the town among them which did some execution, but did not much disturb them; the rest of the night both the armies lay upon their arms. As soon as it was light in the morning, the Highlanders in two bodies, ye. one on the west, the other on ye. east of the town, attacked Sir Jno. who was on a plain a little below them, they fired twice before our men returned it—Hamilton's Dragoons, it is said, stood but one of them—Gardener's Dragoons did great execution, till their Coll. was wounded in the thigh, and many of ym.selves cut to pieces,—after which they retired. The Foot, in the mean time, made 5 regular fires, but at last being surrounded by the enemy and deserted by the cavalry, all that remained were taken prisoners. Lowdon's Highlanders are almost all killed, and ye. baggage all taken. The

Highlanders returned towards Edinbrough, Sir Jno. Cope was at Laudor when I left Kelso, with ye. Earls of Hume, Loudon, and the Dragoons with them, on his road to England. It is thought that the Highlanders will follow him soon by Berwick—their numbers are magnified to 10,000, which I dare say is above ye. truth. By another account the Highlanders seem to have surprised ym. in the morning before they knew what they were about. And Sir Jno. having lighted a great many fires gave ym. an opportunity of seeing his motions in the night."

"*September*, 21*st*, 1745.—The above account was taken from one who was waiting in Cope's camp for intelligence and saw the battle from the town. We hear Murray, of Broughton, is killed."

"*Dr. Waugh to the Dean of the Arches.*

"2nd Oct., 1745.

"Good Mr. Dean,—

"Had the intelligence given by the people in power in Scotland, to the people in the administration at London, been the same we received here from the beginning from my correspondent, I believe they had prevented much of the mischief that has happened by the rebels being too much despised; indeed it looks like a dream, that 36 persons, at most, should land in an obscure island, be so long concealed, and in so short a time make such a progress as that to alarm all England, and so far have conquered Scotland. But I have long apprehended that the truth of matters is thus:—When this affair broke out first all the party, instead of drinking bumpers to favourite healths, and braging of their strength and power, lay all quiet in appearance; talked of nothing but the madness of engaging in such an enterprise; that they had not forgot the year 1715, &c.; all which was swallowed by those that should have been more on their guard, who represented every thing done by the rebels as a mad piece of folly, which they thought they could easily put a stop to, and make great merit of doing it themselves; they therefore would consult with none but their own set of people, and did not care Lieutenants should be appointed, for fear not of their own party. All the loyal people, which certainly they are about Glasgow, Dumfries, and several parts of the country, were therefore from the first under terrible apprehensions, as they were left without arms or defence; and if Cope was worsted, tho' they never could expect such a blow as this, they knew not what would become of them. When he got on the wrong side of the rebels (and why he passed them or did not sooner return none can tell, unless for the same reason he did not fight them) they were sure, for all the pretences, Edinbrough would be betrayed, which would give them arms they had not before; and the consequences of that march were in their fears before they happened, but it is too late now to reflect upon that: God be thanked the whole nation is now alarmed, and the noble spirit that appears in it will give, I hope, a good turn to the melancholy prospect.

"I enclose you a copy of a letter I received this morning, and a copy of the young Pretender's demand upon the town of Dumfries. The same is sent to all the Burghs. The Provost of Annan, but 12 miles from us, was here this day. They all keep out of the way, and I am told will not pay till exacted by a military force, which they hope the King's army will prevent. An express went through this morning, being sent this way from Edinbrough, as I was told, from the magistrates, to petition not to have the town destroyed. The Castle have had provisions sent till now. On the rebels forbidding any more, General Guest sent word to the town, that if his provisions were stopped he would fire upon them, having loaded all the battering canon towards the town for that purpose.

"The magistrates and the castle had a conference, and Guest has given them six days to consider what to do. The Provost hopes the King will save the town, though at the hazard of the castle, at his request. This I had only from the gentleman who came to forward the express, and said he apprehended this to be the case. I wrote to the Duke of Newcastle this morning all the intelligence of the rebels that was in my letters. Accounts of the battle are so hard from all hands of the commanders that they must be known in time, and what is the truth—I thought it not proper from me that any thing should come more than the intelligence of what is doing. Surely never any thing was like it, and all is confirmed by the soldiers and officers that have escaped this way.

"All agree that our men had orders not to fire till they had the word from their officers, but that no orders were ever given by the General, or he seen after the first fire. The general officers being gone, the men fired at random, some one shot, some more, not any above two; they say they were well used, but are all sent prisoners to Perth, the officers on parole; one of those mentioned in the enclosed copy was your neighbour, Mrs. Wilson's son, Captain Tatton. All accounts agree in this, that Gardner did not quit his horse, but died like a man of honour, as did his Lieut.-Coll. behave till he was wounded, Lord Lowdon, and some others; and I think there seems no doubt but that if the superior officers had done their duty, they would have given an end to this rebellion, by vanquishing these ruffians. A clergyman of the Church of Scotland, with whom I am a little acquainted by his having desired the use of my study sometimes, I applied to to give us intelligence if any partys came the midland road, near which he lies; he went himself to see what could be learned, but got not into Edinbrough; however he met with the same accounts of the battle, and I cannot help telling you a story he relates of old Lord Mark Kerr, who was in Berwick when Brigadier Fowlks, and Coll. Lasselles come there; he saies the night of the battle, this old General asked them very gravely where the army was,—they looked confounded, and said, totally routed;—he held up his hands, "*Good God! I have seen some Battles, heard of many, but never of the first news of a defeat being brought by the General Officers before.*" In short, sad it is to say, but we learn no account but that the General Officers being run away at the first fire of the Highlanders, the men were almost left to themselves, made a little resistance, and submitted, so that all was over in a quarter of an hour. On Sunday was sen-net none of the ministers of Edinbrough preached, tho' they had liberty, provided they did not pray for the King *Nominatim:* but there was a sermon in the West Kirk out of the city, which lays under the protection of the guns of the castle,—there we are told Mr. Mc. Vicar, the minister, prayed as follows,—'*O Lord, bless and direct our King, we mean King George the Second, our only lawful and rightful King; but as for this young man who is come here seeking a crown, and disturbing the peace of the country, disappoint his designs against us, but for a' that* '*Give him a crown of glory, good Lord.*' There was on the other hand an officer of the name of Cameron, who was wounded in the battle, and soon after died, but had time enough to desire his friends to carry his duty to his master and to tell him his grandfather had died fighting for his grandfather: that his father had lost his life at Sheriff Muir in the service of his father; and that he was dying of the wounds he had received in his service; and his last desire was that he would send for his only son about twelve years old, put his sword into his hand, and let him know it was his desire he should spend his life in the same service. So deeply is this evil rooted in the Highlanders! The strength of the rebels cannot be known whilst they stay in Edinbrough, they take so many stratagems to magnify their numbers, as sending them out in the night to come in in the morning with any new men, and calling them all fresh supplies, and several other such tricks. The clergyman I mentioned tells me that Kelly who was in Bishop of Rochester's plott is the only confidant of this young man's secrets.

"The Dragoons were mostly Irishmen; many run to the enemy, and have listed, as a soldier tells me who came in to-day that escaped from Edinbrough last Sunday; and very likely they are Irish Papists. I fancy I have tired you as well as myself, but I love to obey your commands to the utmost of my power; that you do not hear more constantly is from the continual hurry I am in, every thing material you shall have from,

"Good Mr. Dean,

"Your most obliged and obedient servant,

"JOHN WAUGH.

"Carlisle, October 2, 1745."

"P.S.—The demand on the City of Glascow has been renewed, and compounded for 5000 pound, and £500 in Tartins,—it was at first £15000.

"The officers I talked with did not know Brigadier Fowlks, he having only joined them at Dunbar; nor has his name, that I remember, been mentioned particularly in any letters but that from which I tell you the story, only he should have commanded the horse. Lasselles and General Cope are named by all."

[FIRST INCLOSURE.]

"To the Provost of Dumfries.

'"Holyrood House, 26th Sept., 1745.

"'Sir,—

"'You are hereby ordered upon ye. receipt of this to repair to the Secretary's Office in the Palace of Holyrood House, there to have the contribution to be paid by the Town of Dumfries for his Highness's use ascertained, which shall be done according and in proportion to the duties of Excise arising out of the said town of Dumfries; for the payment of which said contribution the said duty shall be assigned. This you are ordered upon pain of rebellion forthwith to obey.

"'By his Highness's command,

"'J. C. MURRAY."'

[SECOND INCLOSURE.]

"'Mr. Goldie to Dr. Waugh.

"'Reverend Sir,—

"'My last private accounts from Edinbrough bear yt. they have reason to believe very great body's are coming from the North, tho' few are yet arrived. Several people of Estates there will also join; tho' my correspondent dares not yet venture to name them, till he knows farther. He adds that a great many of the best sense there now judge it a country cause, and will either join privately or publicly so soon as they hear of a landing; at any rate he believes these folks will proceed to London if they can make out 10,000 effective men. He says farther, no rising will be in England till they get there, and yt. he understands many are at London waiting the event of the engagement with Cope, and then to declare. That some part of the Highlanders have deserted with the booty they got at the battle, and that they have no open pillaging at Edinburg yet, but a good many private robberies. Thus far my correspondent who, I fear, begins to have some symptoms of the Epidemical madness yt. prevails at present; however, he is extremely honest, and I dare venture to say this is the language of the party. The *Mercury* of Friday last, published by authority, contains some alterations in the accounts formerly published of the battle and their proceedings. 'The Princes army found £4000 sterling in General Cope's military chest. Several serjeants and corporals, with a vast many private men have entered into ye. Prince's service, so that with the volunteers who come in, the clerks of the office have not leisure to eat, drink, or sleep, by enlisting. Those Sergeants and Corporals are now beating up for volunteers to serve P—— Ch——s. A great many of the Dragoons of Hamilton and Gardner's Regiment's have also enlisted, and we hear all are to be incorporated with the Prince's squadrons. Ou Wednesday the following persons, who were prisoners in Canongate, were brought up and committed to ye. City jail, suspected to have diswaded the private men prisoners from enlisting in ye. Prince's army, in all 50, being sergeants, corporals, and some other private men. The army is encamped or encamping at Dudingstown, are forming several troops of horse, and have sent into ye. country several detachments of Horse and Foot.

"'They have been from their first rising highly favoured with glorious weather. The season even in this month of September is more mild and comforting than it has been in June for the last half century.' N.B. The battle was termed at Gladsmuir, and we have this puff about the weather to bring it within a Rhapsody called the prophecys of Thomas Learmouth, commonly called Thomas the Rhymer 'His R——l H—— s, whose robust and hardy constitution supports his natural inclination to fatigue and hardships, lay all last night in a soldier's tent, at the camp, preferring that tent to the Royal Palace of Holyrood House' Follows an extract of a letter from *Berwick, Sept.* 25:—'Coll. Herchet is landed here from Holland, with 7,220 Dutch forces; they seem mostly Papists, use the Romish ceremonies, and ask where they may have mass: they are tolerable men, but much fatigued Since Gen. Cope arrived here with a part of 2 Regt. of Dragoons from the battle in East Lothian, we have been in the utmost consternation. Some give out that they were attacked with 16,000 men, 10,000 of which were French in Highland dress; but others affirm that know the French yt. they were not capable of attacking or acting as the Highlanders did upon that occasion. Gen. Lord Mark Ker is here, as is ye. Master of Forbes, and Coll. Lascelles, who is said to have escaped after being taken at the battle by putting up the White Cockade; people talk variously of the reasons of the defeat of Gen. Cope's army, tho' there are who quietly ascribe all to the strength of Steel.' All advices from the North agree, that there is nothing to be seen in town or country but people with White Cockades, and even the ladies have fixed them on their head-dress. Several private men and some of the volunteers that were with Gen. Cope, as also two officers of Lee's who have broke their parole, are come forward to you: they got a letter from our provost to your Mayor, and expected one from me; but this I shifted, as I could by no means approve of their couduct, equally contrary to the rules of war and honour; and I could not refrain from asking the gentlemen whether they did not think the other prisoners would be more severely treated on their account, but could get no satisfying answer to my question. However, they, one and all agree that there was no conduct in our General, that they were made to believe ye. Highlanders would only give one fire, and then run off, but when they saw their behaviour a panic seized the whole army, indeed such of them as I have seen seem to carry the remains of it about with them; they wanted bread, had no manner of intelligence. So that they were persuaded the Highlanders had in the night moved off towards Hadington, and were not sparing of giving the epithets of cowardly rascals, &c., when they were just upon them; they all agree that none of their drums beat, nor was one word of command given; and, in short, it is true (tho' incredible when the enemy was at hand) they were surprised, and before they could recover themselves the affair was over. Our men complain that they wanted their swords, which had been all left at Stirling; but if they could not defend themselves with screwed bayonets, the swords, or rather cutlasses, used in the army would have stood them in little stead. I am ignorant in these matters, but am humbly of opinion that if the first rank had some long instruments wherewith to keep the Highlanders at bay, till those behind them had time to load again, they would do great service; for I am told they beat down the bayonets, and being once entered, these can be of no great use. The other officers are to be confined at Perth. Letters are sent by common Edinburgh Cadys from the new Secretary of State to all the Provosts of Burghs in this corner of Scotland, requiring them to repair to the Secretary's Office immediately to settle the contributions to be paid by the several Burghs, under the pain of rebellion. This is carrying matters with a very high hand, but what can be done, to comply or refuse are equally hazardous. Are the mighty promises of making us a free and happy people to be thus fulfilled? I believe the demand will not be complied with till it be renewed with an armed force, nor indeed can it without exposing to the rigour of the law.

"'How will the English like our Scotts way of levying money? You got once a King from us, will you long for such another? If a party come here your humble servant must retire. They know us all by head mark, and it is not unlikely, but on second thoughts, two or three of us may come your way.

"'I am ever, Reverend Sir,

"'Yours sincerely,

"'Oct. 1st, 1745. "'J. G.'"

"*For Dr. Bettesworth, Dean of the Arches—These.*

"Good Mr. Dean,—

"I have been from home all this week, setting forward an address from the Bishop, Deputy Lieutenants, Justices of Peace, Gentlemen, Clergy, and Freeholders of the Countys of Westmoreland, and Cumberland; as the Bishop could not attend the meetings, I was obliged to do it in his name, which has prevented my writing to you since my last. The blockade was soon taken off the Castle of Edinbrough after the Castle had fired on their works and made two successful sallys, and a lodgement on the Castle Hill which commanded the street; so that there can be no reason to be in pain for the Castle. We hear nothing of the Rebels stirring from thence, they are said to be joined by numbers, but the accounts are very uncertain. Kelly, who, I think, all now agree was chief-confident to this young pretender, went, I am told, soon after the battle to France, but is not yet returned. Mc. Donald and Mc. Cleod are said to be coming up with their clans to join; I hope soon to be able to send you better news from Scotland, as the King's forces by the accounts we have will be able to march forward next week through Yorkshire; when they get as far as Newcastle, I hope our fears will be over. All the prisoners taken at Tranent are sent into the Highlands. I doubt they will be in a terrible situation.

"I am, good Mr. Dean,

"Your most obliged and obedient servant,

"JOHN WAUGH.

"Carlisle, October 12, 1745."

"A letter yesterday, dated the 10th, from Newcastle, said the forces were not arrived from Holland, but hourly expected. P.S. Since I wrote this I have seen a letter from Edinbrough; the Rebels, by the account given, are growing strong, tho' their numbers cannot be known whilst they stay, nor their motions guessed at, they keep their secrets so well; the post will not allow me to give you any more particulars."

The county addresses to which Dr. Waugh alludes in his preceding letter were as follows:—

"*To the King's Most Excellent Majesty.*

"The humble address of the Bishop of Carlisle, the Deputy-Lieutenants, Justices of Peace, Gentry, Clergy, and Freeholders of the County of Cumberland.

"We, your Majesty's most dutiful and loyal subjects, the Lord Bishop of Carlisle, the Deputy-Lieutenants, Justices of Peace, Gentry, Clergy, and Freeholders of the county of Cumberland, humbly beg leave to approach your royal throne with hearts full of the warmest gratitude and joy for your most seasonable and safe return to these your dominions. With equal ardour and sincerity we offer our congratulations on the success of your Majesty's arms in the reduction of Cape Breton, a conquest not less glorious than important to us; and in the happy event, under God, your Majesty's consummate prudence and continued labours to restore the liberty and tranquillity of Europe have produced, in placing the imperial crown upon the head of one who, we have the strongest reason to believe, will be both able and inclinable to establish such a balance of power as may sufficiently defend our allies from all the insults of the common enemy.

"A deep sense of the many blessings we enjoy under your Majesty's just, mild, and gracious government, obliges us to express our utter detestation and abhorrence of each wicked effort to deprive us of them; particularly of the present absurd and unnatural attempt to impose on us a foreign, Papish, frequently abjured Pretender to the crown of the realm.

"On this extraordinary occasion we most humbly intreat your Majesty to accept our fresh assurances of duty and unshaken loyalty; our solemn engagements of endeavouring to exert our utmost zeal for the protection of your Majesty's most sacred person; the support of your government; the preservation of our happy constitution in church and state; and we shall not fail to implore the divine favour to continue their invaluable blessings to us thro' the prosperity of your illustrious house, in which we firmly trust they are included; and thereby perpetuate the same to our posterity."

The following address was also sent up from the city. The tone of it forms a rather laughable contrast with the account to be hereafter given of the doings of the citizens.

"The humble address of the Mayor, Recorder, Aldermen, Bailiffs, Clergy, and Citizens of the City of Carlisle.

"May it please your Majesty—We your Majesty's most dutiful and loyal subjects, the Mayor, Recorder, Aldermen, Bailiffs, Clergy, and Citizens of the City of Carlisle, beg leave to congratulate your Majesty on your safe arrival into your British dominions; and on the success of your Majesty's arms at Cape Breton; a conquest which we hope will be as lasting and beneficial to these kingdoms as it has been glorious to your Majesty's forces.

"Permit us also, dread Sovereign, to express our grateful acknowledgements for your unwearied care and pains in settling the balance of power in Europe, by placing the Grand Duke of Tuscany on the Imperial Throne; an event which, we hope, by the blessing of God, will be the means of baffling the ambitious designs, and reducing the exorbitant power of France, and humbling the pride of its perfidious monarch, the inveterate enemy of the Protestant interest, and the common disturber of the peace and tranquillity of Europe.

"We are truly sensible of the many great and invaluable blessings we and all your Majesty's subjects enjoy under your Majesty's mild and auspicious government.

"The preservation of our holy religion, our laws, and liberties, and whatever is dear to us is, under God, the happy consequence of the establishment of your illustrious house upon the throne of these kingdoms; every attempt therefore against your Majesty must necessarily fill the hearts of all true Englishmen with the utmost horror. Permit us then, great sir, to express our indignation at the audacious and unnatural rebellion that the son of an abjured and Popish pretender is now fomenting and carrying on in Scotland; and our greatest abhorrence that any of your Majesty's Protestant subjects who have experienced the fruits of your royal clemency and enjoyed the blessings of your and your royal father's reigns, should basely desert to the standard of that insolent invader.

"Upon this extraordinary and unexpected occasion, we beg leave to give your Majesty fresh assurances of our sincere attachment to your Majesty and your Royal Family; and that we will, to the utmost of our power, contribute our endeavours to defend your Majesty's person and Government against the Pretender and his adherents, and against all your enemies whatsoever.

"And we cannot but look upon it as a distinguished happiness that we have an opportunity of returning your Majesty our sincerest

thanks for that particular share of confidence reposed in us at this dangerous juncture, in being honoured with your royal mandate for arming ourselves against the disturber of your Majesty's reign. And we hope, should the public enemy approach us, that this important trust will not have been bestowed in vain; but that it will enable us to give a surer proof than words can convey, of our firm attachment to your majesty's interest.

May your Majesty's reign be long and prosperous; and that the British sceptre may never be wrested out of the hands of your august and illustrious family, is the ardent prayer of your Majesty's most dutiful and loyal subjects."

These addresses were presented by Lord Lonsdale, together with one of similar import from the county of Westmoreland.

On the 11th of October, Colonel Durand arrived at Carlisle, to take the command of the King's forces there.

"Dr. Waugh to the Dean of the Arches.

"Good Mr. Dean,—

"By some accounts I had last Monday night, from one of the ministers of Edinbrough, and some other gentlemen from that place, who were volunteers there, and forced, on that account, to leave the country, I hoped the rebels had been dispirited and out of hopes of foreign assistance; but our letters, yesterday, bring that their numbers increase daily, and that they are in constant expectation of a landing of foreign forces: that there had been taken out of a ship, come into Montrose, Monday night, the 7th inst., eighty cartload of arms, ammunition, &c.; and it is believed money also, which is all on the way to Edinbrough—the certain particulars not yet known; and that the Master of Strathallan, with eighty officers are landed out of that ship. Seventy gentlemen are said to come up from Bamfe, Aberdeen, and Buchan, with the Lord Pitsligow; and that others are come and coming, who seem to be very resolute to die or conquer. Lord Lovat's people are coming up, he having wrote that he can hinder neither them nor his son from joining; and in his letter saies many of the clans are arming—as

Mc.Creas, Mc.Cleans, Mc.Phersons, &c.—a long catalogue. A few days after the battle Kelly is now said to have sailed from Montrose in a small vessel. Another letter saies, "We have yet no certain account when the army will march, or the route they will take to England; they are in daily expectation of a landing of the Irish brigade and other two regiments from Dunkirk, several of the officers having landed last Monday at Montrose, and with them a great many arms, ammunition, &c.; and it is believed, money." We were alarmed yesterday with a party of seventy or eighty horse, sent to this side to levy contributions; but after taking what they could find for their purpose from Duke Douglas, they returned to Edinbrough, which does not look as if they intended to take this route. I think I have no more news of importance to send you this post, and not much time to spare. We are making all possible preparations for the defence of this town, under the direction of Coll. Durand. We did not hear from Newcastle the forces are landed, but hope they are.

"I am, good Mr. Dean,

"Your mo. obed. Servt.,

"JOHN WAUGH.

"Carlisle, Oct. 17, 1845."

"For the Dean of the Arches.

"Good Mr. Dean,—

"All the news we have from Scotland by this post is that two Gentlemen of Dumfries who have been some days in Edenbrough to try to learn something certain of the Motions of the Rebels are returned and say "that the Rebels are still about Edenbrough, but give out that they are to march very soon; that to conceal their rout, they send part of their Baggage back the way they came, and parties of their men a quite contrary way." These are the words of the provost of Dumfries' letter. As we have no account from any hand of their making any considerable Motion since the party to Dalkeith, we conclude they are still in their old quarters.

"I am Sir,

"Your most obedt. Servant,

"JOHN WAUGH.

"Carlisle, Oct. 31st, 1745."

"*For the Dean of the Arches.*

"By a letter this morning from the Postmaster of Dumfries I have the following accounts. That his Majestie's Birth Day was celebrated with great solemnity at Glascow, and that a party of Highlanders that were in that Town went off the night before to avoid a scuffle with the mob. That it was said Dundonald went in on Saturday and had his horse wounded and his guide killed at ye. west port. That we should soon hear of a considerable body drawn together by my Lord Lowdon at Inverness. That it was talked in Edenbrough the Army would move on Thursday last. This is taken from a letter he saw that came, as I apprehended, from Edenbrough that day; but in a postscript he saies a person is just arrived from thence with an account that the army of the Rebels marched to Dalkeith on Thursday. The provost of Dumfries writes last night 'that a Gentleman of that Town was just arrived from Edenbrough, who came out last Thursday about 12 o'clock at noon, and brings advice that the Baggage, Artillery, Ammunition, &c., were upon Waggons and Carts going to Dalkeith, and that the whole army were in motion and preparing to march Southward; that they gave out they were to go by Kelso, and were resolved to meet Marshall Wade and give him Battle."

"Good Mr. Dean,—

"The above is a copy of what we have received this morning; I apprehend our danger is now at the height; they must move directly either this way, or back to the Highlands. I have no notion of their meeting Marshall Wade's army; as this is our situation, I have been in much hurry this morning, having sent to Dumfries to desire fresh accounts whether their intelligence is confirmed or not; and I have got a very intelligent Clergyman of the Church of Scotland to send proper persons to Selkirk, &c., to learn what can be known from that side; which, with my other letters, has taken up so much of my time that it will be my excuse for this letter.

"I am, Good Mr. Dean,

"Your most obedient servant,

"JOHN WAUGH.

"Carlisle, Nov. 2nd, 1745."

"*To the Bishop of London.*

"My Lord,—

"We are in great hurry and confusion here on the receipt of the inclosed letters, which came in in the night, and this morning we have sent an express to M. Wade with copies, and I have sent the Duke of Newcastle copies likewise; we are all preparing for the defence of this place, though we have no garrison but the Militia of the two countys, the Townsmen, and two Company's of Invalids. Your Lordship will pardon my writing in some confusion as I have been up most part of the night being called up at the first express's arrival. I am, my Lord, begging your Lordship's prayers for our deliverance in this time of danger,

"Your Lordship's most dutiful and obedient humble servant,

"JOHN WAUGH.

"Carlisle, Nov. 4th, 1745.

"No. 1.—Is from the Duke of Buccleugh's Chief Steward at Langholm.
"No. 2.—Is from the Provost of Annan.
"No. 3.—From the Postmaster of Dumfries.
"No. 4.—From the Provost of Dumfries.
"No. 5.—From a Merchant in that Town."

[INCLOSURE 1.]

"'Dear Sir,—

"'This moment I have an express from Moffat, advising that my correspondent there has certain information this morning that 1,800 Highlanders were at Peebles last night, and that a great many gentlemen were at Broughton, which is Mr. Murray's house, six miles from Peebles, escorted by 60 horse. He informs that the whole are moving, and that he is apprehensive this country will certainly receive a visit. This according to my promise, I send you by express, and remain,

"'Dear Sir,

"'Your most affectionate humble Servant,

"'JO. BOSTON.

"'Lang. Castle, Sunday, 7 at night.

"'To John Goldie, Esq., at Carlisle.

"'To be opened by Dr. Waugh, Chancellor of Carlisle.'"

[INCLOSURE 2.]

"'Moffat, 3rd Nov., 1745, 8 o' the morning.

"'I this moment have got notice which seems to be pretty certain, that 1,800 men of the Highlanders were last evening at Peebles, and that their whole army was in motion. There were also several persons of distinction at John Murray's house at Broughton, who were escorted there by 60 horsemen; this news comes to me by a gentleman who came from the Crook this morning, which I thought convenient to notify to you by this express, as I am afraid they are all to be this way.

"'I am in haste, yours,

"'J. G.'"

"'Rev. Sir,—

"'The above is a copy of a letter I have this night received from Jo. Graham at Moffat, which I think proper to acquaint you of; I have also a letter from a gentleman in this neighbourhood this afternoon wherein he says,—

he is sorry to hear that the rebel's train of artillery is arrived, and a very large one it is; I have wrote to him to know what particular information he has of this, but have not yet got his answer. Our magistrates have just now despatched two persons Northward for intelligence of the rebel's motions, and upon their return either Provost Johnson or I shall write you,

"'I am, with due respect,

"'Yours, &c.,

"'B. B."

"'Annan, 3rd Nov., 1745.

"'To the Rev. Dr. Waugh, Chancellor of Carlisle.'"

[INCLOSURE 3.]

"'November 3rd.

"'This serves chiefly to enclose the within papers. You'll have all the news no doubt from other hands, that about 4,000 or 5,000 of the Highlanders came last night to Peebles, first 1,800, and then about 3,000, with 150 cartload of baggage and artillery. This makes it pretty plain that notwithstanding all their boasts, they do not intend to meet our troops, but to get past them into England either by Kelso or through this country. My compliments to the Chancellor. I received his last night.

"'J. G.

"'To John Goldie, Esq., at Carlisle.

"'To be opened by Dr. Waugh, Chancellor of Carlisle.'

(Note by Dr. Waugh.)

"The papers mentioned were the Edinburgh newspapers sent to Mr. Wade."

[INCLOSURE 4.]

"'Dumfries, 3 Novr., 1745.

"'Sir,—

"'I have the favour of your's of last post. The enclosed is a copy of the intelligence I have just now received. One of the gentlemen are with me who says he sent an express from Moffat to Genl. Wade with the same account. But in case that express should be stopt by the way, pray do you dispatch another messenger, as there will now be more safety on your borders; as I have so much to write and so many expresses to send off, I have only to add that I am with the greatest respect, Sir,

"'Your most obedient humble servant,

"'GEO. BELL.

"'Please communicate this to the Gov. and the Mayor.

"'To the Revd. Dr. Waugh, Chancellor of Carlisle.

(The inclosed is as follows):—

"'Two gentlemen, who can be depended on, in riding between Moffat and the Crook, on Saturday, 2nd Nov., after five at Night, met a countryman about three miles from the Crook, who said he was going to Annandale. Upon asking the news of him he told them he had come from Peebles, and that before he came away the Provost had got a message sent him by the rebels, to prepare meat, drink, and lodging, that evening, for 1,800 men. That great preparations were also that night making at Broughton, where some persons of distinction were arrived, escorted by 60 horse, one of these gentlemen proceeded on his journey towards Edinbrough, and the other returned to Dumfries, who relates that on Sabbath the 3rd, at ten o'clock, forenoon, he was overtaken at Moffat by another man riding express from Peebles, of whom his friend had taken the opportunity of writing a letter, that he might call upon him at Moffat, and there that express told him, He left Peebles about two o'clock, Sabbath morning, and that the above-mentioned 1800 men, with 150 carts, with baggage, ammunition, &c., were come there on Saturday night, and a little before he left the town a larger body came up, which he was informed were to the number of 4,000 men, and of this an express was immediately sent to General Wade from Moffat. A gentleman who had gone from Galloway to Stirling for intelligence in his way home on Sabbath forenoon, further reports that as the French baggage, arms, &c., that had come into Montrose had been brought to Perth, horses were there pressed, under pain of fire and sword, to convey it to Aloa, on Sabbath, the 27th October, and that night began to ferry over their baggage with great joy, and continued doing so to Monday and Tuesday; but General Blakeney having notice that the rear was to pass on Wednesday morning, despatched Capt. Abercrombie, with some soldiers and countrymen to attack them, which they accordingly did; wounded some; took 14 or 16 prisoners (ten of whom the gentlemen saw); took 14 cows, 3 or 4 horses, and a great deal of baggage, arms, &c.; stript the prisoners; got several purses of gold and money, and a vast deal of letters, which it's supposed will afford Genl. Blakeney some useful discovery: a great deal of Highland wives were there, whom they also stript and got letters and money on them; they were all brought into Stirling on Wednesday, between 7 and 8 at night, and carried to the Castle, where the General saw them next day. He further adds that there were along with the baggage from the Montrose ship 24 engineers, who us'd the countrymen very rudely who carried it into Aloa, that Glengyle with 150 men and 7 ps. of canon that had been mounted on the Highlander's battery at Aloa was gone to take possession of the castle of Doun 5 miles beyond Stirling, and that Genl. Blakeney was resolved to go there and attack them.

[INCLOSURE 5.]

"'Dumfries, 3 Novr., 1745.

"'We have advice this day that 1,800 Highlanders were at Peebles yesterday with a large quantity of baggage, and were followed by 3,000 more. Several coaches and chases were come to Broughton with a good many of their principal men and officers. We shall have a fuller account of this matter to-morrow morning. Wednesday last Genl. Blakeney detached from Stirling Castle a party of the garrison with a number of country people to a foard above Stirling where a body of Highlanders were passing with a good deal of baggage, arms, money, and ammunition, which they took from them and brought to Stirling Castle with 16 prisoners.

"'Yours, &c.

"'To James Ferguson, Esq., at Carlisle. To be opened by Dr. Waugh, Chancellor of Carlisle.

The Provost of Dumfries to Dr. Waugh.

"Dumfries, 4th Novr. 1745, at 5 in the Evening.

"Sir,—

"The enclosed is a copy of a letter just now received from my correspondent at Jedburgh—please forward copys to Whitehaven, Penrith, &c., which will very singularly oblige, Sir, your most

"Obedient Servant,

"GEO. BELL.

"I send you General Wade's proclamation, copies whereof please cause fix on your publick mercat places.

"Excuse haste."

[INCLOSURE.]

"'Jedburgh, Nov. 3, 1745, Eleven at Night.

"'Dear Sir,—

"'I was obliged by yours which came to hand yesternight. The two gentlemen with whom it came went for Berwick this morning. In obedience to your orders I have just now dispatched an express where you directed. As I now run the bearer to you to acquaint you that the whole Highland army have marched, the last of them from Dalkeith and Newbottle this morning—lie this night at Lawder—their main body moves from Peebles to Selkirk tomorrow, and so forward by Langholm for the west of England, whether they'll visit you by the way, and whether the party at Lawder will hold thence to Selkirk or come this length before they turn west that they may the better cover and conceal the march of their main body, is more than I have learned. But as this intelligence I can depend upon, I thought it worth while to run this express with it.

"'I am, &c.'"

"*The Provost of Dumfries to Dr. Waugh.*

"Dumfries, 5th November, 1745, 8 at Night.

"This moment I have advice, by an express from Moffat, that a Quarter Master belonging to the Highlanders came there about one of the clock this day to secure quarters for 4,000 Foot and 600 horse, and the messr. says he saw them within half a mile of the town before he came away. We expect them or a part of them this way to-morrow. I beg you will dispatch expresses to Penrith, Kendall, Lancaster, and Whitehaven; and am most respectfully your most obedient servant

"G. B.

"The messr. says this party is commanded by the Duke of Perth, Lord Geo. Murray, and Lord Kilmarnock.

"To the Rev. Dr. John Waugh,
Chancellor of Carlisle."

Dr. Waugh to the Dean of the Arches.

(No date.)

"The clergyman mentioned sends word they advance this way very fast. Send no letters."

The season for preparation was now closed, and the hour of trial at hand; yet little or nothing had been done by the Government for the defence of Carlisle during the six weeks that had elapsed since the defeat of General Cope at Preston Pans gave a formidable character to the rebellion. This apathy, it is difficult to account for. It might be that Carlisle was not considered a place of importance, and there is a note by Dr. Waugh on the minutes of the Court Martial upon Colonel Durand, by which it appears that the Secretary-at-War did hold such an opinion; yet it seems to be inconsistent with a due knowledge of the position and history of the town. Or it might be that the prolonged inactivy of the Prince after his victory at Preston Pans induced a notion that he would not venture upon an invasion of England. It is certain that his delay at Edinburgh was most fatally inconsistent with the character of his enterprise. He had taken the Government unawares. His conduct in first eluding and afterwards signally defeating Cope had dispelled the belief at first entertained that he was a rash inexperienced youth, who was madly rushing on certain ruin; and had suddenly re-acted in producing a general apprehension of his considerate and successful daring. Had he marched to England on the heels of Cope's defeated force, the result of his enterprise might have been different; but he paused, and suffered the opportunity to

CARLISLE, FROM STANWIX BANK, 1745.

pass away, never to return. The delay was fatal. It impaired the moral effect of his victory; it unsettled the growing impression of his able conduct; it confirmed the timidity of the English Jacobites, which the prompt advance of a victorious army might have overcome; and it gave time to the Government to collect and concentrate its scattered force, and to re-assure its friends. If it also produced an impression that an invasion of England would not be hazarded, that was comparatively of little moment.

When at length it was resolved to take that step, the route became a question for debate.

It was at first the wish of the Prince to march straightway to Berwick, and to meet and fight Marshal Wade in Northumberland; but he yielded to the advice of Lord George Murray to take the western line of road by Carlisle. Accordingly, on the 3rd of November, the Highlanders broke up from Edinburgh and marched southwards, in three divisions: one by Broughton and Peebles; one by Lauder, Selkirk, and Hawick; and one by Kelso. On the 7th, the last-mentioned division had reached Stonegarthside, on the border of Cumberland, and was supposed to be intending for Brampton through Bewcastle, but turned to the right towards Longtown. On the 8th, the middle division joined, part of the Cavalry came to Longtown, and that night the Prince was at David Murray's house, at Riddings. On the 9th, about three o'clock in the afternoon, a party of 50 or 60, well mounted, and supposed to be officers, appeared on Stanwix Bank, immediately opposite to Carlisle; it being the Martinmas Saturday, market day, and the country people thronging the road on their return from market, the garrison could not fire upon the party for fear of injuring the market people also. They, therefore, had time to reconnoitre in safety for about half an hour; when, the country people having dispersed, the garrison fired from the ten gun battery of the Castle, and obliged them to retire. That afternoon, part of the Peebles division, with the artillery, came up. The Prince, with part of the army, marched down the right bank of the river Eden to Rockliff, crossed there at the Peat Wath, and was at Moorhouse that night: next day, Sunday, the 10th, the remainder of the Peebles Division came up; two more regiments, under Lord Ogilvy and Gordon of Glenbucket, crossed at Cargo and Grinsdale; and the city was invested on all sides—one body, under the Duke of Perth, approaching by Stanwix Bank; another, under the Marquis of Tullibardine, by Shaddongate; and a third under the Prince himself by Blackhall fields and St. Nicholas. A thick fog, which prevailed during the morning, cleared off about mid-day, and disclosed to the garrison the three bodies thus approaching the the town. They immediately opened a fire from the four-gun-battery upon the Marquis of Tullibardine's division in Shaddongate; and he was heard to say:—"*Gentlemen, we have not metal for them. Retreat;*" which they did. The Citadel guns were fired on the Prince's division, and the white flag was observed to fall; the ten-gun-battery fired upon the Duke of Perth's division,—which also retired. The fog then came on again, and obscured their movements from the observation of the garrison, who remained in expectation of a general assault. That, however, was not attempted. The Prince learning that Marshal Wade was expected to advance from Newcastle, determined to march to Brampton, where his Highlanders might have hilly ground for fighting, should the Marshal come on. He slept that night at Blackhall, and next morning marched with the bulk of the army, by way of Warwick Bridge, for Brampton. The force at Stanwix also retired on the north side of the river, in the same direction; and on the 12th all was quiet about Carlisle.

This general movement had the effect of deceiving both the garrison and Marshal Wade: the latter appears to have thought that the Prince was coming to attack him, and remained where he was instead of advancing to the relief of Carlisle: the former seem to have fancied that the Highlanders were gone. Mr. Pattinson, the deputy Mayor, flattering himself that he had turned the Highlanders, lost no time in making known to the government so important a piece of service. He immediately wrote off to the Lord Lieutenant, and the following announcement forthwith appeared in the *Gazette*:—

"*Whitehall, November* 15.

"A Letter dated the 12th Instant, from Mr. Thomas Pattinson, Mayor of Carlisle, brings Advice, that on Saturday Night, the 9th Instant, that City was surrounded by about 9,000 Highlanders; that at Three o'Clock that Afternoon, he the Mayor had received a Message from them, to provide Billets for 13,000 Men, and to be ready that Night; which he refused. That the next Day, at Three in the Afternoon, he received a Message in Writing from the Person stiling himself Prince Charles, and subscribed *Charles P. R.*, in the following Words:

"*Charles Prince of Wales, Regent of the Kingdoms of England, Scotland, France, and Ireland, and the Dominions thereunto belonging.*

BEING come to recover the King our Father's just Rights, for which we are arrived with all his Authority, we are sorry to find that you should prepare to obstruct our Passage: We therefore, to avoid the Effusion of English Blood, hereby require you to open your Gates, and let us enter, as we desire, in a peaceable Manner; which if you do, we shall take Care to preserve you from any Insult, and set an Example to all England of the Exactness with which we intend to fulfil the King our Father's Declarations and our own: But if you shall refuse us Entrance, we are fully resolved to force it by such Means as Providence has put into our Hands, and then it will not perhaps be in our Power to prevent the dreadful Consequences which usually attend a Town's being taken by Assault. Consider seriously of this, and let me have your answer within the

Space of two Hours, for we shall take any farther Delay as a peremptory Refusal, and take our Measures accordingly.

"*November the* 10th, 1745.

"Two in the Afternoon.

"*For the Mayor of Carlisle.*"

"That he the Mayor had returned no Answer thereto but by firing the Cannon upon them: That the said Pretended Prince, the Duke of Perth, with several other Gentlemen, lay within a Mile or two of the City; but that their whole Army was, at the Time of dispatching the above Advice, marched for Brampton, seven Miles on the high Road to Newcastle."

On Monday the 11th, the Prince's Life Guards are stated to have been at Naworth Castle, a seat of the Earl of Carlisle, three miles eastward of Brampton. Lord Carlisle's family were not resident there. The guards are described as being well dressed, good-looking men; and behaved with complaisance. On the 12th, Captain Hamilton came to Naworth to demand billets for 6,000—on which the guards began to look blank, and to secure their portables. About noon, several hundreds, described as a wretched, ill-looking, shabby crew, armed with targets, broad swords, muskets, &c., arrived; and seemed angry that no deference was paid to their flag. These, no doubt, were the "*Walie Dragles*" mentioned in Mr. Goldie's letter of the 15th September. That afternoon and next day they spent in shooting sheep, geese, &c., and robbing on the highway; their chiefs expressed great dissatisfaction, but could not restrain them. After two days spent in the neighbourhood of Brampton, finding that Marshal Wade did not move, a Council of War was held. The Prince, according to Lord George Murray's account, was inclined to march on and attack Wade. Some were for returning to Scotland till they were joined by a greater body of their friends, many having left upon the march. Lord George Murray himself proposed that a part of the army should go and besiege Carlisle, whilst the remainder should stay at Brampton. The Duke of Perth seconded this; and offered to undertake the Battery, if Lord George Murray would the blockade. This was unanimously agreed on, and forthwith carried into effect. On the morning of the 13th, six regiments of Highlanders, besides the Duke of Perth's, were mustered at Warwick Bridge. About one o'clock, came the Prince with his Guards, Lord George Murray, the Duke of Perth, with others of the leaders, and formed them in marching order; headed by the Prince and his Guards, who were 110 in number and well mounted, they marched to Warwick Moor, where they halted and attentively viewed the city. The Prince then returned, with his Guards, and the seven regiments marched straightway down to Carlisle, before which they arrived about three o'clock in the afternoon. Lord George Murray established his quarters at Harraby; the Duke of Perth with his regiment opened the trenches in the evening against the Eastern side of the town; and he himself and the Marquis of Tullibardine wrought at them in their shirts to inspirit the men.

In the Prince's household book there is a note that "*when the Prince was at Brampton he went one day to Squire Warwick's house and dined there.*" This was no doubt on the 13th, when the above muster was at Warwick Bridge. The family at Warwick Hall were of the Roman Catholic faith, and at heart attached to the Stuarts; but at this critical time the Squire, like the generality of the English Jacobites, timidly held aloof; and, with more of prudence than chivalry, was out of the way. Not so his lady; indeed, by all accounts the ladies in general were much more decided than the gentlemen. Mrs. Warwick was daughter of Thomas Howard, of Corby Castle, of a family which had fought and bled for Charles the First, and had retained its ancient faith, religious and political, spite of all reverses of fortune. Mr. Howard had been under suspicion in 1715; and though nothing tangible could be then found against him, yet his people appear to have acted. His huntsman, Oliver Hamilton, was out with Lord Derwentwater; was taken, and confined in Lancaster Castle for six years; and it was supposed that he could have implicated his master, but he faithfully resisted all solicitations to turn king's evidence. Mrs. Warwick, inheriting her father's principles, cordially hailed Charles Edward when he visited Warwick Hall. She received him in the "Oak Parlour," and entertained him with such shew of genuine affection and loyalty, that the young Prince, touched by the contrast it afforded with the cold backwardness of those from whom he probably had received invitations and promises of support, observed that these were the first christian people he had met with since he passed the border. At parting, Mrs. Howard was heard to exclaim, "*May God bless him.*"

The delay at Edinburgh, the apparently determined resistance of Carlisle, and the seeming retreat of the Highlanders from before its walls, no doubt deterred many from showing themselves at this period, who in their hearts wished well to his cause: yet, making allowance for every drawback, it must be confessed that the English adherents of the House of Stuart, when the opportunity was thus given them of rallying round their Prince, gave occasion for the remark that their loyalty to the exiled line was but speculative—a thing to talk of—to cabal, and plot about in opposition, and to embarrass the government; but not to peril their lives and property. It is generally believed that their *promises* of support were so numerous that the publication of them even at this day would astonish and offend too many families.

It is tolerably clear that on resuming their purpose of besieging Carlisle, the Highlanders did not anticipate an easy or a bloodless conquest. They had made preparation for an attempt by escalade; and the following letter of their Commander-in-Chief, Lord George Murray, written on the morning after the besieging force had commenced operations, shows that he did not expect to succeed without a struggle:—

"*Lord George Murray to the Duke of Athole.* *

"Haroby, 14th November, Five of the morning.

"Dear Brother,—

"I posted the men in the Villages so as to stop the communication to and from Carlisle, according to the note I gave to his Royal Highness; but I believe there must be some alteration this day, for I think of calling of Shian from Butcherby (where there is no occasion for a party) to reinforce this post and that commanded by Lord Nairn, as both will be pretty much exposed if the enemy should attempt to sally, and as they will be some miles distant from one another, so that no succour could go in time from the one post to the other, and quite at a distance from the rest of the army.

"Lord Nairn who is now at Blackhall must go to some place nearer Carlisle, and upon the road from thence to Whitehaven; but I can say nothing certain till the places be viewed this day after daylight.

"I am sorry to find that it is impossible to go on so quick with the battery of cannon as would have been wished. By the report of those I sent there the ground is marshy, and vastly too much exposed; and notwithstanding all the pains taken by the Duke of Perth, who is indefatigable in that service and who meets with unnumberable difficulties, I suspect the place pitched upon will not answer. But if the thing be prosecuted, I think it my duty to tell you, so as you may represent it to his Royal Highness, that the men posted upon the blockade of Carlisle will not expose themselves either in trenches or all night in the open air, within cannon shot, or even musket shot of the town, except it be in their turn with the

* The Marquis of Tullibardine. This nobleman in 1715, being then eldest son and heir of the Duke of Athol, was attainted for his share in the insurrection that year. The Duke his father obtained an Act of Parliament to settle the title and estate on his second son, who accordingly at this time enjoyed them; but the Marquis of Tullibardine was styled Duke of Athol by the Jacobites.

rest of the army, and that to be decided by lot who to mount that guard, first night, second, and so on. The way I would propose, if it be approved of by a council of war, is as follows: that 50 men be drafted out of each of the battalions that are at Brampton with proper officers, and at least two majors out of the six battalions, and be sent to quarter at Butcherby, which I believe is within a mile of the battery; and as I suppose 150 men will mount guard at the battery, these six battalions will furnish two guards; your men will furnish one; General Gordon and Lord Ogilvie's one; which in whole makes four guards or reliefs; and I think by that time the town will be either taken or the blockade removed. I don't mention the Duke of Perth's regiment because they have more than their turn of the duty already, besides furnishing workmen, &c., and for Colonel John Roy Stewart's regiments I suppose they have the guard of the equipage, &c., and they will perhaps be better able to furnish some workmen. If any thing be done of this nature, the sooner I hear of it the better. I am, ever dear brother, your most affectionate brother and faithful humble servant,

"GEORGE MURRAY."

This letter being laid before a Council of War, at Brampton, the same day, produced the following determination:—

"So soon as the whole body that now forms the blockade has taken their turn of the guards, the division of the army now here will march in a body and form the blockade; but no detachments can be sent from the different corps, nor do they think it fair to require them to do so, as they had all the fatigue and danger of the blockade in Edinburgh.

Brampton, 14th Nov., 1745."

Upon which Lord George Murray addressed the Prince thus:—

"15 Nov., 1745.

"Sir,

"I cannot but observe how little my advice, as a general officer, has any weight with your Royal Highness ever since I had the honour of a commission from your hands. I therefore take leave to give up my commission. But as I ever had a firm attachment to the royal family, and in particular to the King, my master, I shall go on as a volunteer, and design to be this night in the trenches as such, with any others that will please to follow me, though I own I think there are full few on this post already. Your Royal Highness will please order whom you think fit to command on this post and the other parts of the blockade. I have the honour to be, Sir, your Royal Highness's most faithful and humble servant,

"GEORGE MURRAY.

"Lord Elcho has the command till you please appoint it otherwise."

This resignation of the commander was not however persisted in. The speedy success of the operations against the town, no doubt had its healing effect for the time. On the morning of Friday the 15th, the trenches were pushed within 80 yards of the wall. An assault by escalade appears to have been intended; but before any thing was attempted the white flag was hung out, and an offer made to treat for surrender of the city. An express was despatched to the Prince at Brampton; who replied that he would not do things by halves; and that the city had no terms to expect unless the castle surrendered at the same time. In the afternoon this was acceded to. The terms were: That the town and castle with the artillery and magazines should be delivered up; that the men should lay down their arms in the Market Place; after which they should have passes to go where they pleased, on taking oath not to carry arms against the House of Stuart for a twelvemonth; that the city of Carlisle should retain all its privileges,—that they should deliver up all arms, &c., and also the horses of all such as had appeared in arms against the Prince. And that all deserters, particularly the soldiers that had enlisted with the Highlanders after the late battle at Preston Pans, and had fled to Carlisle, should be delivered up. The Duke of Perth immediately entered and took possession, and the next day proclaimed King James, attended by the Mayor and civil officers in their robes, with their sword and mace. It is stated that on this occasion the health of Prince Charles Edward as Regent being drunk, Mr. Dacre, who had commanded the troop of horse in the city, deliberately proposed the health of King George. The keys of the city were presented to the Prince at Brampton by the Mayor and Corporation on their knees; and on Monday the 18th November, Charles Edward made his entry into Carlisle seated on a white charger, and preceded by not less than an hundred pipers.

It is now proper to revert to those whom we left within the walls on the 9th, awaiting the Highlander's first approach; in order to explain this sudden and unexpected falling away of their apparently resolute determination to hold out.

CHAPTER II.

THE surrender of Carlisle, a walled and garrisoned town, with its Castle, artillery, and stores, before a battery was raised against it, was an event as unexpected as it was at first inexplicable. The news of the capitulation followed so closely upon Pattinson's announcement of the retreat of the Highlanders to Brampton, that the two appeared almost irreconcileable. No action, no assault, no accident had intervened. It went forth to the public almost in the same page of the *Gazette* that the rebels had quailed under the vigorous fire of the cannon of Carlisle, and yet had become masters of the place without bloodshed

Marshal Wade, who, on learning the return of the Highlanders from Brampton to invest Carlisle, had marched from Newcastle in order to give battle and relieve the town, and had proceeded as far as Hexham, there received advice of the surrender of the City and Castle, and immediately retraced his steps. The road southwards was therefore opened for the Prince, and his communication with Scotland secured.

The particulars of what had passed within the town to occasion this untoward result, were not fully nor accurately made known till some months afterwards. Meantime, the blame was cast by one upon another; it being on all hands admitted that much pusillanimity had been displayed.

Colonel Durand, the Commander, quitted the town immediately after the surrender, and proceeded to Bowes, on the Yorkshire road, from which place, on the 20th of November, he made the following report to General Folliot, the Governor of Carlisle:—

"Bowes, Nov. 20, 1745.

"Sir,

"The following is a short and true account of the manner by which the Rebels became possessed of Carlisle.

"On Saturday, Nov. 9th, the Rebels first appeared before Carlisle; and Nov. 14th, in the morning, I received a message in writing, signed by the officers of the Militia of Cumberland and Westmorland, acquainting me that having been lately extreamly fatigued with duty, in expectation of relief from his Majesty's forces, and it appearing that no such relief is now likely to be had, and not being able to do duty or hold out any longer, they were determined to capitulate; upon which I immediately went to them, with Capt. Gilpin and the rest of the officers of the Invalids, and did all that lay in my power to perswade them to change so rash a resolution, by representing the fatal consequences that might attend it, and the dishonour of treating with Rebels whilst they were in a condition of defending themselves; and solemnly protesting that I would never join in so unworthy an action; and some of them having taken notice of an intrenchment which the Rebels were that morning throwing up about 300 yards distance from the Citadel, I answered that I had carefully viewed the intrenchment they spoke of, and thought it was at too great a distance to be of any consequence; and besides, as it was not usual to carry on works in the day time, I imagined it was only done to intimidate the garrison; assuring them that if they would but stand by me, it was my opinion we might defend both City and Castle for some considerable time longer against the whole force of the rebels, as by the best accounts we had of them they had no cannon large enough to make a breach, and they knew all the ladders within seven miles round had been brought into the city; but they still continued fixed in their resolution, alledging that several of their men had deserted the preceding night over the walls, and the rest were so fatigued and intimidated, that they could not much depend upon them; and therefore they would send to capitulate immediately—for should they defer it till next morning, the City might probably be stormed that night and they all be put to the sword; and then sent to the Mayor to know if he would join with them. The Mayor upon that applyed himself to me to know what I would do; I told him I was determined to defend both the

City and Castle as long as I could. He answered he would do the same; but the Militia still persisted in their resolution, and said if the Mayor and inhabitants would not joyn with them, they would send and capitulate for themselves upon the best terms they could get. This struck such a pannick into some of the townspeople that they desired the Mayor would summons the inhabitants at the Town Hall, to consult what was proper to be done, which he immediately did; and the opinion of the majority then present was to defend the town; but the Militia still persisting in their resolution to capitulate, the townspeople at last agreed to join with them, and to send away to the rebels to desire a capitulation; upon which myself, Capt. Gilpin, and the rest of the officers of the Invalids, after protesting against it in the most solemn manner, retired into the Castle with the two Companys of Invalids and about 400 other men, who all then said they would join with me in defending the Castle to the last; but before eight o'clock the next morning they changed their resolution, and all left us to a man. Before I entered the Castle, and before the Mayor and the officers of the Militia could send out to capitulate, I took care to nail up ten pieces of cannon from 4 to 2 pounders that were placed upon the ramparts of the town; which, being light and easily moved, might as I apprehended have been of great service to the rebels. I had also taken care to lay in the Castle a sufficient quantity of provisions.

Nov. 15th, about 10 o'clock in the morning most of the principal inhabitants and officers of the Militia came to me to acquaint me that they had received an answer from the Rebels that unless the Castle was surrendered at the same time with the town they would immediately destroy the city with fire, and put all the inhabitants and militia, without distinction, to the sword; and desiring, for God's sake, that we would take it into consideration; and that the garrison of the castle might march out with all military honours, and both officers and men be at liberty to go wherever they pleased. I told them I would call a Council of War, and then we would give them an answer. I accordingly did call a Council of War whereof the following is a copy:—

"'*At a Council of War, holden in the Castle of Carlisle, Nov. 15th*, 1745.

"'The militia of the countys of Cumberland and Westmorland, as also the militia of the town of Carlisle, having absolutely, to a man, refused to defend the Castle; and the garrison consisting only of two companys of invalids, amounting to about eighty men, many of whom are extremely infirm, and the Castle very large, so that there are neither men to manage the guns nor man the walls; and the Mayor and inhabitants of the town, together with the officers of the militia, having sent to treat with the rebels, against the opinion and protest of Colonel Durand, Captain Gilpin, and the rest of the officers of the garrison, and being refused any terms, and threatening to destroy both town and Castle with fire and sword unless the Castle be surrendered—it is our opinion that, the Castle being not tenable, it is for his Majesty's service that it be abandoned; as it will be absolutely necessary for the preservation of the lives of his Majesty's subjects, who would otherwise be exposed to inevitable ruin. Given under our hands at Carlisle, this 15th day of Nov. 1745.

(Signed) "'J. DURAND.
"'JNO. BERND. GILPIN.
"'JNO. COWLEY.
"'JNO. HUTCHINSON.
"'JNO. SMITH.
"'FRAN. GATTON.'"

"I shall make no remarks upon this plain account of facts, but that when I speak in general of the militia of Cumberland and Westmorland I would except some officers who, I believe, would willingly have staid in the town if they could have prevailed upon the rest.

"I know nothing of the terms of capitulation, as I had no hand in it; but on the contrary solemnly protested against it, nor have I so much as seen it.

"I am now going to Marshal Wade to give him an account, and shall then return to London.

"As myself and the rest of the officers of the garrison flatter ourselves that we have done all that lay in our power for His Majesty's service for the preservation of the city and castle of Carlisle, we hope we shall have the honour of your approbation, which will be an infinite pleasure to us all, and in particular to, Sir,

"Your's, &c.,

"J. DURAND."

Dr. Waugh and his family, together with Mr. and Mrs. Tullie, his wife's relatives, and some others of the principal people of Carlisle, had also quitted the town; and had gone across Stanemoor to Barnard Castle, in order to keep clear of the Highlanders, who advanced into England by the Lancashire road. The following letter from Capt. Hutchinson, of the Invalids, to Dr. Waugh, at Barnard Castle, shows the reception of Colonel Durand's report in London:—

"*Capt. Hutchinson to Dr. Waugh.*

"Dear Sir,—

"Col. Durand desires his compliments to you, and would have writ to you himself; but having a great many other letters to write has not time; therefore desired me to acquaint you that he had the pleasure, at his arrival at this place, to receive a letter from General Folliot, whereof the following is a copy :—

"'Sir,—

"'I received your express from Barnard Castle last night, and immediately took it to the Duke of Newcastle, who carried it to the King, which gave great satisfaction to the King and Duke, and all of us; and they think you acted quite right, and that nobody else could have done better, tho' you were by all here condemned as capitulating with the rebels, which till this express came we had no certain account of. But I am proud now to find you right, and to have the occasion of answering your express in the manner above-mentioned—as for my part, I rested myself satisfied that you would act like yourself, and was certain you had more sense, prudence, and conduct than to be guilty of what was alleged of you, and defended your character to the last. This morning the 1st battalion of our regiment and the 1st battalion of the 3rd regiment marched from this place, and to halt at Lichfield, the 3rd Dec., till further order. His R. H. sets out on Tuesday next for the same place.

"'I am, Sir, your most humble Servant,

"'JOHN FOLLIOT.'"

"'London, Nov. 23rd, 1745.'"

"Col. Durand would be glad if you would send to his grace the Duke of Newcastle, as soon as you conveniently can, a full account of the late transactions at Carlisle, so that your letter may be in town before he arrives, which he thinks will be on Saturday next; and he will then take an opportunity of doing you all the justice and service that lays in his power, in acknowledgement for the many favours, civilitys, and services which he has received from you. Col. Durand joins with me in compliments to Mrs. Waugh, Mr. and Mrs. Tullie, and all friends. Col. Durand begs a thousand pardons for not waiting upon Mrs. Tullie, when at Barnard Castle, and hopes that she has forgiven him before this, for at that time it was not in his power, as I can witness. Col. Durand would be obliged to you if you would favour him with a line, directed to him at London, to acquaint him what time you writ to the Duke of Newcastle, that he may know whether he has received your letter before he waits upon the Grandees.

"I am, dear Sir,

"Your most obedt. humble Servant,

"T. HUTCHINSON.

"York, Nov. 30th, 1745."

Dr. Waugh accordingly addressed to the Duke of Newcastle the following letter :—

"*Dr. Waugh to the Duke of Newcastle.*

"Your Grace has great reason to be surprised that since the Rebels came before Carlisle I have never done myself the honour to give your Grace any account of what passed at and near ye. city: but I hope I shall be excused when your Grace is acquainted that till this post I have hardly had an opportunity to write a letter to your Grace; for during ye. time ye. Rebels were before us Mr. Pattinson denyed to me yt. he could send any expresses to London. After the Rebels got possession I was detained in town till near night on Sunday ye. 17th, to try me whether I would allow prayers to be read in ye. churches without naming the King; two messages from the Pretender's son, and one from their Duke of Perth being sent to me for that purpose, tho' I absolutely refused (and hope no such irregularity either has or will be committed at Carlisle). After the usual time of evening service was passed I was suffered to come away; I was on foot, and in a deep snow, and got a fall which gave me a little fit of the Gout in my hand; and before I reached Penrith I was again surrounded by the Rebels, so yt. it was with great difficulty I got to this place last Tuesday; till I arrived here I had no opportunity to send any letter; and since that I have been to wait on Field-Marshall Wade, which prevented my writing by the last post.

"The surrender of Carlisle in the manner it was done, and the difficultys that were made in the defence of it, are subjects yt. were so much to my dissatisfaction that I know not how to write upon them; tho' I am clear, as I was present at the material transactions, that ye. blame that is due lays in a very narrow compass. The Militia had undergone a good deal of fatigue; but so had the townspeople; and there were few gentlemen in town that had not bore as much as any one of their officers; would they have been directed by the gentleman who commanded us, none need have been so much fatigued; nor should we have had a fourth part of the alarms that were given, which indeed kept us on duty not only for six nights together, but allowed us little rest in the day time. We had once drove the Rebels off with honour, and were persuaded from all we could learn yt. whilst they believed we were resolved to make a vigorous defence they had no design to return. Whether they got accounts out of the town that some of the Militia officers were for retiring in the night of the 13th if Col. Durand would have suffered them, we can't be certain: but on the 14th they surrounded us again. I am no proper judge how long we could have defended the place against such a number of men; and know we had very small, if any, hopes of being relieved. But I am confident Col. Durand would have bore the last extremitys; and yt. the inhabitants would have held out as long as they could if the Militia officers would have stood by them; and that nothing could have prevailed on the town to capitulate when they did, but the impossibility of defending themselves after ye. Militia officers had assured them they would do no more duty, and would capitulate without them in the best manner they could for themselves, if the inhabitants would not join in the capitulation. Then indeed it was thought most advisable to save the town; and to prevent the inhabitants from, at best, being made prisoners. The misfortune was yt. most of the Militia officers came to our defence with great reluctance, and staid there from the first with as great unwillingness, and were constantly objecting ill usage from the Corporation, who I can't say did anything to oblige them: the art and address of Col. Durand in a great measure prevailed with them to do what they did. I wish he could have got them to have stood to their arms till a capitulation had been granted that might have procured them more honourable terms than they are said to have submitted to; as it was, all was at the mercy of the Rebels; and they soon showed that they had no more design to defend the Castle than the town. I don't know what the terms of the capitulation are, as I could not get a sight of it; but no promises of any kind that I heard of were required of the inhabitants; nor was any thing but arms, unless some horses, taken from them by authority,—tho' their effects are yet in danger, very little being removed before the Rebels came, great discouragement being given to the carrying things out, as it was thought the people's having their effects in town would make them more resolute in the defence of it; and we hoped we should be able to defend it till we could have been relieved. Your Grace's commands require me to give you an account, and justice to my townsmen and the gentleman who commanded us with the greatest prudence, temper, and resolution, oblige me to speak out: a disagreeable task it is to say what may throw blame on any gentleman; I wish I could have informed your Grace that all the Militia officers had behaved with as much resolution as some of them would have done could they have prevailed on the rest to have joined them. Then I verily believe I should have had a pleasing subject. Had we been assisted with a few regular forces, in all probability this had not happened."

Dr. Waugh also subsequently drew up a more detailed narrative of the whole matter; which, together with the proceedings of the Court Martial held upon Colonel Durand at a later period, may properly be here introduced, as more fully detailing the transactions within the city during the siege:—

"*Dr. Waugh's Narrative.*

"The first account we had, with any certainty, of a Rebellion being broke out in the Highlands of Scotland, was about the time of the Assize at Carlisle, held for the county for the year 1745. At which time we had a meeting of the gentlemen of Cumberland, and of several Scotch gentlemen about a turnpike road that was proposed to be carried from the Scotch Border through our County. I having pretty much acquaintance among the gentlemen that live on the Scotch Borders, had a good deal of conversation with some of them on the subject of this Rebellion; and finding from one gentleman in particular, whom I esteemed as a very honest, sensible man, that there was more reason for fears than was at that time apprehended by most people, I entered into an agreement with him to give him intelligence of every thing material in relation to any insurrections, &c., that should happen in England, and he to inform me of every thing that came to his knowledge of that sort in Scotland; which correspondence we all along carried on to our mutual satisfaction, as well as to the service of the Government. When he informed me that the Rebels got together in such numbers as to become formidable, and (as I remember) had sliped Sir John Cope, so that the magistrates of Dumfries, &c., began to be apprehensive of their coming towards England, and proposed sending their arms to, and some of them coming themselves for protection to Carlisle, I acquainted the Duke of Newcastle with their proposal, with the correspondence I had held upon this occasion; and sent him up an association that the Chapter of Carlisle, members of the Cathedral Church, and inhabitants of the precincts of the same, had entered into to do every act and thing in their power by themselves, servts., and dependts., for the defence of the City and Castle of Carlisle as long as it should be thought defenceable by the Government or Commander-in-Chief appointed by His Majesty—in return received an order to send all the intelligence I could get to be laid before the King, &c. Pattinson, the Deputy Mayor, and Capt. Gilpin, who commanded the Garrison of Invalids at that time, with some others, had assembled a day or two before and made something like an assosiation of the same sort; but this I never could see, nor could I learn from any that had signed it any perfect account what it was. I had had no correspondence with Pattinson for many years; but finding the people not satisfied, and knowing all depended upon unanimity, which as the town had long been divided by party interests could no way be brought about but by my joining with Pattinson, I talked to Capt. Gilpin and then went to Pattinson, and settled with him to carry all things on amicably for his Majesty's service, by laying aside all animositys and disputes till these troubles were over, which I thought Pattinson (tho' I knew the man) for his own sake would strictly comply with.

"Things being settled as well as we could in this manner, Capt, Gilpin trusting to the assistance the town would give him did all in his power to prepare for a defence in case it should be attacked; in which he was assisted by all the inhabitants and neighbours in every thing in their power—some works were made about the Castle, and Guns sent for by the Corporation for the walls of the town from merchants of Whitehaven. Subscriptions were raised to pay all out pensioners that could be brought in; and all the men that escaped from Prestonpans were stoped, payed, and maintained, &c., by some gentn. of the town.

"Accounts were taken by the Magistrates of the town and county of all stores of powder, lead, &c., in private hands. All persons passing were stoped and examined; for which purposes the gentlemen met constantly every day; and all precautions that could be thought of were used. After the news came of the defeat of the King's army under the command of Sir J. Cope, I wrote to the Duke of Newcastle and told him the inhabitants were ready to have held the town against an irregular mobb, but they could not consider the Rebels who had defeated one of the King's armys in that light, and that I feared they would never be prevailed upon to make a defence unless they had some assistance, or some superior officer sent to command who might say whether the place was tenable or not; upon which Col. Durand was immediately sent down. The inhabitants able to bear arms by the best computation I could make (for Pattinson would shew no list, nor ever turn them out, tho' often desired by Col. Durand) were about 400; what they had been represented by Pattinson I dont know, but have been told above 700. These were by the D. Mayor formed into nine Companys, of which officers were appointed and had commissions from Pattinson who said he had received a power from the Duke of Newcastle to grant them; Guards were immediately set at the gates of the town. The Militia of the two countys were raised about this time; the Genl. Muster of them was held at Penrith, where I was desired by the Bishop to attend the D. Lieuts. and gentlemen assembled on that occasion to propose an address, and a meeting for signing it by the gentlemen, Clergy, and Freeholders. I therefore was desired by the D. Mayor (for young Mr. A. the real Mayor never came into the town) and Capt. Gilpin to carry letters from them and to apply to the D. Lieuts. for all or part of the Militia to be sent to Carlisle, (the Lord Lieut. being absent in Yorkshire); with great difficulty they were prevailed upon to send the Troops of Light Horse (wch. then had no officers, tho' Col. Dacre was soon after appointed) and two Company's of Foot to Carlisle, viz., that commanded by Major Farrer, and that commanded by Capt. Roger Wilson, of Casterton, in Westmoreland. The Westmoreland Company came very unwillingly. The rest were placed at Whitehaven, Cockermouth, Workington, Penrith, Appleby, and Kendal.

"In this situation Col. Durand found us when he came to Carlisle, on the 11th day of October. He brought me a letter from the Duke of Newcastle, recommending him to me, and desiring me to give him all the assistance in my power, which I did to the best of my abilities, during the whole time he staid in the town. The day after Colonel D. came into Carlisle he viewed the walls, &c., opened embrasures, and made platforms, and mounted the canon that came from Whitehaven upon such parts of the Citadel and town walls as he thought they would be of most use. He applied to the magistrates of the county, that were in town, to give directions to all the country for six or seven miles round, to bring in their ladders, which we immediately gave them notice to do, and they all readily complied with; as also a list of all pick-axes, spades, &c., was brought in, and desired Pattinson, who still acted as Mayor, when he thought fitt, tho' at Michs. one Backhouse was sworn Mayor, and was resident, to give orders about not suffering any but the officers of the garrison and gentlemen well known, to go upon the ramparts, &c. He sent an express to the Ld. Lieut., in Yorkshire, to desire all the militia to come into Carlisle; which produced a letter from his lordship to the Dep. Lieuts., that brought them all in at once, in obedience to his lordship's request; but a few days after they came, their month being near expired, they were for returning home, upon which some of the Dept. Lieuts. wrote to the Ld. Lieut. for directions: it appeared by his lordship's answer he did not care directly to give any.

"We were then at a great stand what to do; a meeting of all the gentlemen, magistrates, clergy, &c. that could be got, was desired; and that the Dept. Lieuts. would send out notice for it; Col. Durand, I, and some others pressed this very hard; no one could make any reasonable objection, and I was desired to draw up the form of notice; but at last every one drew off and left the room by one and one, and none signed it; upon which I went to Pattinson and Mr. Aglionby, the elder, who had sliped from us; we agreed to have this notice engrossed, and sent it round to the D. Lieuts., who signed it; and a meeting was accordingly held, to which the Bishop and several gentlemen that could get notice on so short warning came; all agreed that the Militia ought to be kept up, and after some talk we sent an order to the Clerk of the Peace to advance money for their pay which we would see re-imbursed, and which all the country came readily into. In this manner some of the Militia officers were in some sort compelled to stay, tho' much against their inclinations or real intentions; others of them were ready and willing to do their best service for the defence of the place; the former were always complaining of ill usage; and all of them thought they were not treated as they ought to be by the Corporation; and that Pattinson was only seeking his own gain, which indeed was very plain, and his insolence to be dispensed with by nothing but real and hearty zeal for the publick, and for his Majesty's service, which made it necessary to avoid all disputes at this time.

"Several little houses that had been built by the Corporation near the City Gates were thought by the officers of the Militia to render their posts upon the walls more dangerous, which they insisted ought to be pulled down. This Col. Durand had before desired to have done; now Pattinson pretended to have them viewed and taken down; but after valuing of them at £150, he only took off the slates. A jealousie was kept up between the town and castle which all these disputes heightened, so that it was difficult to do what was necessary for the defence of the Castle, especially on that side next to the town, without giving offence to the inhabitants of the town; and whenever any little accident offended some officers of the Militia, they talked of not caring for the town, but that they would be very resolute to defend the Castle.

"Col. Durand, soon after he came into the town, desired leave of the town magistrates to wall up the Scotch and Irish gates; but they would not comply: said it would do great prejudice to the town, (tho', as there is a communication on the out side the walls, I never could find any reason why, tho' it might a little affect the trade of the Bush, Pattinson's House, which he seemed chiefly sollicitous about.) The Col., however, had materials laid for doing it at all the gates, and agreed with workmen to be ready to do it at 12 hours' notice; accordingly when we had accounts of the rebels having marched from Edinbrough, they were immediately walled up, both on the outside and inside of the wooden gates. The battlements round the walls having been lately removed, when the walls were last repaired, Col. Durand ordered several sand baggs to be made, and centry boxes placed along the walls, and desired some hedges near the walls (under which he apprehended the rebels might cover themselves) to be cut down; the Spring Garden hedge, belonging to Mr. Pearson, the Town Clerk, was accordingly cut down; but some others the militia officers had complained of (one in particular, which the rebels did get behind to make the battery they were afterwards erecting against the Cittadell) were not touched. At this time we heard the rebels were marching from Edinbrough, but what route they would take, we were very uncertain, as we were assured from all our intelligence that they came different roads; so that whether they designed to go towards Newcastle, where Marshal Wade lay with a great army, or between us and Newcastle, or by us directly into Lancashire, we knew not.

"We had received some supplys of military stores, arms, &c., but no men. Two companys of soldiers, new raised men, had been removed from us, and we were not very clear whether the Militia would stay with us or not; it required great skill and address in Col. Durand and others, to please and keep men under no military command, and who never showed any inclination to stay; as to the inhabitants, they had been persuaded, advised, and taught, by the example of the chief people in the place, not to send out or conceal their effects, so that with the greatest part of them all was at stake; and as they saw all the chief people ready to defend the town, and under no apprehensions about success, they seemed all, very few excepted (for I really don't know how to suspect above three or four of them of the least disloyalty) resolute and determined to defend the place to the last extremity.

"We now kept a very good look out—had strict watch and ward in all parts of the county,—partys of the Light Horse were sent out for intelligence. Messengers were sent also every way, and accounts sent to Marshal Wade. Col. Dacre had ventured to Gretna, and searched some houses there for arms; and on Friday, the 8th of Nov., Mr. Kilpatrick, his Lieutenant, with a party of men advanced beyond Ecclefechan, and came within sight of a great body of the Rebels which was advancing by that road towards us. There he took a Quartermaster, one Brawnd, of the Rebels who was coming to Ecclefechan to demand quarters, and brought him prisoner to Carlisle. He was sent with a party the next day to Marshal Wade to carry Brawnd prisoner. The Rebels were provoked with this, and the next morning, viz., Saturday, Nov. 9th, a party of their horse came to Stanwix and sent in one Atkinson, a farmer's son at Drawdikes, in the parish of Stanwix, son of an old fellow who had a suspicious character as being inclined to the Rebels, (as Pattinson, who knew him, told me) to demand quarters for 13,000 foot and 3,000 horse, to which no answer was sent, but the guns from the Castle were fired upon the Rebels who immediately retired. Now we were informed that the party with the Pretender which had come the road towards Newcastle and advanced as far as Wooler in Northumberland, those that had come by Kelso and the midland road, were joining those that came by Moffat, Ecclefechan, &c., and were all advancing towards us; so that the resolving to stand to our defence began to be very serious: all the militia men, most of their officers, and the townspeople, now showed a good spirit, and were in all appearance in very good earnest; and all people were assigned their proper posts and dutys.

"The gentlemen that were volunteers did duty where they pleased, part of them in the Castle and part of them in the town; as there had been some disputes between some of the townspeople and some of the Militia officers, it was necessary that persons of credit and some influence should be appointed to act in the capacity of Aid de Con's. to the Commanding Officers, especially as Col. Durand was lame with the gout, and would not move so nimbly as he otherwise would have done. The clergy on my proposing it to them undertook this part, and all executed it with a coolness and resolution yt. became them. Mr. Wardale, Mr. Bennet the Dissenting Minister, and myself attended Col. Durand in that capacity. Mr. Wilson, Mr. Brown, and Mr. Farish attended Capt. Gilpin. Col. Durand likewise desiring two men might be placed in the day time on the Cathedral Church Tower with a large spying glass to make observations on the motions of the Rebels, the clergy undertook this duty,—that is, such of them as were able to go up, which I was not. Col. Durand proposed to the Militia Officers that they should do duty by detachments from their several companys; but they would draw lotts for their posts, and stick to them as they first took them; then he proposed to divide the whole garrison into three reliefs, but they would not consent to it; but would be upon the ramparts every night all or none, and insisted likewise on all the townspeople doing the same duty,—so that it was with difficulty he prevailed to have a body of reserve of 80 men kept about the Main Guard: as he had no command over them, he was forced to submit to let them do every thing in their own way, tho' he often represented the great inconvenience that must attend their fatiguing their men at that rate. This night we finding it was very inconvenient stirring in the streets, at Col. Durand's request orders were given for all the inhabitants to put lights in their low windows next the street, which we found of great use. On Sunday the 10th the main body of the Rebels were seen passing at a distance from the town, having crossed the river Eden below the town; we were told the Pretender himself had lodged the night before at Moor House. That day there being a thick fogg we could not see them so distinctly from the batterys as we might otherwise have done; but when we saw them, which we sometimes did very plainly, they were fired upon from the Castle, Citadell, and every part where the guns could bear upon them; we were assured from numbers of country people that our guns did execution, particularly that one person of distinction, who was called a lord, was killed and buried at Warwick with much seeming regret: that the same ball killed two others at the same time.

"About 3 o'clock that afternoon, one Robinson, a countryman who said he was compelled to come, brought in a letter directed to the Mayor, from the young Pretender, setting forth that he was 'come to claim his father's rights, and was sorry to find the Mayor was preparing to resist him; that if he was quietly admitted, he promised protection to all; if not, he must use the means God had put in his hands, and could not be answerable for the consequences that must attend the entering the town by force; desired him to consider of this, and demanded an answer in two hours.' This was the substance of the letter, which was immediately shown to the Governor, the officers of the Militia, and Garrison, the Magistrates, &c.; who were all called together at the Bush, and without the least hesitation agreed, that no answer ought to be sent, that the messenger should be detained, and the Rebels fired upon wherever they were seen; which was accordingly done, and several parties that appeared this day were fired upon. This night the guard at the ramparts by the Tile Tower challenged some people with horses that came about the

Irish Gate; who, giving no satisfactory answer, were fired upon, some of their horses wounded, but the men not hurt; at break of day they were fetched into the Castle, and found to be people that had been pressed with horses from Scotland to bring the Rebels' baggage, and running away from them were pursued, but the fire from the walls prevented the Rebels coming up to them; they were however detained in the County Gaol for the present.

"Upon this alarm a running fire went round the walls; and continued, notwithstanding all that could be done, the greatest part of the night; so that had the Rebels attacked us in the morning, it is much to be doubted whether the men had any cartridges left, but others were all the night at work making up more ready to be filled as soon as it was light: and this work, I mean a perpetual firing round the town, continued every night more or less for the two following nights. Several parties that were seen about the town were fired upon the next day, Monday the 11th, particularly a party that came to Stanwix, said to be commanded by Glenbucket; who entered my little Vicarage House there, plundered the goods and cloths of the farmer, (who being an old soldier, I had brought in to bear arms for me in one of the town companys for which my name was set down) gutted the house, pulled the glass out of the windows, destroyed the parish books and registers, and did all the mischief they could; threatening what they would do to me when they got into town. I was told of this, and desired the guns to play upon the house which was in a good measure destroyed, but no great harm done to the Rebels in it. On Tuesday all was quiet, and several accounts from spies we sent out and others agreed that the main body of the Rebels had gone over Warwick Bridge towards Brampton; the party above mentioned under Glenbucket went on the other side the water likewise towards Brampton; and we were told that as they found we were resolutely determined to defend the place, the Rebels would not return to us. But on Wednesday the 13th, several accounts were brought us that a party about Warwick were very busy making scaling ladders, having cutt some tall firr trees at Warwick Hall and Corby Castle for that purpose and I think there were some accounts of their making some more of deals and other materials they had seized upon at Rockcliff. About 4 or 5 o'clock this afternoon I was sent for to the King's Arms, where Col. Durand was at dinner, with several of the Militia officers, when he received an answer from Marshal Wade to a letter he had sent him by an express, to acquaint him what we had done for our defence, and with the whole force of the Rebels being then before us. This answer was directed to Col. D— and the gentlemen at Carlisle, and was in these words:—

"'Newcastle, November 10th, 1745, 7 o'Clock.

"'Gentlemen,—

"'I have just now the favour of your letter by express, with an account of the Rebels' approach near your City. The spirit and resolution with which you exert yourselves is very commendable, and I hope will contribute to disappoint the Rebels of any design they may have formed against you, especially since they must take a great circuit, before they can bring their artillery to make use of against you, and I do not hear they have any sufficient to make a breach in your walls. They give out that they intend to proceed to Lancashire—if so, they will probably pass by you, not to lose time or disappoint the friends they expect to meet there; I cannot follow them the way they may probably take, being impassible for Artillery, and the country will be uncapable to furnish so considerable a body with provisions after they have ravaged and consumed what they find in their way; but I hope to meet them in Lancashire, and cause them to repent of their rashness. Lieutenant General Ligonier is marching with a considerable body of troops in order to put a stop to their progress southwards; and I hope in a short time you will hear good news from Edinburgh, the Lords of the Session being set out for that place, to re-establish the civil government, supported by a body of his majesty's forces. . I wish you all imaginable success in so just a cause as that of liberty, and the defence of your country.

"'And am, Gentlemen your

"'Most obedient humble servant,

"'George Wade.'"

"Col. Durand could not refuse to show this letter to all the gentlemen present who had signed the letter to the Marshall. Upon the reading of it, several of the militia officers were so struck with this letter (or with the reports of the rebels being likely to return, making ladders, &c., and so made this letter a handle for retiring) tho' Col. Durand, Sir John Pennington, myself, and some others, said all we could to give it another turn; that they desired the Col. would open the gates and let them go out in the night, in order to save themselves and their men; which, he refusing absolutely to comply with (and we having reasoned a great while with them, hoped this pannick was over) they were again prevailed with to stand to their arms that night; and did their duty more regularly, making fewer alarms than any night before. This evening ten of the chief inhabitants of Wigton threw themselves into the town to assist us, and 50 more were coming the next day, with 70 from Cockermouth, and 150 from Whitehaven; but the rebels having surrounded the town before they could get in, were prevented joining us. The Rebels, before morning, were returned, and a party of them were working at a trench for erecting a battery, behind a hedge opposite to the Cittadell. In the morning of Thursday, the 14th, Col. Durand, with some of the officers of the Invalids, myself, and some other gentlemen that attended him, the engineers, &c., having been to view that work (from which we were soon convinced there could be no immediate danger) received a paper from the militia officers, of which the following is a copy:—

"'The Militia of the countys of Cumberland and Westmoreland having come voluntarily into the city of Carlisle for the defence of the said city, and having for six days and six night successively been upon duty, in expectation of relief from his Majesty's forces, but it appearing tnat no such relief is now to be had, and ourselves not able to do duty or hold out any longer, are determined to capitulate, and do certify that Col. Durand, Capt. Gilpin, and the rest of the officers have well and faithfully done their duty.

"'Given under our hands this 14th day of Nov., 1745.

"'J. Pennington.
"'M. Farrer.
"'Jos. Dacre.

"'H. Senhouse.
"'J. Dalston.
"'J. Hopper.
"'Ed. Wilson.
"'Geo. Crawle.
"'Fle. Fleming.
"'Jno. Ponsonby.
"'Jos. Crackenthorp.
"'Richd. Cook.
"'Giles Moore.'

"Col. Durand went immediately up to the room in the King's Arms where these officers were met; and (as it appeared from what passed after they came out of that room to all of us that were in the house) had been endeavouring to induce them not to think of giving up when there was so little appearance of danger. Those that had signed in the first column persisted in saying they were resolved to treat for themselves, and gave notice to the inhabitants that they might be included in the capitulation if they pleased. The other three gentlemen were, as it appeared to me, very unwilling to sign. Major Farrer had given us notice, and left them when they first proposed it on Wednesday night; said he would draw up his company and fire on any that offered to go out; that their men were willing to stand, if their officers would, which I believe was true, &c., but at last they were prevailed upon to join with the rest: who, after many things said to prevail with them to stand to their arms, and Ensign Bowes of Capt. Ed. Wilson's company having refused to be sent on so dishonourable an errand as to offer to capitulate with the Rebels, still persisted that they would capitulate. Some of them, particularly Capt. Senhouse, told me, *that they had all agreed, had shaken hands upon it, and would do it; if some spoke more than others, they were all of one mind and resolved, so it signified nothing to talk or argue about it.*

"In short they had now all left their posts, many of them had thrown down their arms in such a manner that they could not easiely have returned to them, and nothing that could be said could prevail with them to stand to their arms any more,—not even till they knew whether terms would be granted them or not, or what sort of a capitulation would be given them. All being thus from a hopeful situation, of defending his Majesty's town and castle, of giving a great and honourable shock to the enemies of our religion and liberties, &c., &c., being thrown into the utmost confusion; occasioned a distress in all the inhabitants beyond almost any thing I had ever conceived.

"To think we were safe if we would defend ourselves,—that it was not our our fault we did not—and yet what we were to expect if we gave up,—to be surrounded by the people crying, 'Sir what must we do? you persuaded us we were safe, &c.; what will come of us now?' was certainly the utmost scene of misery; all were afraid and ashamed to give up, but none knew how to defend; for the Militia having thus peremptorily refused to do any more duty, and resolved to capitulate for themselves on the best terms they could if the townspeople would not be concerned in it, and threatened to make their way out by force if they were refused leave to go out, there was no hopes of defending the place. The number of the Rebels, by the best accounts we had, of all sorts were 8,000; of which we supposed there were 7,000 fighting men, which I apprehend to be the truest calculation that was made of them. The inhabitants able to bear arms, as I have said before, about 400; the Militia, &c., near 700. If they had been out, we could not have guarded the walls; whilst they were in nothing but confusion could be in the place. In this situation we had a meeting in the Town Hall, where many of the people seemed quite desperate, as thinking they were ruined and undone in case the Rebels entered. Pattinson came there, took the direction on himself, and behaved with great insolence as usual; said the question was, *Whether we should open the gates to the Rebels, or not open the gates?* Mr. Tullie, the Recorder, Mr. Wilson, myself, and many others, told him that was not the question; the thing we came there to consider was, what could be done in the present situation, as the Militia would do no more? That we were determined for ourselves, and only were to give our opinions for other people, *Whether, as the Militia were determined to capitulate for themselves, which could not be prevented, it was proper that the inhabitants should be included,* to save the town and people from destruction: that all that now appeared to us rational to be done for the service of the Government was to retire into the Castle, to defend that, which we were resolved to do, but could not advise those who would not run that hazard to refuse being included out of mere bravo. This was no part of Pattinson's scheme, which reached no farther than securing his own property; so we (that is, most of the gentlemen) went directly to the Castle, which he would never have anything to do with, come near, or suffer any of his people to be concerned about it; would never send the ladders in his possession into the Castle, or issue any orders, tho' often desired by Col. Durand to do it, for other people to send in theirs.

"I don't know what passed afterwards in the hall, or who came there; but it was given out that there was a majority of the inhabitants against being included. We immediately removed what valuable effects we could into the Castle, which was pretty well supplied with stores of provisions, &c., which had been provided by the officers, Col. Durand, Captain Gilpin, and some gentlemen and others; and all the beginning of the night we were bringing in wine, coals, and every thing we thought might be of use. Col. Durand also sent out what money he had left to purchase everything in the town that would be of service, or that he feared would be of dis-service if it fell into the hands of the rebels. After the meeting in the hall, I was no more in the town that day, for after I had gone to my own house to settle some affairs—given orders to bring in some few valuable effects and what stores, as before, I could remove in the time, I went to the Castle, where my wife had been some time, and from whence I never expected to come out unless taken by force, which we did not fear, as we hoped we should be able to defend it till it could be relieved. Some of the principal of the Militia officers having joined us, as we hoped with a full resolution to defend it as long as we were able; and having brought in about 400 men, as was said, which, with the volunteers and the invalids made a sufficient Garrison, and with which we were so confident that we were able to make a good defence, all agreed to Col. Durand's sending Mr. Backhouse, an officer of one of the Town Companys, to Mr. Wade with an account of our resolution, and of the steps that had been taken;—which I was told afterwards by the Marshal and the general officers under his command caused his march to Hexham. Some time after we were in the Castle, towards evening, the Mayor came to demand the keys of the town, as Col. D—— had retired into the Castle; and John Davinson, merchant, John Graham, apothecary, and Doctor Douglass, a physician, were sent out; as I apprehended, the two former at the request of the Mayor and inhabitants, and the last at the request of the Militia officers, he being a volunteer in Sir J. Pennington's Company. About the time they went out, Col. Durand sent the engineer to spike the guns on the Town Walls and the Cittadell. One of those on the Cittadell had been levelled in the morning at the hedge where the trench was making *and going off now by accident (or fired by Mr. Dobinson)* in the nailing, shot the engineer who was at work in the enemy's works in the trench, and killed him on the spot; they said he was the best they had.

"But to return to the Castle: we were very sanguine we should make a good defence there, and that all the people who were come in were in earnest, till about four o'clock in the morning, when in the guard room, where we were, we had an account that some of the Militia officers, who had not showed the most spirit from the beginning, were got into the Castle, and were at the Master Gunner's house; that some of the Militia officers, on whom we relied a great deal more, began to talk as if they had come that night into the Castle for their security, for fear the town should be stormed in the night, there being now no guard on the town walls, and many of the men being now, but not before, run away over the walls; that if they could have terms they would go out in the morning with their men—that they had sent out a power to treat in their names, and if they afterwards staid in the castle they might be hanged by the rules of warr—that they had done enough, &c. I was sent for out of the guard room and told this, as was Mr. Wilson; we immediately acquainted Col. Durand with it, and that we found, upon inquiry, it was too true; soon after this many of the Militia men came down, and would force their way out of the Castle; which was, by this means, by break of day, abandoned by all except the garrison of Invalids and some few gentlemen, who then saw it was to no purpose to stay there, the place being very weak towards the town, and a much greater force than was left in it being necessary for its defence. As it was, in the opinion of all, it was absolutely unteneable. The approach from the town to the Castle is much the easiest, and the Castle much the weakest on that side of any. This, Col. Durand proposed to remedy by setting all hands at work at break of day to throw up a retrenchment and make some other works, which the jealousie that had all along been kept up between the town and the Castle prevented being done before; but that was now all over for want of hands.

"About ten o'clock the messengers who had been sent out by the Militia and the Mayor being returned, said that the flags had been sent to the Pretender's son at Brampton, and that the answer was—*That he would grant no terms to the Town, nor treat about it at all unless the Castle was surrendered; likewise if that was done all should have honourable terms; the inhabitants should be protected in their persons and estates, and every one be at liberty to go where they pleased.* These were the words as near as I can remember that were told me both by Dr. Douglass and Davinson. No mention of any parole or any other terms. None of the Militia or townspeople were now in arms; all were looking after their affairs; and all thoughts of fighting over with them. I was gone to my own house, and was burning some papers, for which I was to be searched, when I received a message from Col. Durand to desire I would come to the Castle. I met as I went into the guard room most of the Officers of the Militia, and several of the principal inhabitants coming out; was told by Col. Durand that they had acquainted him what the answer was from the Rebels; and that they had begged he would take it into consideration, that the Garrison was to be at liberty to march out with all military honours, and both officers and soldiers to be at liberty to go where they pleased; that he had called a Council of War, at which I might be present; the result of which was that the Castle was not to be held. It was in these words:—

"'*At a Council of War holden in the Castle of Carlisle, Nov.* 15, 1745,

"'The Militia of the Countys of Cumberland and Westmoreland, as also the Militia of the town of Carlisle, having absolutely to a man refused to defend the

Castle, and the Garrison consisting only of two companys of invalids, amounting to about eighty men, many of them extremely infirm, and the Castle very large, so that there are neither men to manage the guns nor man the walls, and the Mayor and inhabitants of the town, together with the officers of the Militia, having sent to treat with the Rebels, against the opinion and protestation of Colonel Durand, Captain Gilpin, and the rest of the officers of the Garrison, and being refused any terms, and threatening to destroy both town and Castle with fire and sword, unless the Castle be surrendered, it is our opinion that the Castle being not teneable, it is for his Majesty's service that it be abandoned, and it will be absolutely necessary for the preservation of the lives of his Majesty's subjects, who would otherwise be exposed to inevitable ruin.

"'Given under our hands at Carlisle, this 15th day of Nov., 1745.

(Signed) "'J. Durand.
"'Jno. Bernd. Gilpin.
"'Jno. Cowley.
"'Jno. Hutchinson.
"'Jno. Smith.
"'Fran. Gatton.'

"The same morning another paper was issued in the same place, viz., 15th Nov., 1745:—

"'We, whose names are hereunto subscribed are of opinion that the Castle is not teneable, the Militia of the countys of Cumberland and Westmoreland, and the inhabitants of the City of Carlisle having absolutely refused to defend the same.

"'Joseph Backhouse, *Mayor*.
"'Richd. Colthard.
"'R. Cook.
"'Fran. Gatton.
"'Fle. Fleming.
"'Robt. Fisher.
"'Giles Moore.
"'Jno. Holme.
"'J. Dalston.
"'Richd. Jackson.
"'Israel Bennett.
"'John Davidson.
"'John Waugh.
"'J. Pennington.
"'J. B. Gilpin.
"'Jo. Dacre.
"'Jno. Douglas.
"'H. Senhouse.
"'J. Tullie.
"'Will. Tate.
"'E. Wilson.
"'Geo. Crowle.'

"After these Councils were over, and Col. Durand had consented to abandon the Castle, as it was by all judged not to be teneable, Sir J. Pennington, Col. of the Militia, J. Dacre, Esq., Col. of the Light Horse, and the Mayor, went out to settle the treaty. When they opened the gates to go out, as I have been informed, for I was not there present, the Rebels entered the English Gate, (none being under arms to prevent it,) and took possession of it; and afterwards the person called by the Rebels the Duke of Perth came to one Taylor's, out of the Scotch Gate, and made a treaty on such terms as he thought fit to grant. I have never seen it."

PROCEEDINGS

OF

THE GENERAL COURT MARTIAL,

HELD FOR THE

TRIAL OF LIEUTENANT COLONEL JAMES DURAND,

The 15th and 16th of September, 1746.

"*At a General Court Martial, held in the great room, at the Horse Guards, on Monday, the 15th, and Tuesday, the 16th days of September, 1746, by virtue of his Majesty's warrants, dated the ninth day of the said September, to examine into the conduct, behaviour, and proceedings, of Lieutenant-Colonel James Durand, from the time he took command in the City and Castle of Carlisle, till the same were surrendered to the Rebels, on the 15th of November last, and to proceed in the trial of the said Lieutenant-Colonel James Durand.*

"Lieutenant-General WENTWORTH, President.
"Major-General POULTENEY.
"Major-General CHURCHILL.
"Brigadier-General POWLETT.
"Colonel FRAZER.
"Colonel WARDOUR.
"Colonel Earl of HOME.
"Major-General JOHN LORD DE LA WAR.
"Major-General WOLFE.
"Brigadier-General BYNG.
"Colonel Lord HENRY BEAUCLERK.
"Colonel Lord GEORGE BEAUCLERK.
"Colonel KENNEDY.

"The Court being duly sworn proceeded to the said trial as followeth :—

"*Lieutenant Colonel Robert Napier*, being duly sworn, says that he can depose no other than that he was ordered by His Royal Highness the Duke to put Lieutenant Colonel James Durand in arrest for having surrendered the Town and Castle of Carlisle to the Rebels sooner than His Royal Highness apprehended the said Lieut. Colonel Durand ought to have done.

"*Lieutenant Colonel Durand* was then asked what he had to say in his defence. He desired leave to give into the Court a Narrative in writing of his conduct, behaviour, and proceedings for the time aforesaid, which he desired might be read and received as his defence, and accordingly is as follows :—

"'The Duke of Newcastle having signified to me His Majesty's pleasure that I should proceed to Carlisle to command there in the absence of the Governour and Lieutenant Governour, I accordingly set out post from London, and arrived there the 11th of October last, in the morning; and immediately went and viewed both town and Castle, which I found in a very weak and defenceless condition; having no ditch, no out-works of any kind, no cover'd way,—the walls very thin in most places, and without proper flanks; but agreed with Captn. Gilpin, who was the only person with me at that time, not to mention our opinion of the weakness of the place for fear of discouraging the Militia and inhabitants; but on the contrary, to speak of it as a strong place and very teneable.

"'Examined the disposition of the several guards, and the orders that were given out by Captain Gilpin before my arrival, and found them very proper, and to the purpose.

"'Examined the Garrison, and found it to consist of two companys of Invalids, making about eighty men, very old and infirm; two companys of Militia, about one hundred and fifty men; one troop of Militia Horse, about seventy; and the town's-people, whom the Deputy Mayor inform'd me he had divided into nine companys of about thirty men each; but whether they consisted of that number, or not, I cannot tell,—as I could never see them out, tho' often ask'd, in order to examine how they were armed, and to teach them a little discipline; but was always answered, that as most of them were poor labouring people, who served without pay, it would be taking them from their work, by which their familys would starve; but they should be forthcoming whenever His Majesty's service required it.

"'Captain Gilpin had also appointed eighty town's-men as gunners, for the service of the artillery in the Castle.

"'These appearing to me to be too weak a garrison for town and Castle (especially as they were only Militia) and being informed there were five companys more of Militia, disposed in the open towns and villages, I sent that night an express to Lord Lonsdale, the Lord Lieutenant, who was then in Yorkshire, to represent to his Lordship, that I thought it would be more for His Majesty's service for those companys to march into Carlisle, and reinforce the garrison, than remain where they were; and accordingly his Lordship sent a letter to the Deputy Lieutenants who brought them all in.

"'But some few days after, the month for which the Militia were raised being expired, many were for returning home, as there was no more money to pay them; and some of the men did go away, but were brought back by a detachment of Militia Horse, who were sent after them; upon which Sir John Pennington, the Chancellor (who took a great deal of pains to bring it about) myself, and several other gentlemen, propos'd a meeting of all the gentlemen of the country, to think of some method for keeping up and paying the Militia, for some time longer.

"'Accordingly a meeting was held at Carlisle, at which the Bishop and several other gentlemen attended. The Bishop said every thing he could to engage them to keep up the Militia, and had great influence upon them. I offered to subscribe fifty guineas, or more, towards paying the Militia; but the gentlemen would not allow of it, and came to a resolution to order the Clerk of the Peace to advance the money, and they would be answerable to him for it.

"'Finding ten pieces of ship cannon, from four to two pounders, which Capt. Gilpin had just sent for from Whitehaven, I gave orders to open embrasures and make platforms, and mounted those cannon upon the walls of the town, where I thought they could be of most use; and desired the Deputy Mayor that forty men might be appointed as gunners for the service of those cannon, which was immediately complied with; and then gave orders to the Master Gunner to instruct them, as also the eighty men already appointed for the service of the artillery in the Castle, in the best manner he could. I also gave orders to repair the Ramparts, and for many other little things, the detail of which I won't trouble the Court with; and as they had sent only six rounds of shot with the said cannon, I sent an express to Whitehaven for all the shot they could spare me, and they accordingly sent me six cart load full.

"'Enquired into the quantity of provisions there were in town, and was assured they had sufficient for two months or more; I also examined the water, and whether it could be cut off from us, but found there were several wells in the town which afforded very good water and in sufficient plenty.

"'Gave orders for no person to be permitted to walk upon the Ramparts but the Officers of the Garrison, Magistrates, or such Gentlemen of the town as were well known; and if any body was perceived taking observations, drawing plans, or asking any particular questions about the state or condition of the town, except the Officers, &c., to be immediately secured for further examination.

"'I apply'd to the Magistrates of the County to issue warrants, for bringing into the town all the ladders within seven miles round, or farther, which was immediately comply'd with, and the ladders brought in.

"'I also desired they would give strict orders to the constables to take an exact account of all the spades, pick-axes, and other tools for moving of earth, that were in the possession of the several farmers, which was also done.

"'My reason for it was, that if it appeared any farmer had a larger quantity than was necessary for his affairs of husbandry, they might be seized and brought into town.

"'I proposed to the Magistrates to wall up the Scotch and Irish Gates, as they were only single gates, without draw-bridges, or any outworks to cover them; and to leave only the English Gate open, which having an outward iron gate, and being in some measure flank'd by a round tower, where I had mounted a small cannon, could not have been so easily forced; but they objected, and said it would be an infinite prejudice to the city; and as I might depend upon having two or three days' notice of the approach of the Rebels, I should always have time enough to do it.

"'I then ordered materials to be laid ready at the gates, and agreed with several workmen to do it, at twelve hours' notice; and as soon as I heard the Rebels had left Edinburgh, I gave orders for walling them up, and it was done.

"'Ordered a large number of sandbags to be made and fill'd, and bought up all the cloth there was in town that was fit for that purpose.

"'Desired a large quick-sett hedge, that was too close to the walls, and might have afforded cover to a large body of the Rebels, to be taken down,—which was done.

"'I applyed to the Magistrates to pull down some small houses and sheds, that I thought were built too close to the walls; but they objected, and said it was private property, and they could not do it.

"'However, upon my further strong representations, and insisting upon it, they pull'd down some part of them.

"'It would have been of service to have pull'd down some more, but was what I could not do myself; as I had no military force to support me but a few Invalids, and also for fear of disobliging the town, upon whose inhabitants I partly depended for my defence; but I often declared my intention that if the Rebels once took possession of them, I would immediately beat them down with some cannon I had mounted upon the Spring Garden Turret and the Tile Tower for that purpose, or have set them on fire, as I thought I could then answer it.

"'The Militia were out every morning at exercise, and having taken notice that their arms were of different bores, so that it was impossible to fit them out of the stores, I desired every man would make a sufficient quantity of ball according to the size of his piece, and ordered lead to be delivered out for that purpose.

"'I desired that two men might be posted upon the high Tower of the Cathedral, with a very large spying glass I had brought with me, and to send me a report of what they observed in the country.

"'The Chancellor proposed to the Clergy to take this duty, which they readily did, and were very exact and vigilant; and when the Rebells came before Carlisle, they took up arms as Volunteers, most of whom served under me as Aides-de-Camp.

"'We sent Marshal Wade, by express, the best intelligence we could get; for which we were chiefly obliged to the Chancellor, who had established a correspondence in Scotland for that purpose.

"'Ordered about four hundred hand-granades, which were all we had, to be loaded and primed.

"'Being informed that the two additional companys of Major General Howard's Regiment were on their march from Newcastle to reinforce the garrison of Carlisle, and having received certain intelligence that the Rebells were advancing towards Annan, I sent away an express to the commanding officer of those two companys, to acquaint him with the intelligence we had received, that he might take his precautions; and desiring him to march, and join us with all possible expedition.

"'Soon after my express was gone, the Chancellor brought me a letter he had just received from Major-General Howard, by which it appeared the companys intended us were not yet march'd from Newcastle; nor did they ever come to us.

"'As the Rebells approached to Carlisle, false alarms became very frequent in town; which, as it served only to fatigue the garrison, and make them less attentive if a real one should happen, I earnestly desired that no drum might beat to arms without my orders; but as that was not regarded, I desired that the only signal for a general alarm might be the ringing the great bells in the Cathedral; and the Chancellor appointed two men to attend constantly for that purpose, and never to ring without orders; and, to prevent their being imposed upon, acquainted them that the person who brought them the order, should likewise bring with him a ticket, of which they had always a duplicate.

"'When the Rebells were advanced to the neighbourhood of Annan, by which our correspondence with Dumfries, and other places from whence we received intelligence, was cut off, I desired Colonel Dacres, who commanded the Militia-horse, would send out some small parties to all the avenues leading to Carlisle, with orders to send back a man every six hours, or oftener as they saw occasion, to give us the best intelligence they could get.

"'One of these partys took prisoner a Quarter-Master of the Rebells; whom, after examination, we sent to Marshal Wade.

"'As the nights were excessively dark, I desired the magistrates would give orders to put out lights in the streets; that in case of an alarm in the night, the men might see their way, and prevent confusion; which orders were carefully observed by the inhabitants.

"'When I had received certain advice that the Rebells were within a day's march of Carlisle, which was on the 8th November, I desired the whole garrison might be divided into three reliefs, with a picquet, and one relief only to be upon duty at a time; and had made disposition accordingly, and acquainted Sir John Pennington, who commanded the regiment of Militia, with my design, which he approved of; but the militia would not consent to it, and would be every night upon the walls, all of them or none; and also insisted upon the townspeople doing the same duty, tho' I often represented it was quite unnecessary, and that many and great inconveniencys would attend it; but all to no purpose; and it was with a great deal of difficulty I could get a reserve guard, of about eighteen men, kept at the Main Guard.

["'N.B.—The invalids were thus divided.]

"'As they said they were volunteers, and would not allow I had the command over them, I could do no more than endeavour to persuade them to act as I thought most for his Majesty's service.

"'As the next day was market day, desired the magistrates would give orders that the market might not be be kept in the city as usual; but in the suburbs, without the gates, which they accordingly did.

"'Appointed rounds to go constantly upon the ramparts from dark to day-break.

"'Some of the Clergy and Volunteers offer'd themselves for this service, and were very diligent.'

"'JOURNAL

"'OF THE SIX DAYS THE REBELS LAY BEFORE CARLISLE.

"'*Saturday, Nov.* 9.—Perceiving many country people had got into the town, it being market day, I ordered the drums to beat to arms, and turn'd out every person but the inhabitants, Militia, and Volunteers.

"'About twelve o'clock the watch upon the tower gave me notice that they saw a party of horse at Grimber-Hill, about two miles distance from the town; and about one o'clock that party appeared above Stanwix Bank, and sent in a country fellow, with a verbal message to the mayor, to provide quarters that night for thirteen thousand foot and three thousand horse, or the town should be reduced to ashes, to which no answer was returned; and the whole garrison appeared in the highest spirits, and seem'd resolved to defend the town to the last; and the cannon from the Castle firing upon the Rebells partys, they retired.

"'That night we sent an express to Marshal Wade, to acquaint him with the Rebells approach to Carlisle.

"'*Sunday, Nov.* 10*th*.—The morning was so dark and foggy we could not discern any thing; but learned from the scouts we sent out that several large bodys of the rebells were advancing towards us; and it clearing up a little about noon, we perceived a large body of the Rebells marching towards the Irish Gate, —but firing upon them, they retreated. We also perceived large bodys of the Rebells marching over Carlisle Fields; and some of them coming within reach of our guns, we fired upon them, and as we afterwards heard, did some little execution, which made them retire to a great distance.

"'About three o'clock in the afternoon, a country fellow, who said he was forced, brought the Mayor the letter which was published in the *Gazette*; which he shewed to me, the officers of Militia, and chief inhabitants of the town, who were then assembled at the Bush; all treated it with the contempt it deserved, and unanimously agreed not to return any answer, and to detain the fellow who brought it.

"'*Monday, Nov.* 11*th.*—About two o'clock in the morning, there was an alarm, occasioned by the trampling of horses under the walls, near the Irishgate; but the night was so dark we could not distinguish anything; but the men upon the walls, having challenged, and receiving no satisfactory answer, fired as well as they could judge, upon the places where they heard the noise; and as soon as it was day light, and I had examined the ground thereabouts, sent out a detatchment, who brought them and their horses into the Castle: some of the horses were wounded, but the men not hurt. Upon examination they said they were people of the low country in Scotland, whom the Rebells had forced to carry their baggage, and had taken that opportunity of deserting from them; however they were confined.

"'About noon, a party of the Rebells appeared at Stanwix, but the Castle firing upon them they soon retreated; we were afterwards informed by some people of the village, that upon our firing upon them, they had retired towards Brampton, and that we had killed one of the Rebell's principal officers.

"'That day some of the Rebels baggage was brought into town, by some people of the country; particularly some arms and two waggon load of biscuit.

"'*Tuesday, Nov.* 12*th.*—We could not perceive any of the Rebells, and were informed by some scouts we sent out, that their main body was marched to Brampton with their artillery and baggage, leaving some partys behind them at Warwick Bridge.

"'*Wednesday, Nov.* 13*th.*—We had accounts from several country people, that the partys the Rebells had left behind them, at Warwick Bridge, had cut down some fir trees at Corby Castle and Warwick, and had seized upon a quantity of deal, and were very busy in making a great number of scaling ladders, and had pressed all the carpenters they could find.

"'About three o'clock in the afternoon, as I was at dinner with several officers of Militia, and some gentlemen, an express was brought from Marshal Wade, directed to me and the gentlemen at Carlisle, in answer to the express we had sent him, dated the 9th of November, acquainting him with the Rebells' approach to Carlisle.

"'As by the direction of the letter, the gentlemen who had signed the express had a right to see it, and as it was brought to me in that public manner, that it was impossible to conceal it, the contents were soon generally known; and most of the Militia officers, who were then at dinner with me, said it implied it was not in his power to come to our assistance, and therefore they could not answer exposing their men any longer; tho' Sir John Pennington, the Chancellor, and myself took a good deal of pains to persuade them the letter did not mean so much as they seemed to apprehend.

"'I thereupon, earnestly entreated them to continue to do their duty, and endeavoured to the utmost of my power to persuade them to do it; assuring them they had nothing to fear from the Rebells; that we were in a very good condition of defending ourselves; and that if they would continue to behave with the same spirit and resolution they had hitherto shewn, the Rebels would never take the town; or words to that effect.

"'Soon after, hearing the Militia officers were assembled in an upper room, and were going to take a resolution of abandoning the town that night, I went up to them,—when they ask'd me to open the English Gate for them, which I absolutely refused; and after expostulating with them, I thought I had prevailed upon them to stay, as I heard no more of it that night, and they all went to their posts as usual.

"'That afternoon we perceived the Rebels were returned back from Brampton, and had again surrounded the town; we immediately dispatched another express to Marshal Wade, to acquaint him of it; but as the Rebels were in his way, he could not proceed on his journey, so he returned to us again.

"'*Thursday, Nov.* 14*th.*—At day break the Rebels were perceived throwing up a small entrenchment about three hundred yards from the Citadell; which being informed of, I immediately went to view it, and there found a great crowd of people, who seemed to be alarmed at it; upon which I said everything to encourage them to do their duty, assuring them it was nothing but a poor paltry ditch, that did not deserve the name of an intrenchment; that the Rebels had no cannon large enough to make a breach in our walls; that as it was not usualto carry on works of that kind in the day time, I imagined it was only done to intimidate them; and that if they would but stand by their walls, the Rebels could never take the town: or words to that effect; and gave orders to fire upon them.

"'After staying there some time, I went to the King's Arms, where the Militia officers where assembled, and there received the paper marked A; upon which I made use of every argument I could think of, to induce them to change so rash a resolution, by representing the fatal consequences that would attend it, and the dishonour of treating with Rebels, whilst they were in so good a condition of defending themselves; assuring them I would never join in so infamous an action; and that if they would but stand by me, the whole force of the Rebels could not take us, as by the best accounts we had, they had no cannon large enough to make a breach, and with the garrison we had it was impracticable to scale our walls, or words to that purpose, and said a great deal more to the same effect. But they still persisted in their resolution to capitulate, and said it was to no purpose to argue any longer about it, for they were all resolved, and had shaken hands upon it.

"'Against which resolution of the Militia, myself, Capt. Gilpin, and the rest of the officers of the Invalids protested in the most solemn manner.

"'They then asked the inhabitants if they would join with them, and gave them notice that they might be included in the capitulation if they pleas'd; but if they would not, they were determined to capitulate for themselves upon the best terms they could get.

"'The Deputy Mayor asked me what I would do; I answer'd I was determined never to capitulate with Rebels, but would defend both Town and Castle as long as I could.

"'Most of the inhabitants then present endeavoured to perswade the Militia not to capitulate; but not being able to prevail, such a general distraction and confusion ensued as no tongue can describe.

"'The men by this time had left the walls, and most of them had thrown down their arms, so that I began to apprehend if the Rebels should hear the confusion we were in, they might immediately scale the walls, as there was none to oppose them: and went to the Castle to give some orders there.

"'When I was at the Castle, I perceived two large bodys of the Rebells marching off toward Rowcliff; and as I was then very lame with the gout, and could move but slow, desired Lieut. Hutchinson, who was with me, to run to the King's Arms, to acquaint them with it, and that I would follow him as fast as I could walk, to endeavour again to perswade them to change their rash resolution,

"'During this time the Mayor had assembled the inhabitants at the Town Hall, to consult what they should do, in relation to the proposal of the Militia; what passed there I can give no account of, as I was not present.

"'But soon after I was returned back to the King's Arms, the Mayor came to me and acquainted me they had agreed to join with the Militia, to send out to the Rebells to capitulate; saying at the same time, to the best of my remembrance, that as the Militia had determined to capitulate, they were obliged to join with them, or words to yt. purpose.

"'Upon which myself and the officers of Invalids, after protesting against their capitulation, retired into the Castle with the Invalids; and, in a little time afterwards, were followed by most of the Militia officers, and about four hundred of their men, and several gentlemen and clergy of the town, who all declared they would join with me in defending the Castle to the last; and agreed to my sending Mr. Backhouse, one of the officers of the Town Companys, express to Marshal Wade, to acquaint him with their resolution.

"'I then said every thing I could to encourage them to do their duty, acquainted them with the quantity of provisions we had, the disposition I intended to make, assuring them, with the garrison there was then in the Castle, the Rebels should never take it; and said a great deal more to that effect.

"'Before I entered the Castle, I gave orders to nail up the ten pieces of cannon upon the ramparts, as I had not time to remove them; I also gave orders to bring into the Castle all the small arms and ammunition that had been delivered out to the Militia and townspeople; all the hand-granades, sand bags, &c.

"'Sent into the town to buy up all the bread I could get for the men that night, till we could bake the next morning, as also for many other little things I thought might be wanted; and particularly desired Lieut. Hutchinson to send and buy up all the gunpowder there was in town, for fear of its falling into the hands of the Rebels.

"'I had put two ovens in the Castle into thorough repair, as also the well; I had fixed up a hand-mill for grinding of wheat, belonging to the Dean and Chapter, which the Chancellor had procured me; I had also erected a smith's shop with a forge; and all necessary tools: and had done many other little things.

"'*Account of Provisions, &c., in the Castle.*

"'About 130 bushels of meal, and 210 bushels of wheat.
"'270 bushels of potatoes.
"'Between 700 and 800 weight of cheese.
"'500 pound weight of butter.
"'Half a ton of salt.
"'400 load of coals.
"'A large quantity of candles, and all the straw we could get.
"'15 anchors of brandy, and 2 casks of rum.
"'2 chests of medicines.
"'About 27 bullocks, and between 30 and 40 sheep, and many other things.
"'Necessary utensils for dressing of victuals.
"'A large quantity of poles and deal boards.
"'Besides wine, and other provisions, sent in by the gentlemen, or brought in by the Militia.

"'*Friday, Nov. 15th.*—About one o'clock in the morning Captain Gilpin informed me that there were none of the Militia upon the walls; upon which I went with him to Sir John Pennington, who was at the Gunner's house, to acquaint him with it, and to desire he would order some men upon the walls; Sir John immediately went with us to the place where the men lay, and with great difficulty prevailed on about thirty to take their arms and go centrys, promising them they should be relieved in an hour, as it was a very bad night; but in a very short time they were all gone from their posts.

"'Soon after a mutiny begun among the private men of the Militia; who all declared they would do no more duty, nor would they stay and defend the Castle upon any account whatsoever.

"'A general confusion ensued, numbers went over the walls; others forced their way out the gates; upon which I earnestly entreated the Militia officers to go to their men and endeavour all in their power to prevail upon them to stay and do their duty, which they promised me they would, but without effect; for before eight o'clock in the morning, they had all left us to a man; and we remained with only our few Invalids, who from their great age and infirmities, and from the excessive fatigue they had undergone, occasioned by the frequent false alarms we had, which had kept them almost continually upon duty, were rendered in a manner of no use.

"'About ten o'clock most of the Militia Officers, and Inhabitants came to us, and told us the Rebels had absolutely refused to grant them any terms, unless the Castle was surrendered; and had declared they would immediately destroy the city with fire, and put all the Militia and inhabitants, without distinction, to the sword; and desired for God's sake we would take it into consideration; but if the Castle was surrendered, everybody should be at liberty to go wherever they pleased, the City be preserved; and all be protected in their persons and estates.

"'I said these threatenings were words of course, and meant very little; and repeated what I had often told them before, that I was determined never to capitulate with Rebels; and would still, if possible, have procured a garrison to defend the Castle; but they persisted in saying their men had all refused to do any more duty.

"'I told them, as to what they had mentioned of surrendering the Castle, I could give them no answer to it, till I had consulted my officers; they soon after drew up and signed the paper mark'd B.

"'I called a Council of War marked C.

"'About a fortnight before the Rebels left Edinburgh, I was seized with a very severe fit of the gout, and still very lame and full of pain when the Rebels came before Carlisle; yet in that condition I was every where I thought I could be of use, and was six nights following without going to bed.

"'(Signed) J. DURAND.'"

"[N.B.—The papers marked A, B, C, are inserted afterwards.

"The said narrative being read, Lieutenant-Colonel Durand produced his witnesses, in support of the several matters therein set forth.

And first :—

"*Captn. John Barnard Gilpin*, commanding one of the companys of Invalids at Carlisle, being duely sworn, was required to inform the Court, what he knew of the strength and condition of the Town and Castle of Carlisle, and what passed in conversation between him and Lieutenant Colonel Durand, after viewing it.

"He says that on Lieutenant Colonel Durand's coming to take upon him the command of the Town and Castle, he desired this deponent to go with him round them, to examine their condition, which he did, and they found them very weak and defenceless. He farther says that the Castle of Carlisle is an old, irregular building, near 700 yards in circuit, and has 20 pieces of iron cannon of six pounders; and as it has no ditch (except on the town side the small remains of one, which time has near fill'd up, and is passible in almost all places), has no outworks of any kind, nor flanks, the Rebells might have approach'd to the foot of the walls wherever they pleased, without any possibility of hindering them, or dislodging them when they were there, as we had no fire that could bear upon them, nor any men to make a sally; and then, by mine or sap, might have thrown down any part of the wall they thought proper.

"For about sixty yards round the summer house battery the wall is very low, and might have been scaled with great ease.

"The wall to the right of the gate is about seventy-four yards long, very old, thin, and decayed, having several very large cracks in it; the inside facing entirely taken away, and no rampart behind it; and being so very weak, might have been easily thrown down.

"The gate towards the town is not covered by any outworks; and tho' it has a draw-bridge before it, yet that bridge is of no sort of use, as there is a free passage both to the right and left of it; which gate might very easily be approach'd, especially in the night, as the nights were then excessively dark, and be forced by a petard, or burnt with tar barrels, as it is only a single wooden gate; and from the gateway are stair-cases, that lead up to the top of the gateway, as also into the inner Castle, which would at once have given the Rebells possession of it.

"The wall over the Lady's Walk is about sixty yards in length and very low, has no parapet nor any flank to defend it; and might have been scaled with great ease, especially as, at about seventy or eighty yards from the said wall, there is a large bank of earth, and a hedge, which run parallel to it, and would have afforded cover to a large number of Rebells, who, by a continual fire upon the said wall, might have made it impossible for any men to have stood there, as there was no parapet to cover them; and under cover of this fire, the Rebells might have advanced several detachments, both to the right and left of the ditch, with scaling-ladders, and taken possession of the Lady's Walk, where we could not bring any fire to bear upon them; and immediately, with great ease, have scal'd the wall.

"At the foot of the said wall is an old gateway, wch. had been just wall'd up, and might have been open'd again in a very little time, as it was not defended by any flank, and consequently not in our power

SOUTH, OR MAIN ENTRANCE OF CARLISLE CASTLE AND DRAWBRIDGE, IN 1745.

to give them any interruption; from whence the Rebells might have forc'd their way into the inner Castle, or have blown it up.

"Against all which attacks, which would probably have been made at once, with the whole force of the Rebells who then surrounded us and were computed to be seven thousand strong, we had nothing to oppose them, but four Gunners and a few Invalids; who from their great age and infirmitys, and from the excessive fatigue they had undergone by their being almost continually upon duty, by the frequent false alarms we had, were in a manner rendered useless; so that it appeared to Lieut. Colol. Durand, and to ye. officers of the Invalids, impossible to make any defence, and thought it was more for his Majesty's service to abandon it, to preserve the city from ruin, and the great number of gentlemen of the best estates and familys in the two countys of Westmoreland and Cumberland, who were then in the city, from at least being made prisoners of war; which we apprehended would have been, in many respects, an infinite prejudice to his Majesty's service.

"He farther says, that after having review'd the town and Castle, and finding the bad state of them, Lieutenant-Colonel Durand declared to him upon that occasion, that he desired the weak state of them might not be known, lest the people should be intimidated or discouraged; and he accordingly chose to give it out as a teneable place, especially the Castle; the rather, finding that the people of the town thought it so to be.

"*Lieutenant John Hutchinson*, of one of the companys of Invalids at Carlisle, being duly sworn, and examined, confirms the state and condition of the Castle of Carlisle to be as set forth by Captain Gilpin.

"These two witnesses were desired by the Court to inform them whether Lieutenant-Colonel Durand had any means and time to throw up any works to remedy the weak part of the Castle.

"They both say it was impossible; he having neither men sufficient, nor materials, nor time.

"*Lieutenant General Folliot*, Governor of Carlisle, was desired to inform the Court what he knew of the state of the town and Castle. He says that it is seven years since he has viewed them; at which time it was in a very weak condition, there being neither ditch, covered way, nor flankers; and does not know that any alterations or amendment has been made since that time. That he remembers as he went up on a part of the Rampart, between the town and the Castle, he was advised not to go too near the wall, for fear it should break down.

"*Captain Gilpin*, being again examined, says that he has resided at Carlisle about eight or nine years: and that no material alterations have been made in that time to the works either of the town or Castle; that the whole inside facing of the Rubble Wall on the right of the Gate, between the town and the Castle, was taken down in order to be repaired, but never was repaired; so that it is now in a worse condition than when General Folliot was there; there being several cracks in it, which he believes are quite through.

Captain Gilpin, and *Lieutenant Hutchinson*, further say, that the numbers of the Garrison in the town and Castle consisted as set forth by Lieut. Col. Durand in his narrative; and that there was no certainty of the numbers of the townspeople, which the Deputy Mayor had divided into nine companys, those companys having never been review'd, for the reasons Lieut. Col. Durand has given.

"*Dr. John Waugh*, Chancellor of the Diocese of Carlisle, being duly sworn and examined, says, that the nine companys, into which the town's people have been said to be divided, being all labouring people who received no pay, he believes they never were reviewed: having often heard it given as a reason, that it was calling them off from their labour, by which they subsisted, and would therefore be a loss to them.

"*Capt. Gilpin* and *Lieut. Hutchinson*, being further examined, say that there were eighty townsmen appointed as gunners, who were not skill'd in gunnery, to assist the four gunners that were upon the establishment; of which four two of them were townsmen, who had never been regularly brought up as gunners; the other two had formerly been on service; but one of these last was very old and and infirm.

"*Capt. Gilpin* being examined as to the number of companys of Militia that were out of the town of Carlisle, and which, at Lieut.-Colonel Durand's request, were brought into the town, as the said Lieut.-Colonel alledges:

"He says he believes there were five companys, of about seventy men each; that their arms consisted of different kinds of fowling pieces, and old muskets, which were but in a very bad order; and those companys were, at Lieut.-Colonel Durand's request, brought into the town.

"And further says, that the County Militia, pretending the month was expired, for which they were engaged, began to be very uneasy, and mutinous, and resolved to retire home, and some of them did go home. That a detachment of the Militia Horse was sent after some of those that had thus gone away, in order to bring them back, which they accordingly did.

"*Dr. Waugh* also declares that the month for which the County Militia had been engaged, was expired a few days after they came into the town; and thereupon a meeting of the gentlemen was had, in order to think of some means of keeping up the Militia some time longer; and a voluntary subscription was proposed, to pay the Militia, to which Colonel Durand did offer to subscribe; but it was not allowed of, and an order was drawn up to the Clerk of the Peace for the County of Cumberland, and he believes also to that of the County of Westmoreland, to advance money to pay the Militia, which the gentlemen signed, and thereby engaged themselves to be answerable for the repayment of it, upon whch the money was sent, and the Militia did stay.

Capt. Gilpin, and *Lieut. Hutchinson* being further examined say, that ten pieces of ship cannon, which they believe, to the best of their remembrance, were from four to two pounders, were in the Castle of Carlisle upon ship carriages when Lt. Col. Durand came; and there were then only six rounds of shot, that had been sent with the cannon, upon which Lt. Col. Durand sent to Whitehaven for more, and there were five or six cart loads sent him from thence, and in a day or two after, Lt. Col. Durand ordered these cannon to be placed on the Ramparts of the town, in the most proper places; and as there were not a sufficient number of gunners, Lt. Col. Durand did apply to the Mayor of the town, who did appoint forty townsmen for that service, over and above the eighty that had been already appointed for the Castle, whom Lt. Col. Durand ordered the Master Gunner to instruct in the best manner he could.

"*Dr. Waugh* being examined as to the quantity of provisions in the town, says that he often heard Lieutenant Colonel Durand enquire of the Deputy Mayor about the quantity of provisions in the town; and the Mayor assured him there was a sufficient quantity, there being a great number of cattle about the town, which could easily be brought in, and the barns in the town were fill'd with corn; and that as the Rebels approach'd, many of the cattle were brought into the town.

"*Capt. Gilpin,* being further examined, says, he verily believes orders were given by Lieutenant Colonel Durand, as he has aledged in his narrative, for no person to be permitted to walk on the Ramparts, but the Officers of the Garrison, Magistrates, or gentlemen of the town who were well known; and if any body was perceived taking observations, asking questions, &c., they were to be secured for farther examination.

"*Robert Fisher*, of New Hall, gentleman, being duely sworn, deposeth that Colonel Durand did give the orders which the last witness has mentioned; and that a friend of his (this witness's) coming accidentally into the town, and asking the number of men the garrison consisted of, was immediately secured in pursuance of those orders.

"*Lieutenant Hutchinson* says those orders were given out, and put up in the Guard Room of the town.

"*Dr. Waugh*, being ask'd whether Lieut. Col. Durand did give any orders about the bringing in the ladders within seven miles round the town, says that Lieut. Col. Durand did desire all the ladders as above said might be brought into the town; that accordingly warrants were made out; and he believes all the ladders that could be found were brought into the town. And further sayes, that at Col. Durand's desire, accounts were brought in by the constables of the number of spades and other tools for turning of earth, that were in the possession of the several farmers and other country people. He also further says that Col. Durand did apply to the Deputy-Mayor to wall up the Scotch and Irish Gates; but for the reasons which Lieut. Col. Durand has mentioned in his narrative, the Deputy Mayor would not consent to it; that Lieut. Col. Durand did order materials and agreed with workmen for walling up those Gates, which upon the Rebells' approach was done.

Capt. Gilpin and *Lieut. Hutchinson* being ask'd, confirm the walling up of the Scotch and Irish Gates at the approach of the Rebels, by Lieut. Col. Durand's orders.

"*Thomas Backhouse*, of Carlisle, Ensign in one of the Town's Companys, being duly sworn and examined, says that he went round the town and suburbs by Col. Durand's desire, with another gentleman, to buy up all the cloth that could be found that was fit for making of sand bags; and they accordingly brought an account of the quantitys and prices, which was afterwards bought up for that purpose; and the baggs were made up and fill'd, and many of them placed upon the Ramparts of the town.

"*Capt. Gilpin* and *Lt. Hutchinson* being ask'd, say they remember a large quantity of sand bags were made up, and fill'd by Lt. Colol. Durand's orders; and many of them placed where there was occasion, upon the ramparts of the town. And being further examined, these witnesses also say, that Lt. Colol. Durand did apply to the Magistrates, to have several hedges and houses pull'd down, which favour'd the approach of the Rebells, by serving as a cover to them, but the Magistrates opposed it, saying they were private propertys, and that they could not do it; but they did in part comply with it, but not so much as Lieut. Colol. Durand would have had. And they also say that Lt. Colol. Durand had placed two pieces of cannon, one upon the Spring Garden Turret, and the other on the Tile Tower, to beat down those houses, if the Rebells should take possession of them.

"*Capt. Gilpin* further says, that Colol. Durand did order out the County Militia to exercise, and found their pieces of different bores; and thereupon order'd them to fit their pieces with the proper balls, but does not remember that Lieut. Colol. Durand did deliver out any lead for that purpose.

"*Lt. Hutchinson* and *Mr. Backhouse* being ask'd, say they remember Lieut.-Col. Durand did order a quantity of lead to be delivered, and balls to be cast by the Militia, which was accordingly done.

"*Dr. Waugh*, being again examined, says, Lieut.-Colonel Durand did apply for two men to be on the Steeple of the Cathedral, to discover from thence what was doing in the country; and this deponent says the Clergy did take that duty upon them. He remembers expresses were sent to Marshal Wade, to give him intelligence, and this deponent had established a correspondence in Scotland for intelligence from thence.

"*Capt. Gilpin* being asked, deposeth that Lieutenant-Colonel Durand ordered all the hand-granades to be loaded and primed, wch. he believes were about four hundred.

"*Dr. Waugh*, being further examined, says, there were alarms in the town so frequent, that there was no rest in the town, as well by the firing of the men from the Ramparts, as by beating of drums; that at last they were not minded; whereupon Colonel Durand did desire this deponent that the signal for an alarm might be by the ringing of the bells of the Cathedral, and not to be rung without the Colonel's orders, which was comply'd with and observed; but the Militia, being under no discipline, continued to make the alarms by their firing and beating of drums as before.

"*Dr. Waugh, Capt. Gilpin, Lieut. Hutchinson, Mr. Backhouse,* and *Mr. Fisher,* confirm what Lieut. Col. Durand has said of sending out partys of the Militia Horse, and the orders given them; as also the taking of a Quarter Master of the Rebells, who was sent to Marshal Wade; and that lights were put out in the town at night, as Col. Durand has related.

"And *Capt. Gilpin* and *Lieut. Hutchinson* also confirm what Col. Durand has related, with respect to dividing the Militia into three reliefs and a picket, and his having made a disposition accordingly; but that the Militia refused to consent to it notwithstanding Lieut. Col. Durand's representations, and would be all at once on the walls of the town.—And they say the Invalids were divided into the said three reliefs and picketts.

"All the above witnesses say they heard the Militia often declare they were Voluntiers, and not under the direc command of Lieut.-Colonel Durand.

"*Capt. Gilpin* was required to inform the Court what he knew of the steps taken by Colonel Durand on the approach of the Rebels, or any of their partys.

"He says that as often as any partys of the Rebels appeared near the town or Castle, and were within reach of the cannon, Lieut.-Colonel Durand ordered the cannon to fire upon them, which was accordingly done, and often obliged those partys to retreat.

"*Mr. Israel Bennett,* Dissenting Minister of Carlisle, being duely sworn and examined, says, that on Wednesday, the 13th of November last, there were some country people came in town, and told him that the Rebel partys that were left at Warwick Bridge and Corby had declared they would at all adventures take the town of Carlisle, and that they had cut down a great many fir trees, in order to make scaling-ladders; and he (the witness) saw several fir trees had been cut down at Corby, and as well as he remembers, some of those trees were split for the purpose; and he was informed by several country people that the intended ladders were to be of a particular structure, in joints, of lengths of about six foot; and he further says, that a carpenter or two at Brampton had told him they had been compelled to make the ladders, to the best of his remembrance.

"*Dr. Waugh, Mr. Bennet, Capt. Gilpin, Lt. Hutchinson, Mr. Buckhouse,* and *Mr. Fisher* say that the country people were frequently coming in town, who reported, and it was generally believed, that the Rebells were making scaling ladders, and that they had not only cut down fir trees for that purpose, but had also seized several deal boards, and that they had pressed all the carpenters round about to work at them.

"*Lieutenant Colonel Durand* produc'd a letter from Marshal Wade, dated Nov. 10th, 1745, directed "To Colonel Durand and the Gentlemen at Carlisle;" which the Court declared they were well satisfied from their own knowledge to be signed by the Marshal's own hand, and which letter Lieut. Col. Durand desired might be read, and accordingly it was read, and is as follows:—

"'Newcastle, Novr. 10th, 1745. 7 o'clock.

"'Gentlemen,—

"'I have just now the favour of your letter by express, with an account of the Rebels' approach near your city; the spirit and resolution with which you exert yourselves is very commendable, and I hope will contribute to disappoint the Rebels of any designs they may have formed against you, especially since they must take a great circuit before they can bring their artillery to make use of against you, and I dont hear they have any sufficient to make a breach in your walls.

"'They give out that they intend to proceed to Lancashire; if so they will probably pass by you,—not to lose time, or disappoint the friends they expect to meet there; I cannot follow them, the way they may probably take being impassable for artillery; and the country will be incapable to furnish so considerable a body with provisions, after they have ravaged and consum'd what they find in their way,—but I hope to meet them in Lancashire, and cause them to repent of their rashness.

"'Lieutenant-General Ligonier is marching with a considerable body of troops, in order to put a stop to their progress southwards; and I hope in a short time you will have good news from Edinburgh, the Lords of the Session being set out for that place, to re-establish the Civil Government, supported by a body of His Majesty's forces.

"'I wish you all imaginable success in so just a cause as that of liberty and the defence of your country, and am,

"'Gentlemen,

"Your most obedient humble servant,

(Signed) "'GEORGE WADE.'

"[N.B.—This is the letter mentioned by Col. Durand in his narrative in the Journal of Wednesday, Nov. 13th, pa. 13.]

["Two letters to the Marshall from the gentlemen at Carlisle were read, one of which was the letter mentioned in this answer of M. Wade, tho' they are not entered in the proceedings."]

"*Dr. Waugh* being ask'd what happen'd on the receipt of this letter, says that he was not present when it was received by all the gentlemen who happen'd to be then altogether, among whom were many of the Officers of Militia; but upon receipt of it Lieut. Col. Durand sent for this witness, who upon coming into the room found a great confusion among them, saying that they apprehended by the above letter that Marshal Wade could not come to their relief; that they had defended the town six days and six nights in hopes of being reliev'd, but seeing they were not to be relieved they had nothing further to do, (or used words to that effect); and said they thought the Government did not look upon the place as being of any consequence. And this witness further says, the two additional companys of Major-General Howard's Regiment when the Rebellion first broke out were, one in the town, and the other in the neighbourhood, but were afterwards taken away.

"*Mr. Fisher*, being ask'd, says he was present at the above meeting when the said letter was received, and confirms what the last witness has said; and further says that Lieut.-Colonel Durand spoke many things to them to encourage them, that they were in no danger, and using other words to that effect, and to dissuade them from thinking that the Marshal's letter implyed he could not come to their relief; which the Chancellor also confirms.

"*Dr. Waugh, Capt. Gilpin, Lt. Hutchinson, Mr. Fisher*, and *Mr. Backhouse*, farther declare, that several Militia Officers being assembled in an upper room, Major Farrer, of the Militia, came down to acquaint Colol. Durand that they were met to consult about going out of the town and leaving it; upon which Colol. Durand went up to them, but these witnesses dont know what pass'd then; but Lt.-Colol. Durand came down afterwards and told them what had pass'd above, which was as he has set forth in his narrative; and they did hear several of the Militia agree to the truth of what Colol. Durand had said to those witnesses; and the witnesses did themselves hear Colol. Durand refuse opening the Gates of the town to any of them, and the Militia did again return to their posts that night.

"All these witnesses also say that Lt.-Colol. Durand did all he could to persuade the Militia to stay, or at least a part of them if they would not all; but he could not prevail upon any of them. And these witnesses believe the Militia all acted together in concert, as they had actually declared they had shaken hands together, and what was to be done should be so done by all.

"They also say they were present with Lt.-Colol. Durand upon the walls of the Citadell, having heard the Rebells had thrown up an intrenchment, where there was a great crowd of people who were in great consternation; whereupon Lt.-Colol. Durand did say all he could to encourage them, telling them the work the Rebells were upon was nothing of any consideration—that they (the Rebells) had no cannon to hurt them,—and using other expressions despising what the Rebells were doing; and added that if they intended anything they would not carry on works of that kind in the day time; and therefore this shew was only to intimidate them; and thereupon Lt.-Colol. Durand gave orders to fire upon them, which was done.

"Then Lieut.-Colol. Durand produced a paper signed by Sir John Pennington and others of the Militia Officers, being the paper mark'd A, referr'd to by Lieut.-Colol. Durand in his narrative, on the back of which is a deposition made upon oath by Sir John Pennington before Edward Ashe, Esq., one of His Majesty's Justices of the Peace.

"Before reading the said paper and deposition,

"*Edward Ashe*, Esq., Justice of the Peace for the County of Middlesex and the City and Liberty of Westminster, being duely sworn and examined, saith that the paper signed by Sir John Pennington and this deponent, and now produced, is the deposition of the said Sir John Pennington, duely made and sworn before him this deponent.

"Then the said paper mark'd A, and Sir John Pennington's deposition thereon were read, and are as follows:—

[A.]

"'The Militia of the Countys of Cumberland and Westmoreland having come voluntarily into the City of Carlisle, for the defence of the said Citty, and having for six days and six nights successively been upon duty, in expectation of relief from His Majesty's forces, but it appearing yt. no such relief is now to be had, and ourselves not able to do duty or hold out any longer, are determined to capitulate, and do certify that Colol. Durand, Capt. Gilpin, and the rest of the Officers, have well and faithfully done their duty.

"'Given under our hands, the 14 day of Novr., 1745.

"'(Signed)

"'J. Pennington
"'M. Farrer
"'Jo. Dacre.
"'H. Senhouse
"'J. Dalston.
"'John Hopper.
"'Ed. Wilson.
"'Geo. Crowle.
"'Fle. Fleming.
"'Jno. Ponsonby.
"'Jas. Crackanthorp.
"'Richd. Cooke.
"'Giles Moore.'

"*Sir John Pennington's Deposition as follows:*

"'*Middx. and Westr. to wit.*} SIR JOHN PENNINGTON, Bart., came this day before me, one of His Majesty's Justices of the Peace for this County, City, and Liberty, and made oath that the Declaration on the other side of this paper, signed by himself and the other Officers of the Militia, whose names are likewise subscribed, was the original paper given by him and the rest of the Officers of Militia to Colonel Durand.

(Signed) "'J. PENNINGTON,'

"'Sworn voluntarily before me, this
25th of August, 1746.

(Signed) "'EDWD. ASHE.'

"*Mr Bennet* and *Mr. Fisher* being again examined, say they were with Lieut.-Col. Durand at the Citadell, and return'd with him to the King's Arms, where most of the Militia Officers were assembled; and upon his coming into the room they immediately declared to him, that neither they nor their men would defend the town any longer; which declaration Lieut.-Col. Durand received with a suitable indignation, and used all the arguments he could to prevail with them not to insist on their declarations, but it was to no effect; and they then gave him the paper signed by the Militia Officers, which these witnesses believe to be the same above set forth, desiring it might be read aloud, which was accordingly done; and Lieut.-Col. Durand and the rest of the officers thereupon protested strongly against that resolution.

"*Dr. Waugh* being also further examined, says that when he knew the Militia Officers had taken the above resolution, he endeavoured to perswade them to keep to their duty, till they knew whether the Rebells would treat with them, or what terms they would grant them; but they answered it signified nothing to argue; they were resolved, had all agreed, and would capitulate for themselves, whether the town would join or not; and in general this witness remembers that Lieut.-Colonel Durand used all possible arguments to get the Militia to continue in their duty, but to no effect.

"All the witnesses agree in Lieut.-Colonel Durand's having endeavoured to disswade the Militia from their resolution, but to no purpose.

"*Lieut. Hutchinson, Mr. Fisher,* and *Mr. Backhouse* declare they heard Lieut.-Col. Durand tell the Deputy Mayor, upon his asking him what he would do, that he (Col. Durand) would never capitulate with Rebels, but was determined to defend both Town and Castle as long as he could.

"*The above Witnesses* and *Dr. Waugh, Capt. Gilpin,* and *Mr. Bennett* declare that the Militia had all left the walls in great confusion and thrown down their arms; and some time afterwards the townspeople, on seeing this, apprehending they could not defend the town themselves, forsook the duty they had done before, and were then in a great confusion themselves.

"*Capt. Gilpin* and *Lieut. Hutchinson* being asked if Lieut.-Col. Durand made any and what disposition of the troops, say that he had made a disposition, which they apprehend to have been a very proper one, in case of alarms; having appointed the several alarm posts as well for the Militia and Town Companys, as for the Invalids, and also appointed some guards; but all to no purpose, as the Militia and Town Companys would not observe it.

"*Lieut. Hutchinson* further says, that Lieut.-Col. Durand going up after this confusion into the Castle, and seeing from thence two large bodys of Rebels marching off towards Rowcliff, he sent this witness to the King's Arms, to acquaint the Militia Officers therewith, and said that he (Lieut.-Col. Durand, who was then lame with the gout) would follow him, to endeavour again to perswade them to change their resolution; and this witness says he did himself speak to them to that purpose, to which they answered, it was only a trick of Col. Durand's to draw them on to do more duty, but that they would not do any more.

"*Lieut. Hutchinson* and *Mr. Fisher* say that they heard the Mayor tell Lieut.-Col. Durand that the townspeople had come to a resolution to join with the Militia in capitulating with the Rebels, as they said they thought they were not able to defend the town of themselves, the Militia having left them; and these witnesses heard Lieut.-Col. Durand protest against this proceeding of the inhabitants.

"*Dr. Waugh, Capt. Gilpin, Lieut. Hutchinson, Mr. Fisher,* and *Mr. Backhouse* say that after this resolution of the inhabitants, Lieut.-Col. Durand went into the Castle, and was soon afterwards followed by most of the Militia Officers, and about four hundred of their men (as these witnesses believe as to numbers), and by several Gentlemen and Clergy of the Town; who all declared they would defend the Castle to the last; and that thereupon Lieut,-Col. Durand declared to them as he has set forth in his narrative.

"*Mr. Backhouse* further says that he was sent express to Marshal Wade, to acquaint him with this resolution, which he accordingly did.

"*Capt. Gilpin, Lieut. Hutchinson, Mr. Fisher,* and *Mr. Backhouse* say that before Lieut.-Colonel Durand retired into the Castle, he ordered the cannon of the town to be nailed up, for want of time to take them with him, and which was accordingly done; and the sand bags and hand granades, small arms, and ammunition, that had been delivered out to the Militia and townspeople, were by his orders taken into the Castle. The two first of these witnesses say, they remember Colonel Durand did buy up all the bread in the town, as he has set forth in his narrative; and Lieut. Hutchinson also says, that he remembers orders were given by Lieut.-Col. Durand, for bringing in all the gunpowder that was in Town, and some of it was accordingly brought in.

"*All the above witnesses and Dr. Waugh* confirm what Col. Durand has related of repairing the two ovens in the Castle, and the well, and providing the other necessary conveniences.

"*Captain Gilpin* and *Lieut. Hutchinson* say the quantity of provisions mentioned by Lieut.-Col. Durand in his narrative is, to the best of their knowledge, true; and that there was rather more than less, of what is there mentioned.

"*Capt. Gilpin* being ask'd, confirms what Col. Durand has related to have pass'd on the 15th of November, as to this witness's having told him that there were none of the Militia upon the walls, Lieut.-Col. Durand's going thereupon to Sir John Pennington, and what Sir John did on that occasion,

"All the witnesses above named confirm also what Lieut. Col. Durand has related, of the mutiny among the private men of the Militia, and what they (the Militia) thereupon declared, the confusion that ensued, their going over the Walls, and forcing their way out of the Gates, and the circumstances that follow'd, as mentioned by Col. Durand; and that before eight o'clock in the morning they had all left him to a man, and there then remained only the few Invalids; who for the reasons Lieut. Col. Durand has mentioned, were in a manner of no use.

"*Capt. Gilpin, Lieut. Hutchinson,* and *Mr. Fisher,* confirm, that about ten o'clock most of the Militia officers and inhabitants came to Lieut. Col. Durand, telling him the Rebells had absolutely refused to grant them any terms, unless the Castle was surrendered; and what they further declared thereupon, and desiring him to take it into consideration, in the manner as related by Lieut.-Col. Durand in his Narrative.

"*The above Witnesses, Dr. Waugh,* and *Mr. Backhouse* confirm what Lieut.-Col. Durand answered on that occasion, in the manner as it is related by the Lieut.-Col. in his narrative. And Dr. Waugh says, he was present when the paper thereupon drawn up and signed by several inhabitants and Militia Officers, declaring their opinion that the Castle of Carlisle was not teneable for the reason therein mentioned, was delivered to Lieut.-Col. Durand.

"Whereupon Lieut.-Col. DURAND produced the said paper, to which Sir John Pennington having made a deposition on oath, which is there underwritten, before the same was read.

"*Edward Ashe, Esq.*, Justice of Peace, before-named, being examined on his oath, saith, that the paper signed by Sir John Pennington and this deponent, and now produced, is the deposition of the said Sir John Pennington duely made and sworn before him this deponent.

"Then the said paper, being the paper marked B, referred to by Lieut.-Col. Durand in his narrative was read and is as follows:—

[B.]

"'We, whose names are hereunto subscribed, are of opinion that the Castle of Carlisle is not teneable, the Militia of the countys of Cumberland and Westmoreland, and the inhabitants of the City of Carlisle having absolutely refused to defend it.

(Signed)

"'JOSEPH BACKHOUSE, *Mayor*.	J. PENNINGTON
"'JOHN WAUGH.	JO. DACRE.
"'J. B. GILPIN.	H. SENHOUSE.
"'J. DOUGLAS.	J. DALSTON.
"'JNO. HOLME.	E. WILSON.
"'WILL TATE.	GEO. CROWLE.
"'JOHN DAVIDSON.	RICHD. COOK.
"'RICHD. COLTHARD.	FLE. FLEMING.
"'FRA. GATTON.	GILES MOORE.
"'ROBT. FISHER.	J. TULLIE.
"'RICHD. JACKSON.	ISRAEL BENNETT.'

"*Sir John Pennington's Deposition thereon is as follows:*

"'*Middx and Westr.*' } SIR JOHN PENNINGTON, Bart., maketh oath that the above was signed by himself, and he verily believes by the several persons whose names are thereunto subscribed.

(Signed) "J. PENNINGTON.'

"Sworn voluntarily before me, this 25th August, 1746.

(Signed) "EDWD. ASHE."

"Then Lieut, Col. Durand produced the paper marked C, referred to in his narrative, being a Council of War holden in the Castle of Carlisle, which being shown to Capt. Gilpin and Lieut. Hutchinson, they say is the original Council of War holden as above-said, the 15th of November, 1745, signed by themselves, and the other members who have subscribed their names thereto.

"The said paper was read, and is as follows:—

[C.]

"'*At a Council of War holden in the Castle of Carlisle, on Monday, the 15th of November*, 1745.

"'The Militia of the Countys of Cumberland and Westmoreland, as also the Militia of the town of Carlisle having absolutely to a man refused to defend the Castle, and the Garrison, consisting only of two companys of invalids amounting to about eighty men, many of whom are extremely infirm, and the Castle very large, so that there are neither men to manage the guns nor man the walls, and the Mayor and inhabitants of the town, together with the officers of the Militia, having sent to treat with the Rebels against the opinion and protest of Colonel Durand, Capt. Gilpin, and the rest of the officers of the Garrison, and being refused any terms, and threatening to destroy both town and Militia with fire and sword unless the castle be surrendered, it is our opinion that the castle being not teneable, it is for his Majesty's service that it be abandoned, as it will be absolutely necessary for the preservation of the lives of his Majesty's subjects, who would otherwise be exposed to inevitable ruin.

"'Given under our hands at Carlisle, this 15th day of Nov., 1745.

(Signed) "'J. DURAND.
"'JNO. BERND. GILPIN.
"'JNO. COWLEY.
"'JNO. HUTCHINSON.
"'GEO. SMITH.
"'FRA. GATTON.'

"*Capt. Gilpin* was ask'd by the Court, what number of men he apprehended was necessary to do the ordinary duty of the Castle, when liable to be attack'd.

"He says he thinks it would require not less than sixty men to do duty as centrys upon the Walls, a very great number of men for making a defence, out of a want of proper flanks, which would oblige to have the Walls mann'd all round.

"*Lieut. Gen. Folliot* being ask'd what number of men would be necessary for the ordinary duty of the Castle when subject to an attack, says that not less than sixty men would be required as centrys, and about five or six hundred men to defend the Castle properly. And being further ask'd whether Lieut. Col. Durand had ever applied to him for what appeared to be wanted, says that Lieut. Col. Durand did make application to him for stores and men for the Garrison of Carlisle, and he (the witness) did apply to the Ordnance and to the Duke of Newcastle in consequence of it; and particularly

to have five hundred men out of Sinclair's and Battereau's regiments, as they came from Ireland, to be sent there. That some stores were sent, but does not know whether they arrived at Carlisle; and as to the 500 men, they were never sent.

[*Note by Dr. Waugh.*—" It is to be observed that no part of the evidence given on this trial was taken down by the Deputy Judge Advocate, but what the court thought to relate immediately to Col. Durand's defence. A strong instance of which was in this evidence of General Folliot's, who gave a reason for these men's not being sent, tho' Marshal Wade had consented to it—viz., that the Secretary of War told him, that Carlisle was not (or could not be) of consequence enough to put the government to the charge of sending an express on purpose."]

"Then Lieut.-Col. Durand ask'd all the witnesses, publickly, whether they had anything to object to his conduct or personal behaviour.

"They all declared that he had acted with great spirit and resolution; and that no man could do more, as far as they are judges, for the defence of the town and Castle, than he had done.

"After which all parties withdrew but the Court.

"THE COURT, having duely weighed and considered the several matters now before them, ARE UNANIMOUSLY OF OPINION that Lieutenant Colonel James Durand took the proper means to defend the Town and Castle of Carlisle; and he having fully proved every article set forth in his defence, this Court is also unanimously of opinion, that the said Lieutenant Colonel James Durand has done everything in his power that became an experienced, diligent, and brave officer; and from the bad condition of the Town and Castle, as well as from the resolution the Militia, Magistrates, and Towns-men came to of capitulating with the Rebells, in contradiction to the said Lieutenant Colonel's opinion and protestation, and the said Lieutenant Colonel having no more men under his command than about eighty invalids, and most of them very old and infirm, it was impracticable for him to make any longer a defence than what he did; and do therefore acquit him of the charge laid to him of the contrary.

"THOS. WENTWORTH."

The preceding documents place it beyond doubt that the immediate cause of the surrender of Carlisle was the unlucky circumstance of the Cumberland and Westmorland Militia having been brought within its walls. The Invalids were veteran soldiers, and as such behaved themselves. Colonel Durand, the commandant, did all that the trying difficulties of his position demanded. The townspeople, of every class, appear to have been prepared to stake their all, and to hold their town to the utmost extremity. The Militia it was, officers and men (with some few exceptions), that marred every endeavour of the commandant, garrison, and townsmen, to organize the disposable force for defence of the place; and reduced them to the necessity of surrendering without having incurred the loss of a man.

But what can be said of the Military department of the Government which gave occasion for so deplorable an exhibition? We have it on the authority of Dr. Waugh, otherwise it might well be discredited, that when Colonel DURAND made application through the medium of General FOLLIOT to the Ordnance and the Duke of NEWCASTLE for 500 men of SINCLAIR'S and BATTEREAU'S Regiments to be sent him as they came from Ireland, the Secretary-at-War replied *that Carlisle was not, or could not be, of consequence enough to put the Government to the charge of sending an express on purpose.*

Carlisle not worth the expense of an express—say, £50! How dense must have been the ignorance of history and geography in the war office of that day to have produced such a reply! What must have been the sensations of the Secretary-at-War when he saw the results; the Highlanders within 100 miles of the Capital, and the whole kingdom in consternation! It is no palliation to urge that the Government might reasonably expect the Militia of two counties to have made some stand against the invaders. The Secretary-at-War put the matter on a totally distinct footing; he obviously left Carlisle to its fate as not worth defending: and moreover it must have been within recollection that in 1715, when Bishop NICHOLSON and Lord LONSDALE raised the *posse comitatus* of Cumberland and Westmoreland to the number of 12,000 or 13,000 men, they dispersed and fled at the approach of less than 1,500 Highlanders and Northumberland men under FOSTER and Lord DERWENTWATER; and consequently it might have been foreseen that little dependence was to be placed upon any such local forces. There is no excuse whatever for the disregard of Dr. WAUGH's repeated warnings, and of Colonel DURAND's representations. Five hundred regular troops thrown into Carlisle would have enabled the Colonel to hold it against all the efforts of the Highlanders, who had no artillery to breach the walls. They durst not have advanced into England leaving Carlisle in possession of the King's troops behind them, whilst Marshal WADE also, with a strong force at Newcastle, might co-operate in their rear. It is therefore not too much to say that for the sake of a £50 matter at the outside, the Government in 1745 sacrificed the City of Carlisle; made way for the irruption of a victorious army of Highlanders into the very heart of England; and so not only perilled the very existence of the reigning dynasty for a time, but caused a fearful accumulation of bloodshed and misery amongst the people of both kingdoms.

The conduct of the Militia admits of no defence; yet it is by no means certain that it resulted from cowardice. The people of Cumberland and Westmoreland are of a race whose courage has been proved during centuries of warfare both regular and predatory. In antient times they bore the brunt of many a fierce inroad, and were never loath to return the compliment. With the union of England and Scotland, it is true, this their occupation (as it might once have been termed) was gone, and habits of peaceable employment had ensued; but it would be hard to say that they had thereby become degenerate in spirit. When the tide of success turned against Prince CHARLES EDWARD some pains were taken to repel the suspicion of disloyalty which the Militia had incurred. The alternative, indeed, was an awkward one,—for there seemed none other than cowardice,—yet it was safer at a time when the axe and the gibbet were painfully active in their deadly work. It may be urged with some force that the conduct of the Militia had its origin in a leaning towards the STUARTS, or at least an indifference towards the House of Hanover. The people of the border counties had, through the accession of JAMES THE FIRST to the English throne, obtained immense benefits. Hence in the Civil War they were found steadily adhering to CHARLES THE FIRST. Hence Carlisle, in 1644—5, withstood a siege and blockade of many months by the Parliamentary forces; and in 1648 Sir MARMADUKE LANGDALE was enabled to head a body of 3,000 foot and 700 horse, raised in the Counties of Cumberland and Westmoreland for the King. This shows the affections of the people to have been strongly interwoven with the ancient Monarchy; and it need scarcely be remarked that such feelings are not easily eradicated. In the revolution of 1688 the country people had little share. Lord LONSDALE, by his activity at that period, secured Carlisle for King WILLIAM; and all remained quiet, whilst the change of dynasty was perfected elsewhere: but when in 1715 Lord LONSDALE, with Bishop NICHOLSON, mustered the *posse comitatus* of the two counties, and attempted, with 12,000 or 13,000 men, to face "*the handful of Northumberland fox-hunters*," as Sir WALTER SCOTT termed them, who under FORSTER and Lord DERWENTWATER, had risen and proclaimed JAMES THE EIGHTH, they found themselves unable to bring a single man to measure swords with the insurgents: the whole body broke up and dispersed to their homes.

The truth, therefore, seems to be, that the rural population of Cumberland, never thoroughly weaned from their predilection for the antient line of Kings, entertained in 1745 little or no affection for the Hanoverian family; and could arouse no ardour in its cause against the gallant representative of the STUART line: neither had they the enthusiasm of the Highlanders, nor the influential example and authority of their chiefs, to impel them on the other hand to embrace his cause. They came to Carlisle unwillingly—they pleaded the expiration of their legal term of service—some even departed for their homes, but were brought back by force. What could be expected of men in such a frame of mind? It was not the want of stone walls to cover them that made the yeomen of Cumberland disperse in 1715. It was not the walls of Carlisle that could make them valiant in 1745. In both instances the ingredient awanting was that hearty, generous loyalty to the reigning family which a century previously elicited from their ancestors in the cause of CHARLES THE FIRST efforts of courage and constancy not surpassed in any part of England.

To whomsoever the blame may be properly attributable, one thing is certain, viz., that the weight of it fell on the citizens of Carlisle. They got a bad name, which for many years adhered to them, and at the time subjected them to affronts and indignities. Dr. WAUGH and some other gentlemen of the town effectually cleared themselves individually from all suspicion, and established a claim to the approbation of the government for the vain exertions they had

H 2

made: the Militia officers escaped all inquiry into their conduct, whilst the whole brunt of the odium was directed upon the town by the arrest of the Mayor and some of the Aldermen and citizens, who were kept in custody a considerable time, and then turned out without trial or any opportunity of explaining themselves.

HIGHMOOR'S HOUSE,

In which Charles Edward and afterwards the Duke of Cumberland Lodged, 1745.

CHAPTER III.

THE Capture of Carlisle was in every respect a fortunate circumstance for the Prince. Besides its moral effect, it put him in possession of a number of cannon and a quantity of ammunition, and military stores: besides arms of various other kinds, amongst others are mentioned the broad swords taken from the Highlanders at Preston in 1715. And, which was more important than all, it furnished a basis for securing his further advance into England, affording a safe medium for his communication with Scotland; and a secure point to retreat upon in case of reverse. No time was lost in following it up. Immediately after the surrender, part of the army appears to have marched southwards; for we are told by Dr. Waugh, who quitted the town on the evening of Sunday, the 17th November, that before he reached Penrith, 18 miles distant, he found himself again surrounded by the Rebels. At that time the Prince himself was yet remaining at Brampton. He entered Carlisle next day the 18th, and fixed his quarters at the house of Mr. Highmore, Attorney-at-Law. This was a large white-fronted house on the west side of English Street, nearly in the centre of the city. It stood a little back from the street, which is there wide and spacious. The entry was by an archway in the centre of the building, of sufficient width for a carriage drive, which led through to the garden behind, extending to

Blackfriars' Street. Under this archway were the entries of the house, and on it in front was a large bay window of the drawing-room above, on the first floor. The house was large and commodious. It was antiently called "*The Earl's Inn*"; and was in all probability the property and occasional habitation of the Earls of Cumberland in antient times, when Carlisle was a place of great public importance, and affairs required their presence there; or of refuge from the wasting inroads of the Scots—for in those times scarcely was there a family of consequence in the country that had not its house of refuge in the town. Highmore's House, as it was called in later times, has been converted into shops, and new fronted; the archway which formed the entrance to it is now "Barwise's Court'; and in the garden has been formed a street communicating with Blackfriars' Street: so that it is no longer recognizable as "a house."

Mr. Highmore, at all events, had no reason to lament the occupation of his dwelling by the Prince, since we learn in the "Household Book" that he received twenty guineas for the mere use of it during four days, tho' he furnished nothing,—not so much as coal or candle: neither did it affect his appetite, for we are also informed that, besides this liberal payment, he had every day two dishes of meat at dinner, and as many at supper for himself and his wife, at the Prince's charges.

The terms of the capitulation were honourably fulfilled, and there is no mention to be found of any plunder, violence, or licence on the part of the Highlanders. The effects that had been taken into the Castle for safety were allowed to be removed. It is said, indeed, in Hutchinson's History of Cumberland, that £2,000 was raised by the town to save the houses from being plundered, but no authority is stated for this assertion, and it is believed to be incorrect. Nothing of the kind is mentioned in any of the letters to Dr. WAUGH by his friends left in Carlisle at the time, who would undoubtedly have suffered in the exaction had such a thing taken place, and could not have failed to mention it when writing particularly on the subject of their sufferings. A large map of England taken for the Prince's use, and some two or three dozens of wine, drunk to his health no doubt, formed the sum total of the deficit in Dr. WAUGH's house; Mr. WARDALE, his Curate, found that the door of the wine vault had been attempted and the lock spoilt; but he writes, in a strain of considerable satisfaction, that he had "clap'd two more padlocks on the outside and was satisfied that all was safe within"—a feat which would have been of little avail had there been any thing like violence abroad.

It is alleged that the Prince, whilst at Carlisle, nominated one THOMAS CAPPOCK to be Bishop, and that CAPPOCK was accordingly installed as such in the Cathedral. But there is great reason to question the truth of this. On the trial of CAPPOCK, the witness against him deposed that CAPPOCK joined the Rebels at Manchester; that he was acting as an officer, and marched with them from Manchester to Derby; that he marched with them thence for Carlisle; and the witness heard him preach several sermons. The King's council then asked if he acted as a divine among the Rebels, as well as a military officer? The witness answered, "he did so. I have heard him read prayers a great many times with a hanger by his side, he was called Chaplain to the Manchester regiment, and because he was a great favourite among the Rebels, Mr. HAMILTON, the Pretender's Governor of the Castle of Carlisle, made him a Bishop, and this was done by order of the young Pretender soon after the City of Carlisle surrendered to the Rebels." This account is inconsistent within itself. It is clear that CAPPOCK was not in Carlisle "*soon after the surrender of the City to the Rebels*"—because he joined at Manchester, and came there with them first in their retreat. And it is utterly improbable that his nomination to the Bishopric and his installation in the Cathedral should have taken place at the period alleged without it being mentioned in the correspondence between Dr. Waugh and his Curate, who remained at Carlisle. So outrageous an act of indecency must have excited the strongest indignation in every member of the church, yet it is never mentioned. We may therefore acquit the Prince of it, and safely conclude that it was nothing more than the impudent assumption of CAPPOCK himself, who, having forged his letters of orders, was quite equal to the forgery of his episcopal title also.

Captain JOHN HAMILTON was made Governor of the Castle of Carlisle, and a garrison of about 100 men placed in it. Sir JOHN ARBUTHNOT, an officer in the French King's service, was appointed Governor of the Town, and occupied the house of Mr. TULLIE, in Abbey Street, (now Mr. DIXON's,)—Mr. TULLIE and his family having left the town and taken refuge at Barnard Castle. One Colonel STUART is also mentioned as being left—but it is probable that he marched south, to join the main body, about the end of November, when a battle was expected, and an order came for every man that could possibly be spared to join. Mr. GEO. ABERNETHY, an officer in GLENBUCKET'S regiment, acted as Commissary.

It is stated in the Jacobite memoirs, published by CHAMBERS, that Mr. STRICKLAND, one of the eight gentlemen who accompanied the Prince from France, died at Carlisle whilst it was in the possession of the Highlanders, but no record of his interment is to be found at either of the Churches in the town. It is possible that he might be interred, and yet no entry may have been made on the register during that unsettled period, but as his name is in the list of prisoners taken in the town on its subsequent recapture by the Duke of CUMBERLAND, it is most likely that his death took place during or after the removal of the prisoners to Lancaster. He was probably of the family of STRICKLAND, of Sizergh, in Westmoreland; one of whom, Sir THOMAS STRICKLAND, had been of the Privy Council of King JAMES THE SECOND, and had followed the fortunes of that Monarch when he abdicated, and died in France.

Of Mr. PATTINSON, the Deputy-Mayor, we hear little more. He had contrived successfully to keep himself out of danger; for, whilst he pulled the strings, the Mayor (Mr. BACKHOUSE) was the actor, and bore the blame. The Jacobite song, "*The Mayor of Carlisle*," refers to Pattinson alone:—

"O Pattison! ohon! ohon!
"Thou wonder of a Mayor!
"Thou blest thy lot thou wert no Scot,
"And bluster'd like a player.
"What hast thou done with sword or gun,
"To baffle the Pretender?
"Of mouldy cheese and bacon grease,
"Thou much more fit defender!

"O front of brass, and brain of ass,
"With heart of hare compounded!
"How are thy boasts repaid with costs,
"And all thy pride confounded!
"Thou need'st not rave, lest Scotland crave
"Thy kindred or thy favour;
"Thy wretched race can give no grace,
"No glory thy behaviour."

The ridicule and abuse heaped on him by the Rebels perhaps contributed to clear him of suspicion in the eyes of the Government; for we do not find him amongst those who were afterwards taken into custody. He died in the ensuing year.

On the morning of the 22nd November, CHARLES EDWARD, arrayed in the Highland garb, marched out of Carlisle on foot at the head of his troops, full of hope, and confident of success. Fortune, after a long and unremitting persecution of his family, seemed to have relented towards him. Every step he had taken since his landing on Scottish ground had been signally successful—not less so this his first essay in England. Little did he suspect that it was but the one solitary gleam of sunshine that was destined to enliven his career, as if to render the after gloom more dense by the contrast; or that Carlisle, which he now quitted in triumphant anticipation, was so soon to behold him once more a hasty fugitive, and to witness that bloody vengeance against his devoted followers to which his illusory success was to provoke the English Government.

At the first approach of the Highlanders many of the country people around Carlisle had left their homes in panic, and fled to more remote parts of the country, but this quickly subsided, and they all returned, finding that no violence was offered. By the time of the Prince's march southwards, the prevailing sensation was that of curiosity. As he marched at the head of the Highlanders, the people came on all sides to see him pass. He had given his strict injunction, and it is admitted to have been as strictly complied with, that all respect should be paid to the female sex. The Highlanders "never used so much as a single woman in the whole country with indecency"—hence the women as well as the men did not scruple to indulge their prevailing impulse. And in after times many an old matron was there that could tell how in her young days she had mounted her pony and hastened to Barrock fell to witness the march of "Bonnie Prince Charlie" and his gallant band.

The accounts of what took place in Carlisle after his departure are scanty. The Militia, no doubt, had all made the best of their way home on the earliest opportunity. The townsmen, left to themselves, seem to have in some degree recovered their spirits; and even to have meditated a recapture of the Castle by a *coup de main.* The draft of 40 men from the garrison to join the main body in Lancashire, in the end of November, by reducing its strength, encouraged their design. To what extent it had been matured we are not informed. It was betrayed to HAMILTON, the Governor, by one JOHN CREIGHTON, a smith, as it is said; whereupon HAMILTON craftily invited the Mayor, Aldermen, and others, to an entertainment in the Castle, and there took the opportunity of obtaining their parole, that they would give discouragement to every attempt of the kind. The young men of the City, however, had frequent affrays with the soldiers of the garrison when they found them at a disadvantage—and took some of them prisoners, whom they sent off to Marshal WADE, at Newcastle. The Governor endeavoured to check this disposition by seizing the parents of some who were identified as taking part in the skirmishes; but the hostile spirit of the townspeople was daily more clearly displayed, so that HAMILTON threatened military execution. Yet nothing of the kind was actually attempted. On the contrary, Sir JOHN ARBUTHNOT, the Governor of the town, appears to have ingratiated himself with the inhabitants. Mr. BIRKET, a Prebendary of the Cathedral, became so friendly with him as to bring upon himself the observation of his Diocesan, and the suspicions of the Duke of CUMBERLAND subsequently: and Mr. WARDALE, Dr. WAUGH's curate, who was left in charge of the Doctor's property, evidently looked to Sir JOHN as a safeguard rather than enemy.

When rumours of a reverse in Derbyshire began to reach Carlisle, Governor HAMILTON took measures to prepare for the worst. He seized on the markets; fixed prices on all commodities; laid in supplies; stopped the post office bags, and opened the letters; impressed beds and other necessaries for the use of a garrison. Every thing betokened his apprehension of the retreat of the Highlanders, and of his expectation that Carlisle would shortly have to stand the brunt of an attack by the King's forces.

Meantime Dr. WAUGH had removed from Barnard Castle to York, where the Earl of Carlisle kindly provided him with a house. The stoppage of the post rendered correspondence with his friends in Carlisle difficult. The following letters, however, possess some interesting details.

"*Sir Philip Musgrave to Dr. Waugh.*

"To Dr. Waugh—to the care of the Postmaster, at Penrith, Cumberland.

"Orgreaves, Nov. 16th.

"Dear Sir,—

"As the two enclosed are come into my hands I would not send 'em without assuring you and Mrs. Waugh of my respects, tho' I have nothing else to say; nor if I had would it be prudent to be very circumstantial now that I understand a probability of the posts being intercepted; my Lady Derby brought yesterday to Lichfield an account of Carlisle being attacked with some loss to the Highlanders. You may be sure we are in great pain for the situation of our poor county, now become a scene of confusion; and accounts come so slowly and uncertainly hither that our anxiety is more likely to continue. I understand you have the courage to shut yourself up within the walls of Carlisle. I hope to hear from you when you have an opportunity, nobody being more truly anxious for your safety than,

"Sir,

"Your most obliged Humble Servant,

"P. M.

"All are well here, and much at yrs. and yr. family service."

---

* "*Mr. Nicolson to Dr. Waugh.*

"Hond. Sir,—

"Having no heart to visit poor Carlisle yet, I dispatched a messenger yesterday with some queries to Mr. Wardale, who sent me the inclosed answer, which I hope you'll think a mighty satisfactory one, all things considered.

"We are and shall be extreamly uneasie here till we hear again from you, and would therefore beg a line by the Penrith carrier, under cover either to Mr. Raincock or Dr. Donkin, and I think there will be no hazard of my getting it safe to-morrow sen'night. God send us good news and a happy meeting, and I am ever yours,

"Most faithfully,

"JOS. NICOLSON.

"Hawkesdale, Nov. 25, 1745."

"*Mr. Wardale to Mr. Nicolson.*

"Dear sir,

"I am sorry to hear of Mr. Chancellor, &c., having been confined so long at Hutton, because I fancy it would

---

* Mr. Joseph Nicolson, of Hawksdale, near Rose Castle, the nephew of William Nicolson, Bishop of Carlisle, who died in 1726. He was a gentleman of considerable property, talent, and erudition,—was the manorial steward, auditor, and confidential adviser of the Bishops of Carlisle, and also of other families of importance in the county; and by his zeal and influence appers to have been the main stay of the political interest of the Howard family in Carlisle. In conjunction with Dr. Burn, he published, in 1777, "The History and Antiquities of Cumberland and Westmoreland,"—a work which evinces great research and discrimination.

not be with their inclination. As to his house, goods, &c., I hope he will not think himself badly off, though nobody offered a farthing for what they had. They have drunk about two dozen and a half of wine, two or three bottles of brandy, and eat a good deal of victuals; but done no harm to any thing in the house; nor taken any thing out of it except a large map of England for the Prince's service, (in their tearms.) As to his hay, they have not I think committed much waste in the stable in town; and as to his stable at the garden, and hay stack in the Close, they are untouched: so that his loss that way I think is but trifling. I find they have attempted the wine vault, but by good luck the door and lock have proved too strong for them, for it continues still locked, but the lock so bent that the key will not open it, and I have clap'd two more padlocks on the outside; so I am satisfied all is safe within. I have been at Mr. Tullie's to enquire how all things were there, and I find no harm done; and Sir John Arbuthnot, who lodges there, and is left Deputy Governor of the Castle, has promised me to take all possible care that no harm shall be done to any thing in the house; as he has done also for Mr. Chancellor's, upon Col. Stuart's recommendation. As to the safety of sending clothes, &c.,—I can only say that I can get a protection for them from the Governor, I believe any time, but I fancy the best security is a certainty that the road is clear for I am perswaded there are no more to follow. I have had some little squabbles, but have succeeded thus far; and I do not apprehend much danger for the future. I beg you'll give my duty to the Chancellor and service to all along with him, and all on the other side Stainmore; and do me the favour to pay my best compliments to Mrs. Nicholson, and all the good family at Hawksdale, for whom, I can assure you, I have been much concerned, as I do not doubt they have been for their friends at Carlisle.

"I am, dear Sir,

"Your most obedient humble Servant,

"R. W.

P.S.—I hope Mrs. Tullie, and Mr. Chancellor need not be apprehensive of any future danger to their houses, at least no diligence or care shall be wanting in me to preserve everything."

"*Mr. Wardale to Dr. Waugh.*

"Revd. Sir,—

"I wrote two lines in haste to Mr. Nicholson the other day, which he tells me he has sent forward to you, which will give you some little notion how affairs stand here. Your house is clear and quiet at present; and tho' they talk still of more forces coming up, I am told by some that have travell'd the road there are none between here and Edinburgh. What you mentioned to Mr. Wilson's servant shall be taken what care I can of; and I intend to send a messenger over to-morrow to consult Mr. Nicholson about the best method. Our Governor talks often about Military execution, but has not, and I trust does not, design to do anything that is hard to the town.

"If they should return upon us, we can only do the best we can. If things continue as they are at present, I hope both you and Mr. Tullie may be easy as to any great damage to your houses and goods; and if anything worse happens, I can only say that I trust in God nothing shall be wanting that lies in my power. I think I have nothing more to add to what I wrote to Mr. Nicholson that can be worth your hearing. I am, Revd. Sir, with my hearty prayers for yours and good Mrs. Waugh's welfare, and humble service to all friends,

"Your most dutiful and most obliged humble Servant,

"R. W.

"P. S.—'Tis with great pleasure that all your friends here have heard that your are all pretty well and safe upon Stainmore, out of all danger from straggling parties, which we much feared.

"Carlisle, Tuesday, Nov. 26th, 1745,

"Ten at Night."

"*Lady Annandale to Mrs. Waugh.*

"Comlongon, November ye. 28th, 1745.

Madam,—

"I have felt in the most sensible manner what you and the good Chancellor have gone through since I had the pleasure to dine with you, and sincerely wish you may have found as few ill consequences from such an unhappy affair as the nature of it can admit, and hope this will find yourself and family in perfect health. I thank God I have escaped a visit from these dreaded gentlemen, tho' most of my neighbours of four miles distance from me had one, and some of them lost their horses. I must now return my thanks for the friendly care the good Chancellor and you have taken of my trunk of plate, which I shall among other obligations retain a grateful sense of; and if it's convenient, and the Chancellor and you think it safe to send it back by my servant, Adam Beckton, and Hewert's the carryers, when they come for it, I desire the trunk of plate may be delivered to them. I got a letter to-day by a private hand from Dicky, who tells he and Charles are well, but desire to come home, as the scholars does nothing after this week, most of them being gone for fear of the Highlanders. I am at a loss what to doe till I know if it's safe for them and horses to pass through Carlisle, or if it's necessary to get a protection from the new Governor of Carlisle Castle. The Chancellor's and your opinion of this will add to the obligations of, Madam,

"Your most sincere humble Servant,

"C. ANNANDALE.

"My humble service waits on the Chancellor, and my compliments to Mr. and Mrs. Tully, who I hope are well, and have not suffered from the New Inhabitants."

"*Mr. Wardale to Dr. Waugh.*

"Carlisle, Nov. 29th, 1745.

"Rev. Sir,

"Mr. Wilson's servant having been detained in order to see Dr. Douglas, who was in Scotland, you'll receive with this a letter writ two nights ago. Lady Annandale's servant obliged me to open the letter to Mrs. Waugh, and I write to her to let her know her trunk was safe, &c. We are still pretty quiet. Sir John is still at Mr. Tullie's, but pays for everything he has, as he tells me. He desires his service to Mr. Tullie, and promises all safety. He talks of going to lodge in the Castle. I could almost wish he would stay where he is, but cannot take it upon me to press it, not knowing Mr. Tullie's mind.

"By the bye, I believe all their men here will desert them; some going off every night. Mr. Wilson's servant now stays for me, I have nothing particular to add at present, but that I am Rev. Sir,

"Your most dutiful and

"Obliged humble Servant,

"R. W."

"*Lord Carlisle to Dr. Waugh.*

"Nov. 30th.

"Sir,

"I have been very impatient and uneasy till I received your letter last night. I am extremely glad to hear that you and Mrs. Waugh are well, and got out of the Rebels' hands, though I am afraid you have suffered much every way. I long to hear the particulars of the defence and surrender of Carlisle. The Mayor was in great credit here for a few days, but it was soon over. I have a little house at York—which is quite furnished; if you will make use of it till things are a little settled it is very much at your service, and you will be out of the way there of the Rebels as they are marching on in Lancashire.

The Duke's army must soon meet them, and put an end to those people who have given us so much disturbance. As Nowell got away I have not heard what mischief they have done to me or any body else; but I take it for granted, they have taken every thing that came in their way. My Lady Carlisle desires her compliments to Mrs. Waugh and you.

"Your most faithful humble Servant,

"CARLISLE."

"I have given orders about my house at York, so if it is any conveniency I hope you will immediately make use of it.

"*Mr. Robinson to Dr. Waugh.*

"Chancery Lane, Novr. 30th, 1745.

"Dear Sir,—

"You cannot very easily conceive what satisfaction your letter wch. I recd. yesterday gave to your friends in town, particularly Will. Tullie, Nancy, and I. We heard a very dismal account of your being prisoners to the Rebels for the ransom of Carlisle, which I hope for your own sakes was not true; but you have as great a share of our pity and compassion as if the affair was undoubted. Will. Tullie* has been more particularly affected, and has, I think, confined himself to his chamber ever since he heard

---

* Mr. William Tullie, brother of Mrs. Waugh, was in the Six Clerks' Office, in Chancery.

the report. You cannot be too circumstantial in your accounts of the affair of Carlisle, for we do not yet know the particulars, or who to blame, or who to commend. I mean between the townspeople and the Militia. Everybody condemns the vanity of the Mayor in his letter to my Lord Duke of Newcastle upon the retreat of the Rebels from before Carlisle after the first summons. I dare say as soon as we can look about us he will be called to an account for refusing yr. dispatches a place in his express. I fancy it will be still very old news to give you any accounts we have of the Rebels here; but by the last accounts they were bending towards Manchester; however, considering the inconsiderableness of their numbers, the ill condition of them; and on the other hand considering the high spirit of the Duke and of the soldiers under his command, I think the Rebels entirely ruined, and that the affair is drawing towards a crisis, and must be determined in a little time. The people here will have that the 2d son of the Pretender was on board the *Soleil* privateer, taken by the Sheerness man-of-war. I wish that news may be confirmed, but, as yet, I own doubt of it. Will Tullie, Nancy, and I join in affectionate service to you, Mrs. Waugh, and Mr. Tullie, and all friends, and I am,

"Dear Sir,

"Your's, most affect'ly,

"CHRISR. ROBINSON."

"*Sir Philip Musgrave to Dr. Waugh.*

"Orgreave, Nov. 30th.

"Dear Sir,

"The not having heard from you since the taking Carlisle, and my Uncle Chardin's account from London of your friends there being uninformed of your situation since that time, and therefrom suspecting your being taken as a hostage, has filled me with the greatest concern and uneasiness upon your account, which, I hope, will be removed before I can receive an answer to these, which, to be surer of its coming to your hands some time or other, I shall direct to Mrs. Waugh; and you may be assured that you have no friends more impatient to hear of your welfare than those now at Orgreave, a place in which we think ourselves in the greatest security, as protected by the Duke's Army now in and about Lichfield, which is at this time greatly animated by his presence, and eager to engage the enemy, which were at Preston last Thursday, tho' it was said a party was gone to Liverpool; but I think the rest will hardly attempt to make the coast for fear of being inclosed between the sea and our 2 armies, and bringing inevitable destruction upon themselves. Our Ladies here are perfectly well, and little Pap. improves apace in wisdom and stature. We long to hear some particular accounts from Cumberland, both in regard to our Friends and our own selves; but as I have not heard much of an authorised plundering the country, I hope at least those places which they only passed through are not much hurt, and that the Capitulation for Carlisle was observed. Adieu, Dr. Sir. My Wife and Sister joyn in respects to you and Mrs. Waugh, with your

"Most faithful and obedt. Servt.,

"P. M.

"I understand your daughters stood the seige, and should be glad to hear they neither suffer'd by frights or otherwise. I just hear the Highlanders are beating up for volunteers at Liverpool and Manchester, and have got 50 at the latter. So I suppose the Young Chevalier is still at Preston."

"*Mr. Chardin to Dr. Waugh.*

"Sir,

"I was extremely glad to hear by your letter to my Lord Carlisle that you was at last got safe out of Cumberland: indeed all your friends in town were very uneasy to know what was come of you: here is a letter received yesterday which is intended for you and addressed to your Lady. We are now apprehensive of ye Rebels coming to London, and that they will endeavour to give the slip to both the Duke and Wade,—if so we may have them here in a week. A camp will be immediately formed upon Finchley Common a little beyond Barnet. Lord Carlisle orders me to tell you that he wrote to you last post, and offered his house at York: he hopes his letter did not miscarry; pray be so good as to present my humble service to Mr. and Mrs. Hassell, and that I would have wrote but expect to hear of her return home, tho' not advisable till these vermin are safe some other way. Poor Harry has wrote to me to know what was become of all his Cumberland relations. I beg my respects to your Lady and to all my acquaintances,—refugees at Barnard Castle.

"I am, with respect,

Sir, your most obedient humble servant,

"GEORGE CHARDIN.

"I hear ye. Pretender is very angry with Mr. Sympson and Mr. Martin for not staying at their houses to receive him. I mean no joke.

"To the Rev. Mr. Chancr. Waugh, att

"Barnard Castle, in ye.

"Bishoprick of Durham."

"*Mr. Nicolson to Dr. Waugh.*

"Hond. Sir,—

"After much expectation John Gardiner and his guide from Hutton called here on Friday evening, and we hope you are all well, tho' truly we could get very little out of him; and as he had no letter, made us fear the worst: I sent an old horse with him to Carlisle to bring your goods here and promised to have a letter ready when he came back, but he now desires it to Carlisle, which shall be complied with. I heartily wish you may receive him and his carriage safe; but truly I think him a most idle, trifling fellow, and not fit for these precarious times. I had an account last night from Francy Hewitt that there are certainly 2,000 more Rebels at Perth, and that they expect to be joined by their clans dayly, but my acct. saies that Glascow, Aire, and Irwin, have raised 5,000 men by whom its hoped they'll soon be defeated. Our common country clash saies that there is to be a general battle at Preston this day, and that Wade and Ligonier are certainly joined—God send us a good account of that day whenever it happens. There was an order sent this last week to Carlisle for such of the new garrison there as were able, to march directly to the main body, in pursuance of which about forty left that place on Wednesday and Thursday, and a party of them were attacked about Lowther—one killed, two wounded, and nine taken prisoners, who were immediately sent to Marshall Wade. Our B—— had resolved upon a London journey this winter directly from P——, but I think that scheme is now changed, and he designs for home the latter end of this week.

"Your's, &c.,

"J. N.

"Dec. 1st, 1745."

Mr. Wardale to Dr. Waugh.

"Carlisle, Dec. 2, 1745.

"Rev. Sir,

"I have sent on the other leaf a catalogue of your goods in the two trunks, which I hope will come safe to you, as I hear of no parties now in the road. I shall be very uneasy till I hear of their arrival. A line by the post I believe will come safe. We are much in the same situation as when I wrote last, very little disturbance. Our strangers to day fired the cannons and rejoiced, they say, upon the landing of 10,000 French in Scotland. In fact, I am afraid your effects may still be in danger. I suspend my belief, and can only wish and hope the best. Sr. John is still at Mr. Tullie's and is very civil and obliging, and still desires his service to Mr. Tullie, and assures him of great safety, if he please to return home. Lady Annandale sent for her trunk to-day, and speaks with great regard for you and Mrs. Waugh, and desires her compliments to you when I write. I sent not the letter, because, there is an order to me for the delivery of her trunk in it. I think I have nothing more worth your hearing that I care to write. I beg my compliments to all friends with you, and shall always be glad to receive yours or their commands in anything in my power.

"I am, Rev. Sir,

"Your most dutiful and obliged humble servant,

"R. W.

"Poor Hans only a 2nd Lieut. at last. I hope ye. honest Register is well, I hear he is with you. Your study infects me, I believe. I have writ twenty letters I think this last week.

"*1st Trunk*—A cloth gown cassock, &c., a hat, 2 pr. of shoes, 1 pr. of slippers, a bedgown, a pr. of pink shoes, 12 bands, 1 doz. ½ doz. of shirts, a pr. of breeches, a cloth waistcoat, blew back'd book, 4 fine shifts, 1 lawn, 3 cambrick, 1 muslin apron, 3 pr. of gloves, 1 pr. of clogs, a fan, 1 pr. of pink stockings, 2 pr. of cotton, a combing cloth, a pink handkerchief, 2 pr. of black stockings, 2 pr. of thread, 1 pr. of yarn, a bundle of lawn cambrick, &c.

"*2nd Trunk*—8 shifts, 4 coarse aprons, 6 night caps, 10 handkerchiefs, 10 neckcloths, 2 muslin handkerchiefs, 2 cambrick do., 3 white hoods, a bundle for Mrs. Tullie, a flowered silk night gown, capuchin, stays, a yellow silk night gown, a white quilted pettycoat, a white under pettycoat, a bed gown, necklaces, silk hat; in the box lid 2 canrs. of tea, lipsalve, pins, powder, brushes, razors, strop, a pr. of gloves, nail cutters, cased bottle, wigs, little bl. prayer book."

"*Mr. Nicolson, to Dr. Waugh.*

"I am favoured with your's of the first inst., and am extremely glad to hear you are all well, &c. I cannot help thinking that there is nothing like being a man's own sollicitor; but then the journey will, I doubt, be very expensive, tho' York, in the way proposed, will not be less so. What should you do with your family but send them along with your fellow travellers to Kilton? Mrs. T. has lately complained much to some of her cronies at C——, that Mrs. W. uses her with so much ceremony, form, &c., that it takes away all that pleasure and advantage that ought to accrue from relations living so near one another. Pray let this be now removed and use a little convenient freedom. But if you are resolved against this, what if they should make a shift at *Caldbeck for the remainder of this winter? I see no kind of probability of any disturbance there, and I question not but Mrs. W. wou'd be full as happy as at York without you.

"We expect my ——— home this day, in most extraordinary health, I am told, much better than when he left us. I had a letter from him on Monday, with some franks to be made use of *to you*, and I assure you he expresses great concern for you.

"We were terribly alarmed on Monday afternoon with the firing of 21 cannon at C——, fearing some mighty victory or advantage had been gained; but they say it was for some French landing in Scotland, and most people think it was only a feint to keep up their men's spirits, which flag much, as it's said; but I had never seen C—— since it's change of government, and I suppose you have intelligence from thence pretty constantly: indeed we hardly hear any news either from south or north, tho' we have got some post letters of late, but never regularly. Mr. W. takes most extraordinary care of your affairs at C——; they could hardly have been in so good hands. Pray what is become of Mr. Jackson? But I hope he and all our other runaway friends are included in your *all*. God send us good news of all kinds, for truly the times are now extremely dull and gloomy.

"Yours, &c.,

"J. N.

"Dec. 5, 1745."

---

* Dr. Waugh was rector of Caldbeck, a secluded parish about 15 miles S.W. of Carlisle, which Mr. Nicolson here suggests as a safe place for his family during his purposed visit to London.

R. Diggle to Dr. Waugh.

"London, 5th Dec., 1745.

"Dear Chancellor,

"The letter you gave us from Bowes was an inexpressible pleasure to all yr. friends, at it delivered us, in a great measure, from the violent anxietys we had been under ever since the Rebels came to Carlisle. I hope you will believe me when I assure you I bore a very sensible part, with the warmest of yr. friends, in our concern for you all; and most sincerely congratulate you upon yr. safety, tho' we are not without pain for your health after so much and such an unusual kind of fatigue. However, if we may believe the sanguine people in this town, this cursed affair will soon be put an end to; for by the accounts which came yesterday, the Rebel Army and the Duke were within three miles of each other, near Newcastle, in Staffordshire; so that an account of a battle is expected this day. I pray God grant success, tho' I must own I am not quite in such high spirits, with an assured confidence of success, as I find most people are here. When your health will permit, would not a London journey be, upon many accounts, proper at this time; would not all accounts and reckonings with the Government be made up better, while things are recent and fresh? and might not your interest be pushed with greater vigour and assurance when it is backed with such distinguisht instances of your merit and loyalty? I hope you will excuse my presuming to hint at any thing that looks like advice to you, since it proceeds only from the sincerity of my good wishes to you. My best respects wait on both familys, now altogether, I hope.

"And I am, dear Sir, yr. affect. kinsman,
and humble servant,

"R. DIGGLE.

"I am come to this place to fetch home my son for the holydays; the good wishes of the season attend you all,

"*Ten at Night*—The Rebels are slipt into Derbyshire.

"I have sent the *Gazette Extraordinary*, just come out."

"*The Bishop of London to Dr. Waugh.*

"White Hall, Dec. 6th, 1745.

"Good Sir,—

"It is some time since I waited on ye. Duke of Newcastle, to recommend you to his Grace; which I did in such a manner as I hope will be for your service, upon a proper occasion, if it please God to deliver us from our enemies, and restore us to a regular administration. Then it will be natural for our Governours to look back, and consider how to reward the persons who have distinguished themselves at such a critical juncture; among whom you are justly entitled to stand in the first rank. If the Earl of Carlisle be in town, I doubt not but he has been acquainted by the Duke with what I said to him concerning you and your character: for, as to your behaviour on this particular occasion, I found he was fully apprised of it before, and was sufficiently sensible of it. I congratulate you and your family upon your deliverance from the danger and fatigue to which you exposed yourself in support of ye. government, and upon your being all brought together again, in a place where you may at least sleep at peace. The rebels were expected at Nottingham yesterday, having altered their scheme for Chester and North Wales. It does not yet appear to us here, whether they will bend their course to London or Yorkshire.

"I am, Sir,

"Your assured friend and brother,

"EDWD. LONDON."

The Dean of the Arches to Dr. Waugh.

"Dear Mr. Chanc'lor,

"At ye. same time yt. I should condole with you upon your sufferings at Carlisle, and what you have since undergone, I should from my heart congratulate you on your escape into Yorkshire, if I could think you were in a more secure retreat there, or that you were like to be altogether out of danger by coming up to London. Surely there was never so bold an undertaking as this, for a handful of men in comparison with the great numbers now in arms for the government, to cause so general a panick in both parts of this United Kingdom.

"One would think from what we see and hear that God, for ye. punishment of our most provoking sins and iniquities, had given us over into the hands of our enemies, and made all opposition either to fall before them, or to become ineffectual. The government to prevent the ill influence of ye. many groundless reports rais'd by disaffected persons have come to a resolution to publish all the intelligence they receive both of the motions of ye. enemies and of our own forces by one or more additional Gazettes: accordingly we have one come out this morning acquainting us yt. that the former were gone to Derby, and yt. ye. Duke of Cumberland was to be at Northampton as last night, it being apprehended that ye. others had a design by forced marches to give ye. Duke a slip and gett up to London before him; and we are not without our fears on this account, and a body of troops is said to be forming at Finchley Common by way of precaution. Should you hold your resolution of seeing London this winter, I shall hope for ye. favour of your company as often as you can afford it; in the meantime all our best wishes attend you and yours, and the friends you have left behind you.

"I am, dear Sir,

"Yr. most affectionate humble servt.,

"J. BETTESWORTH.

"Dec. 7th, 1745."

"*Lord Carlisle to Dr. Waugh.*

"Sir,

"I suppose by your letter I had last night that the Militia Officers, and so my Lord Lonsdale, have done ye some ill offices, tho' I am quite a stranger to it, having never heard any thing of it. I am satisfied that your behaviour was perfectly right, and what your profession might justly have excused you from. I am sorry to hear that you have been such a sufferer. It ought, I am sure, and I hope it will be made up to you. I am glad to hear you are coming to town. I think it right upon all accounts, tho' I did not know how to advise it; but especially if you have been misrepresented, it is absolutely necessary to set that in a true light now, which, perhaps, may be very difficult to do some time hence. I shall be very glad if my house is any conveniency to you. York certainly is a very safe place, and I hope you will carry your family there. The Rebels are marching on very fast. The Duke was to be at Northampton as last night with part of the army; therefore, in a day or two we may expect to hear of an action. God send us good success, that an end may be put to these disorders. There is another army preparing about London, so that I think it is impossible these people can escape. The King, I hear, is very well satisfied with Coll. Durand's conduct. I hear some think the Rebels will still get into Wales. No account where they are to-day.

"I am, Sir, your most faithful humble servt.,

"CARLISLE.

"Dec'ber ye. 7."

"*Mr. Robinson to Dr. Waugh.*

"Chancery Lane, Dec. 7, 1745.

"Dear Sir,

"I am extreamly obliged to you for your last letter; Nanny and I have felt a great deal for your sufferings, and sincerely rejoice in your escape, and we heartily wish your effects were as safe as your p'sons. I hope they will soon be restored to you, tho' I am affraid not without considerable loss.

"It gave us great pleasure to hear of your journey to London, where we shall be very glad to see you. If you wo'd bring Mrs. Waugh along with you, and accept of a lodging in our little house, it is most sincerely at your service. We would make no strangers of you but treat you (as we live every day ourselves) with a plain joint of meat; the best part of your fare would be (and that I can assure of) a most hearty welcome. Nanny joins sincerely with me in this invitation, and in affectiouate complim'ts to you, Mrs. Waugh, your family, and all friends; and I am, with the utmost truth,

"Dear Sir,

"Your most affectionate and most hble. sert.,

"CHRIS. ROBINSON.

"P.S.—In your acct. of the affair at Carlisle you have laid the blame where I all along suspected it to be. I am much obliged by your suffering me to see it, to satisfy my own curiosity; and you may rest assured no other use shall be made of it, and that I was very far from taking your caution amiss."

"*Mr. Nicolson to Dr. Waugh.*

"Hond. Sir,

"The Bp. is got home, but not better than when he went away, for he is now in a pretty great cold, which he thinks was contracted at Allonby chapel, where he preached last Sunday. His lop. enquires much after you, and desires to be named when I write. Inclosed you receive what accounts I had on Thursday, as to Scotch affairs; and yesterday we were much delighted with a currt. report that the Rebels had mett with an intire defeat near Manchester, which God grant may be confirmed; but, from many circumstances, I doubt it cannot yet be so. It is said our new governours at Carlisle got the post bagg on Wednesday, and after perusing the letters they burnt them all. It is also said (I believe with too much certainty) that Mr. Salkeld, with three servts., all well armed, went to Carlisle the beginning of this week, and still continue there. We shall now send to Penrith every post day, so that if you write, directed there, letters will come both safe and quickly.

"Yours, &c.

"J. N."

"*Mr. Nicolson to Dr. Waugh.*

"Last night I had the pleasure of your's, but how conveyed I cannot imagine, for Jack got it at the smith's shop, they said from Wigton. Having had several letters already seized by the rebels at Carlisle, I dare not send any more, but will dispatch my nephew to talk with Mr. W. and get your directions performed to the utmost of our power. If you thought your horses safe here I have hay and corn at your service; but truly I cannot tell what to think, not only from our accounts from Scotland, the last of which I send you inclosed, but also from what I have just received from Mr. Dobson, who saies that they had advice at Penrith yesterday from Kendal that the Rebels are certainly marching back again, and had got as far as Manchester on their return; and yesterday I had a messenger from the Borders who said that the French and Highlanders had passed about six miles above Sterling, and were seen in Falkirk Moor, but this I think must be a mistake. All communication with Carlisle being in manner entirely cutt off however as to the post, I have seen no kind of newspaper this fortnight, but hear the foreign accounts do not look more favourable than our home ones, so that our affairs seem more and more gloomy every day. Pray what is become of the honest Register, for I have not heard the least sillable of him since he left this place. Mr. Birket was at Rose on Monday to tell the Bishop how matters stood at C——. I cannot say he was over civilly used. The endeavouring to do duty, at the Cathedral, was mentioned—not taking arms—or if not able to do that, why not at one of his livings, &c. I shall acquaint my lord with your compliments sometime to day, and am your's, &c., *Dec.* 11*th*, 1745.

"The letters which were taken at C——, were all coming here (none from me) and the r—— were not so much as mentioned in one of them except Mr. Pet's."

"*Colonel Durand to Dr. Waugh.*

"London, Dec. 12, 1845.

"Dear Sir,

"Capt. Hutchinson and I got to town last Monday night, and at my arrival I received the favour of your letter, for which I am extremely obliged to you. Yesterday morning I waited upon the Duke of Newcastle, and took an opportuniy of doing justice your merit, by representing to him, in the strongest manner I was capable of, the great and many services you did his Majesty at Carlisle, and shall take care to do the same in all places where I think it can be of any use to you. If it ever lyes in my power to acknowledge the many favours and civilitys I have received from you, you may always command,

"Dear Sir,

"Your most obliged humble servant,

"J. DURAND.

"P.S.—My compliments to Mrs. Waugh, Mr. Tullie and his Lady, and all friends. My sister desires her compliments to Mrs. Tullie."

"*Mr. Nicolson to Dr. Waugh.*

"We are this night much alarmed with account of an express which came from Kenaall this morning, at four o'clock, to Mr. Armitage, at Lowther, signifying that the Rebels returned to Manchester on Monday night sword in hand, got to Wiggan on Tuesday, enter'd Preston about 11 o'clock on Wednesday, and as supposed would be at Garstang that night, and in Westmoreland this: that the Duke's army would only reach Warrington this night, and Marshall Wade's Settle to-morrow; so that we expect another visit from the Highlanders unmolested. I sent to Carlisle this day and have got a couple of your boxes here and will send again to Mr. W. tomorrow to consult about sending for more. But all kind of communication by letter is entirely stopt, and Mr. Cook sends me word this night that I was in great danger of being sent for as a prisoner into the Castle upon account of the letter which was seized coming from Mr. Petrie. They hear nothing at Carlisle of the party of Highlanders which was said to be coming up, so that I hope there is nothing in it; nor is there, as far as I can learn, any thing from that quarter since my last. Last night I had an account from Penrith that the Duke's Army was already joined with between 7 and 8000 Gentlemen Volunteers, and numbers were dayly coming in, wch. raised our spirits not a little.

"We had this day a Christening * at Rose, and my Lord added 'York' to the circle. I would not have you write till you hear from me again, for fear the office at Penrith sho'd be in the same hands that poor Carlisle now is. All happiness attend you and your's, and believe me ever, &c.,

"J. N."

The victorious Highlanders had reached Derby without a check. To use the words of the Dean of the Arches, it seemed as if Heaven "had made all opposition either to fall before them, or to become ineffectual." These words testify most forcibly the powerful effect produced on men's minds at the time by this extraordinary expedition. The sensation in London was intense. It was apprehended that the Prince, evading the Duke of CUMBERLAND and Marshal WADE, would march directly upon the metropolis. And such in fact was his plan. He had received assurances from France that a body of troops should be landed on the Southern Coast to create a diversion in

---

* This was probably the chirstening of Rosemary Dacre, afterwards Lady Clerk, daughter of Mr. Dacre, who commanded the troop of militia horse in Carlisle during the siege. He married the daughter of Sir George Fleming, bishop of Carlisle ; and at the time that he was besieged in the town his lady was at Rose Castle, hourly expecting her *accouchement*. On the 15th November, the day of the surrender of Carlisle, she was delivered of her daughter. The bishop having left Rose Castle for a time, his chaplain was about to baptize the infant, when a party of Highlanders appeared, headed by a Captain Macdonald. An old grey headed servant ran out, and entreated the Captain not to proceed, as any noise or alarm might occasion the death of both lady and child. It seems to have been taken for granted that their object was to plunder the castle. Lady Clerk in her account of the incident published in the Edinburgh Monthly Magazine in 1817, expressly affirms that such was the case. If so, their consideration for Mrs. Dacre was the more remarkable. Captain Macdonald enquired when the lady had been confined? "*within this hour*," the servants answered. Macdonald stopped. The servant added, "*they are just going to christen the infant.*" Macdonald taking off his cockade, replied, "*let her be christened with this cockade in her cap ; it will be her protection now, and after if any of our stragglers should come this way ; we will wait the ceremony in silence,*" which they accordingly did ; and then went into the coach yard and were regaled with beef, cheese, ale, &c. They then went off without the smallest disturbance. The white cockade was preserved with an almost religious care ; and when George the 4th, seventy-six years afterwards, visited Edinburgh, the venerable lady being introduced to the monarch at his desire, narrated the romantic incident of her birth day ; and produced the relic, Macdonald's cockade of the fatal '45.

his favor; he confidently reckoned on being joined by numerous English malcontents; he might well rely on the enthusiastic energies of his troops to enable him to gain a day's march upon the Duke, and deal a mortal blow at the heart of King George's power, already morally impaired by his extraordinary and apparently irresistible inroad. This has been stigmatised as the mere dream of a rash and inconsiderate youth, and as having been wisely over-ruled by the better judgment of his councillors at Derby; but there are who take another view of it. The enterprise of Charles Edward was not, on his part, an inconsiderate act. It had been long contemplated. In a letter to his father, written on the eve of his embarkation for Scotland, he stated it to be his firm resolution to conquer or to die, and that he never intended to come back. These are expressions which, if they were found in a proclamation, might prove little beyond a desire to inspire resolution into adherents; but in the farewell letter of a son to a parent, they import a considerate determination of the writer's energies, mental and physical, upon the object in view. He seems to have been from the first, and throughout, deeply impressed with the conviction that his enterprise was not an ordinary invasion—nor, consequently, to be planned and conducted upon the ordinary rules of warfare. To such, indeed, his means were strikingly inadequate; for he had little more to start with than the cordial affection and prompt muster of his Highland adherents. Beyond that lay the difficulty,—to redevelop the repeatedly suppressed and then almost hopeless loyalty of the English Jacobites; to resuscitate into life and activity their ancient but nearly dormant sympathies with his long exiled race. This could be effected only by extraordinary means; by daring almost to the verge of romance—by working forcibly upon the imagination of men. And if for this, as it is admitted, his personal qualifications were well adapted, much more so were the means he possessed in his faithful Highlanders; the descendants of those who under Montrose a century before had stayed for a time the falling fortunes of CHARLES the FIRST. They constituted an army, the materials and tactics of which were so admirably suited to his occasion that it is scarcely too much to say that his plans were based partly on their peculiar character. They astonished whilst they attacked their foes. COPE's flight from Preston Pans to Berwick shews how their furious charge with the claymore affected the minds of men who had met with undaunted countenance the best troops of France, on the fields of Germany. They were capable also of effecting marches of a length and rapidity at that time almost inconceivable. They were, in short, precisely the men with whom a daring and resolute leader might have set at nought the ordinary prudential rules of regular warfare, have baffled the calculations of his opponents by the eccentricity of his course, and have struck a decisive blow before his mode of warfare could be fully comprehended.

That such were the views of CHARLES EDWARD it may fairly be argued from his constant and anxious desire to push forward to London, regardless of the manœuvres of the Duke of CUMBERLAND and Marshal WADE, except for the purpose of evading them. And with this desire in a most intense degree he had succeeded in inspiring his troops. They had passed Preston, the limit they had once superstitiously dreaded —they had passed it triumphantly under their Prince, and were confident that under him they were destined to enter London.

But it was destined to be otherwise. The brilliant conceptions of CHARLES EDWARD's genius were not in unison with the cooler and more prudential views of his officers. They also had been carried forward to an extent far beyond that which ordinary calculation should have led them. Opposition had fallen before them or seemed to be ineffectual, till they found themselves at Derby with three armies in their front each larger than their own. And it became the question whether they should, in the face of such odds against them, tempt fortune farther, or revert to the dictates of prudence? In this crisis, which peculiarly demanded the decision and energy of a leader, they resorted to the deliberation of a Council of War. The result was easily to be predicted. The question of advance or retreat was debated—or rather speeches were made to break the resolution of retreating to the Prince; he alone being for the advance—all his officers for retreat. Almost broken-hearted by this sudden destruction of his hopes, —the extreme dejection into which this determination to retreat cast him, strongly argues his clear perception that it was fatal to the very principle of his enterprise, —he was constrained to acquiesce. From that moment his character and bearing underwent a change he no longer headed his troops with alacrity—the fate of the STUARTS overshadowed him.

No doubt the decision of the officers in the Council of War at Derby was, on all visible grounds of calculation, and on all ordinary rules of warfare, the only one they could come to. But that is scarcely the whole case. It was not a case of ordinary warfare. They had gone too far for that. And now that time has removed the veil which concealed what was then secretly passing in men's minds, we have become acquainted with enough to induce a belief that the Prince was in the right in his bold conception of an advance on the capital, and his officers the miscalculators in coming to the determination of retreat. Lord MAHON, who possesses the most ample information on the subject, has stated his opinion, that, had they pushed on to London, the STUARTS would have regained the Crown. Certain it is, that the Duke of NORFOLK, Sir W. WYNN, Lord BARRYMORE, and with these, no doubt, the whole body of the English Jacobites, were on the eve of declaring against the government, when the retreat from Derby prevented them. From the moment that movement took place they remained quiet. The French troops, on the eve of embarkation, were countermanded—the Highlanders, bursting with rage and venting loud lamentations, retraced their steps. The Duke of CUMBERLAND became the pursuer—the country people were roused to hostility against a retreating foe—every thing was reversed—and the Prince found himself once more the sport of Fortune at the moment when he fondly imagined that she was about to crown his daring with success.

The retreat was not conducted so orderly as had been the advance. The Highlanders, no longer enthusiastic with hope, were less manageable by their Chiefs. We hear of plundering and affrays with the country people. Horses and shoes appear to have been everywhere sought after and seized. They were closely followed by the Duke of CUMBERLAND, with his now inspirited army. And expresses were forwarded to arouse the country by assurances that the defeat of the main body must speedily ensue, and that the people should be ready to cut off the flying remnants. This had considerable effect in rousing the population in favour of the Government; but, by the extraordinary spirit and physical energies of the Highlanders they effected their retreat in the depth of winter, and in the face of a superior force, without loss—at least with so trifling a loss that it can hardly be named as such, when the length of the march and the circumstances are considered. The principal difficulties they encountered occurred in their passage through Westmoreland and Cumberland, as they once more approached Carlisle, the importance of which as a secure point to retreat upon now became apparent.

[*Extract of a letter dated Appleby.*]

"Dec. 14th, 1745.

"At five this evening we had a messenger from Kendall; who informs us that about 120 of the Rebels' vanguard came in there between 11 and 12 at noon, and yt. the main body was betwixt Lancaster and Kendall. The Duke of Perth and two ladies in a chaise were in this cavalcade—the people of Kendall armed themselves with such weapons as they had; resisted them—and would not suffer them to alight in town,—killed one of them, took three prisoners, and two horses. The messenger also saystheir horses were scarce able to crawl along the street; they got through the town as well as they could, and took the Shap road. An express was sent immediately to Penrith of what happened at Kendall, and we just now hear from Penrith,—viz., eight at night, that as the 116 soldiers were yet there they are resolved to give them a warm reception if they come that way; and the Beacon is now on fire to alarm the country to come in. Several people go from hence to-night, and many more will go to-morrow morning early. It is supposed that many of their chiefs are amongst this party, and their most valuable effects, seeing they had several led horses and sumptures; and some make it a question whether or no one of these fine ladies be not in reality the pretended Prince. If they pursue their journey and go thro' Penrith, I hope they will be taken; they certainly can reach no farther than Shap this night."

"*Mr. Lamb to Dr. Waugh.*

"Brough, 16 December, 1745.

"Rev. Sir,

"This morning I recd. your letter, and also .our packet, for my Ld. Bishop. We have had no post from Penrith since Friday. Soe I have sent your packet to Rose by a servant of my own who I can confide in, and hope it will goe safe to his Lordship's hand. I went over to consult Mr. Hodgson as soon as I recd. your letter. On Saturday the D. of Perth, w'th about 110 horse, went thro' Kendal, not being allowed to light by the mob, who killed one, took two prisoners, and three horses; the rest got to Shap that night, and made for Penrith next morning, but were repulsed there, and were obliged to retreat within two miles of Appleby, then passed over Bolton Water, not daring to come into Appleby; they were soe closely pursued from Penrith that they were forced into Orton last night, and got to Kendall this morning before it was light; otherwise our country, who were up in arms from all parts, would certainly have taken them.* We hear the whole body are got into Kendall last night; and the D. of Cumberland soe near them that we expect to hear of an engagement to-day, when we hope to have a good account of them.

"I am, Revd. Sir,

"Your most obedient humble servant,

"J. LAMB."

"P.S.—The Rebels left Kendall yesterday, and the Duke got into Kendall last night."

"Mr. Nicolson to Dr. Waugh.

"Dec. 16th, 1745.

"Revd. Sir,

"I was extremely glad to find by your's of the 14th inst., (which Lamb sent to Rose this evening by his own servant) that you are so agreeably settled at York, and hope all will yet turn out well; for we are in great hopes that the Rebels are entirely defeated ere this by the Duke at Lancaster. On Sunday we dispatched a messenger to Penrith, who brought a brave packet of news, in substance that there had been a sort of a Battle on Ellelmoor, five miles below Lancaster, the Highlanders having made a sally upon the Duke's Vanguard, who soon made them retreat there again,—

* The Duke of Perth, according to Lord George Murray's account, was sent off from Preston to Scotland to bring up men; Lord George states that when the army reached Kendal two days afterwards they there found the Duke of Perth, who had been obliged to return, having been attacked by the Country Militia, so he could not make his way to Carlisle.

that the Duke of Perth, with 110 Hussars, came into Kendall on Saturday, about tenn o'clock, were attacked there by the mob with stones, &c., for they had no arms, upon which the Rebels faced about, fired, and killed two; but that no ways intimidating them, they pursued again, pulled one off his horse and killed him directly, took two more prisoners, with some horses and baggage. This the thinking part of the town thought a most rash attempt, supposing the rest of the army coming up; but finding afterwards that they were still at Lancaster and in a most hopeful way of being demolished there, greatly regretted that the assailants had not been better supported and encouraged; for had that been done they think the whole party might have been taken, and that there are several people of great distinction amongst them, and most probably the Chevalier himself; which, Penrith being apprised of, fired the Beacon that night, and lay under arms, and next morning went in quest of the Rebels, who durst not make Penrith their route; met with them on Langwarthby Moor, and drove them back to Orton. And this day the whole country for ten or 15 miles round are up, with such sort of arms as they can procure; it being added in the letters from Kendall that the Duke has sent expresses all about to desire the country to rise and take care of straglers, and he'll take care of the main body. These accounts I dispatched last night to Wigton, Annan, Netherby, and Canoby; and this morning got a good many people up at Dalston; as many of whom as had arms proceeded to Armathwaite Bridge upon hearing that was to be their route; and this evening we had a report that they had surrounded the Rebels there; but this, by Mr. Lamb's account, must be a mistake, for he saies that many of the inhabitants of Brugh marched this morning, armed in the best manner they cou'd, to join others in pursuit of the Duke of Perth and his party, who, they were advised at four this morning, were forced into Orton last night by several from Penrith, and hope very soon to have a good account of them; and the messenger adds that as he came along he heard a very great firing thereabouts for several hours together. I was also, this afternoon, at Seburgham Bridge, with about 50 of the inhabitants thereabouts, all in arms to prevent their flying that way, and treated them to half a guinea; in short, I have had a day something like one of your's at Carlisle, and indeed, if I was but capable of executing the office I might be allowed to be your successor in intelligence both as to trouble and expense.

"I have got two of your packing boxes here as I told you before, filled I suppose with linnen, and have since got your iron chest and one other large chest, it looks like the upper part of that in your study; but no more can be done at present, nor dare I send one of your letters into town, for every body is most exactly searched, and no one thing now suffered to come out of town, and the gates only open a very little in the middle of the day.

"The new governor and his crew are most certainly terribly afraid, and a good many of their common folks have deserted. Last night they raised a story that the French and Highlanders had taken Sterling Castle by assault with great slaughter,—that they had also taken Edenbrough in the same way, and put every body to the sword that they found in arms,—that they were 7000 strong, had 20 cannon, 24 pounders, and several mortars; but accounts from Scotland this day (which I send you inclosed) make us pretty easie. The reason of our getting no London news, nor indeed letters of any kind is that our worthy postmaster has absolutely discharged his brother from opening any of the bags; and the present masters of Carlisle threatening his house if they had them not, they are, as its said, all carried to them and generally burnt. I am glad to hear Miss T—— is much improved, pray acquaint her as soon as you conveniently can that her last bill is still by me, for I have never yet had an opportunity of seeing her brother, nor can I learn where to write to him. The bishop desires his service and thanks to you for your letter, and I believe was well pleased with it, tho' it cost him some shillings. If matters goe right at Lancaster you may still safe write to Penrith. We are now again alarmed with an account that this party left Orton last night and have joined the whole body at Kendall, where they got last night with all their artillery; so pray do not write again till you hear further from yours, &c."

"*To Mr. Joseph Nicolson, at Hawksdale (if absent, to the Rev. Mr. Thompson, at Rose Castle.)*

"Wigton, 16th Dec. 1745.

"Sir,

"I came here this evening to wait on the gentlemen and other inhabitants about this place (in obedience to the request in the Duke of Cumberland's express you sent us) to spirit up the people to exert themselves in picking up the straglers from the Rebel army; and upon your further information by the bearer of their motions, I hope a considerable number may be immediately raised to act in such place and manner as may best answer the intention.

"I am (Sir)

"Your most humble Servant,

"JOHN FLETCHER."

"*The Earl of Carlisle to Dr. Waugh.*

"Sir,

"I received your last, and am very glad to hear that you and your family are gott well to York. I wish my horse was better, for your accommodation. As you will not desire to make a long stay in town, I think there is no sort of hurry for your coming, for possibly, by the meeting of the Parliament, after Christmas, the ministry may be a little more at leisure than they are at present. By that expression in my letter I meant nothing more than that I was afraid you had suffered a great deal of fatigue and loss in effects. I am afraid the Rebels will get back into Scotland, and God knows how long the fire may be kept up there. I am sure it is our interest by all ways and means, and at any expense, to put an end to it immediately. We are in great expectations every day of news from the Duke, tho' it is doubted whether he can get up with them; however it will drive them so fast thro' Cumberland that they will do less mischief. My Lady Carlisle joins with me in compliments to Mrs. Waugh, and

"I am, Sr.,

"Your most faithful obedient Servant,

"CARLISLE.

"Dec. 17th."

"*Sir Philip Musgrave to Dr. Waugh.*

"Dear Sir,—

"I have received your favours and am extremely concerned to understand those Rebels have obliged you and yr. family to fly so far from home, but hope the defeat of them had by this time restored tranquillity to our country, as it is strongly reported here that they were surrounded in Lancaster, by two bodies of our forces last Saturday, who wou'd undoubtedly secure 'em all; which, if true, I suppose will alter yr. purpose of spending yr. winter in York, as it will bring my wife, &c. to Edenhall very soon, it beginning to be time for her to think of removing if she is to do it at all this seeson. I hear there is a possibility of yr. being soon in London; I wish it may be so, and that we laugh together at past troubles, as I hope you have received no particular or extraordinary damages. Our ladies joyn in respects and good wishes to yr. self and family.

"Wth., Sir, yr. most faithful

"And obedient Servant,

"P. M.

"Dec. 18th."

To the Rev. Dr. Waugh in Little Else Lane, in the Minster Yard, York.

"Barnard Castle, 20 Decem., 1745.

"Dear Sir,—

"I was called to Egleston, Friday last, upon some necessary busyness that required my attendance for some dayes, and returned Tuesday evening last where I found your most acceptable favour, dated the 14th instant. I deferred giving you trouble of answer from an expectation I could by this post give you some good accounts of the Duke's army which, thank God, has in some instances proved to expectation, for about four o'clock Tuesday afternoon the Duke came up with the rest of the rebels at Clifton, and attacked several partys of theirs that were laid and lined the hedge on the road-side. which the Duke had notice of. Twelve of the Duke's men were killed ; the number of the Rebels not yet known, but sixty taken prisoners. They had left a party at Lowther to plunder and burn the house, who dispersed immediately on the approach of the Duke : he lay all that night at Clifton, but sent a body into Penrith to relieve the town, where a number of the rebels were left, and had begun to plunder, but were all dispersed, a good many killed, and 40 made prisoners. Twelve of the dragoons were killed, and poor Phill Honeywood very much wounded on his head by neglect of putting on his scull capp ; but supposed will recover. It is said they are passed Carlisle, leaving a number in the Castle with three week's provisions, which they had laid up. The Duke it is said cannot fail of coming up to the main body before they pass the river Esk, which is now flooded, that they must be obliged to go a great way round to the small rivers that branch into the river Esk. As you are a good judge of that passage you may judge of it better than any information which I have. I have hinted to Mr. Tully what you desired and refer him to give you an answer, as I had it not from him. I expect further accounts by the west post this day which is not yet come in : and if any thing further matteriall come, you shall certainly have it from

"Your most obt. humble servt.,

"W. HUTCHINSON.

"P. S.—The second party of Marshall Wade's army lay over here to day, Genl. Howard, and Coll. Howard with them. Tho' I have good reason to believe the accounts given you are facts, yet as no information comes by any letters this day over Stainmoor, you must suspend it to next post when you shall hear further from me."

"*To the Rev. Dr. Waugh, York.*

"Brough, 21 Dec., 1745.

"Revd. Sir,—

"On Wednesday morning, I carryed some letters to Genl. Oglethorp at Orton, who the Duke expected would have been with the Rear Guard of the Rebels the night before. I went with them till they took ye. road to Strickland Head, then I went the Shap road, and at Shap-thorn I came in sight of the D.'s army abt. 12; and when we came just by Lowther Park there came advice that about 300 of 'em were in Lowther Wood near the Hall; I was just by when the Duke ordered some of his forces into the Park, in pursuit of them; but they all got thro' the wood on to Clifton, but two that were taken, one Hamilton, a Captain of the Rebels' Hussars, and one Ogden from Manchester. About 3 the D.'s army got into Clifton. So the Duke ordered a party of Bland's men, about ten out of each company, to light and attack them on foott, they being then come out under the hedges. About four they began to fire, wch. continued till about 8; our men forced them beyond Clifton, and then lost them. I then went to Cous. Robinson's at Lowther all night, and next morng. about 8 I went to the Moor again, when it was a most violent storm of wind and rain; I rode thro' Field, and see 7 our men dead, and there was 13 wounded. Amongst whom Coll. Philip Honeywood had three cuts on his head, tho' I hope he will do well again.

"I hear he is now got to Howgill Castle. I only see 4 Rebels killed, but hear that 30 more had been thrown into Clifton Mill dam, and 70 taken prisoners, with more brought to Appleby to-day. Our forces came just in time to save Lowther Hall and Penrith from being burnt, and Penrith has suffered much by their plunder.

"*22nd Mg.*—I have just now recd. a letter from Mr. Cowper by Penrith post, that the Duke's Army are all before Carlisle. The Rebels, he is afraid, are fled, except what they have left in the Garrison. They were playing their cannon last night agt. our brave men. I pray God bless our arms with success. And am,

"Revd. Sir, your most humble servt., in haste,

"J. LAMB."

"*Mr. Nicolson to Dr. Waugh.*

"The concluding paragraph of my last was too true; for yesterday a part of the Re—s entered Carlisle, and the rest this evening.

as I suppose, tho' they had not got in when the messenger came away (about two o'clock this afternoon), which has intirely spoiled all the fine designs of this country; which, I do believe, wou'd have made no small figure, if the Duke had been so lucky as to defeat the main body at Lancaster. We hear that the Highlanders design to march north to-morrow; and that the Duke was at Kendall last night in full pursuit of them, which last is, I think, pretty well confirmed this moment. God send him a happy campaign, and tho' the seat of warr is a most dreadful thing, I cou'd almost wish it here to prevent our forces from being cut off in Scotland, which, I doubt, must be the case if these Rebels are suffered to get there before the Duke. The —— is but poorly; he thinks he has got a little touch of the gout in his ankle—this probably may give him a little relief, however it affects his spirits. I send you enclosed a letter I had this day from Mr. Petrie, as I hope I shall another from Annan, where I sent an express this morning. I have sent your two chests to C——, tho' I dare say we are quite safe from any plunder from the Highlanders. I sent your letter to honest G—'s, and Mr. W. came there and got it, and sends me word most of the things mentioned were come away before. My mother and sister will not stir from Carlisle, tho' I have sent several times to desire it; the former has got her hearing much better, and if she's but so happy as to see the Duke will think it a full recompense for all the trouble she has hitherto had with the Highlanders. You may now safely write to Penrith, as I hope to tell you by the next post, you may to Carlisle, and am, ever your's, &c.,

"J. N.

"I hear nothing of Gardner yet."

"*Mr. Nicolson to Dr. Waugh.*

"Hond. Sir,

"The Duke, with all his horse belonging to his army, are now at Penrith and thereabouts, where they got on Thursday evening, and had a small skirmish with the Rebels about Clifton, in which about 8 only were killed on each side, as was first said, and about sixty of the latter taken prisoners. They never engaged our people openly, but fired from behind the hedges, where Col. Honeywood was wounded in two places, but I hope not dangerously; and this morning I hear that 40 or 50 of the Rebels have been discovered in the river, where their companions had thrown them to conceal their being killed.

"Most of the Highlanders left Carlisle yesterday, and marched directly for Scotland; but we hear this morning that some part of them are returned, which I can hardly believe, tho' I think Esk would stop them all about Netherby, Longtown, &c. I cannot hear they have done much damage at Carlisle. Mr. W. sends me word that there were about sixteen at your house, and all is safe there, and even your hay has suffered very little. It is said they have left a garrison at Carlisle, chiefly English; and some say Sanderson, that was at Whitehall, governor. On Thursday they sold a good deal of coals, beef, and other things, which does not look as if they designed their garrison should long subsist there. They stript most persons they met with about Carlisle of their shoes; which, with horses, are all the plunder I hear of. Whilst things are in this uncertain state, you shall sure to hear every post from,

"Yours, &c.,

"J. N.

"You may write to Penrith, but no further yet. The ——— is much at one; he saies, a better night.

"To the Rev. Dr. Waugh, in Little Alice Lane, near the Minster, York."

Concerning the skirmish at Clifton the accounts are contradictory: on the one hand it has been treated of as a successful attack by the King's troops upon the Rebels in a strong and defensible position, from which they were driven with loss; on the other hand as a decided check given by the rear of the retreating Highlanders to their pursuers. And there is as wide a difference between the statements of the loss sustained on each side. The Duke of CUMBERLAND'S Gazette account making the loss of the King's troops only 12 men; whilst others assert the loss to have been at least 150. Lord GEORGE MURRAY, who was personally engaged, gives the fullest details of the action. They had experienced great difficulty in effecting the retreat from Shap for want of sufficient carriages for conveyance of the ammunition, &c. When they approached Clifton on the afternoon of the 18th, the Duke of Cumberland with his dragoons was close upon them. Lord George Murray says:—

"I now observed small platoons of horse appearing on eminences at some distance behind me, of this I sent word to the Prince, but at Penrith they had taken a notion that it was only Militia. There was indeed a body of two or three hundred light horse, being, I believe, mostly Cumberland people, that drew up in my way, thinking to obstruct our march; but so soon as the Glengary men threw their plaids and ran forward to attack them, they made off at the top gallop and gave me no more trouble. When I came to Clifton, I sent off the cannon and other carriages to Penrith, being two miles further; and as I believed these light horse that had met me would probably be near Lord Lonsdale's house at Lowther, as he was Lord Lieutenant of the County, I went a short way with the Glengary men to that place thro' several inclosures, it being not above a mile. Lord Pitsligoe's horse had joined me, so I was in hopes, by scouring these inclosures, to meet with the light horse. We got sight of severals hard by Lord Lonsdale's house, but could come up with few; at a turn of one of the Parks, one like a Militia officer, clothed in green, and a footman of the Duke of Cumberland, were taken. We understood by them that the Duke, with a body of 4000 horse as they said, were about a mile behind. I sent Colonel Roy Stewart with the prisoners to Penrith, and to know his Royal Highness' orders, and that I wold stop at Clifton, which was a good post, till I heard from him. When I came back to Clifton, the Duke of Perth was there; and besides Colonel Roy Stewart's men, being about 200 that I left there, Cluny with his men and Ardshiel with the Appin men, were with them. The Duke of Perth, who was also there, had been persuaded that it was only Militia that had appeared; but he then saw, upon an open muir not above cannonshot from us, the enemy appear and draw up in two lines, in different divisions and squadrons. His Grace said he would immediately ride back, and see to get out the rest of our army; for as the grounds were strong where I drew up, he did not doubt I could maintain that post till others joined me. I sent an English gentleman with him who had attended me all the retreat, and knew the country perfectly well; who said he would lead them a near way by the left, undiscovered, that they could fall on the enemy in flank; and as there was a lane that lay betwixt Lord LONSDALE's inclosures, which was near a mile in length, and thro' which the enemy had come, if they were obliged to retire they would suffer much by both sides of the lane if we lined it. I only desired 1000 more men than what I had, by which means I could not only maintain the post I had, but send half of my men thro' the inclosures on my right, so as to flank the enemy on that side, if they were attacked on the other side; and if once but 20 of their horse could be killed, it would make such an embarrass in the lane, that it would put them all in confusion, and choke up the only road they had to retreat, except the Appleby road; and that might be also secured, which would give us an advantage that perhaps we should not meet the like again.

"After the Duke of PERTH went to Penrith, I made my disposition in the best manner I could; caused them to roll up what colours we had, and made them pass half open to different places, bringing them back under cover; so that the enemy, seeing them as they were carried forward to different places, could not form any judgment of our numbers. I did this in a manner to make them believe that our numbers were much greater than they were, and they could not know but our whole army was come into the village, and about it. After an hour, they dismounted, as near as we could guess, about 500 of their dragoons, which came forward to the foot of the muir they were upon, and to a ditch which was the last of three small enclosures from the places where we were posted at the village. My men were so disposed that the Glengary men were upon the enclosures on the right of the highway, and APPIN'S men, with CLUNY'S in the enclosures, on the left; Colonel ROY STEWART'S men I placed on the side of the lane or highway, close to the village. I was about 1,000 men in all. PITSLIGOE'S horse and hussars returned to Penrith. The ditches at the foot advanced more towards the muir on the right than on the left; and that part was also covered by Lord LONSDALE'S other enclosures; so that they could not easily be attacked, but had the advantage that they could, with their fire, flank the enemy when they made an attack on our left. The lane, which was the highroad between these small enclosures, was not above twenty feet broad. It was now an hour after sunset, pretty cloudy; but the moon, which was in its second quarter, from time to time broke out and gave good light; but this did not continue above two minutes at a time. We had the advantage of seeing their disposition, but they could not see ours. Our hussars, upon seeing the enemy, went off to Penrith. One of their officers, Mr. HAMILTON, with two or three of his men, had dismounted, (being ashamed of the going off of the others,) and gone in through a hedge, and were taken prisoners; how it happened I cannot tell, for it was before I came back from Lowther Hall. Had they staid near Clifton, they ran no risk.

"Colonel ROY STEWART returned to me from Penrith. He told me His Royal Highness resolved to march for Carlisle immediately, and had sent off the cannon, before, and desired me to retreat to Penrith. I showed Col. S. my situation, with that of the enemy. They were, by this time, shooting popping shots among us. I told him if I retreated, being within musket shot of the enemy, they would follow up the lane, and I must lose a number of men, besides discouraging the rest; that from Clifton it was a narrow road, and very high *walls*, so that I could not line them to secure my retreat; and that, probably, my men would fall into confusion in the dark; and that the enemy, by regular platoons in our rear, being encouraged by our retreat, must destroy a great many; and by taking any wounded man prisoner, they would know our numbers; whereas, I told him I was confident I could dislodge them from where they were by a brisk attack, as they had not, by all that I could judge, dismounted above 500. Their great body was on horseback, and at some distance; and CLUNY and he owned that what I proposed was the only prudent and sure way; so we agreed not to mention his message from the Prince. I had crossed the lane or highroad several times, which only could be done at the foot of the village, by two gates, one on each side. I now went over again to where the Glengary men were placed, and ordered them to advance, as they should observe me do on the other side; and to keep up their fire as much as they could till they came to the bottom ditch; and that if *we* beat the enemy from their hedges and ditches, *they* had a fair sight of them, and could give them a flank fire within pistol shot; but I gave them particular injunctions not to fire across the lane, nor to follow the enemy up the muir. I left Colonel CAR with them; he was one of the Prince's Aid-de-Camps, but had liberty to be mostly with me. He was an excellent officer and was riding through the fields in the time of the fire, as if it had been a review. After having spoke with all the officers of the Glengary regiment, I went to the left of the lane. The dismounted dragoons had not only lined the bottom enclosures, but several of them had come up to two hedges that lay south and north: the others where we were, and the dragoons at the bottom, lay east and west. The Appin battalion were next the lane upon that side, and CLUNY's farther to their left. We advanced and had a good deal of fire on both sides. After the Highlanders on that side had given most of their fire, they lay close at an open hedge, which was the second in these fields. We then received the whole fire of the dragoons that were at the bottom, upon which CLUNY said, '*What the devil is this?*' Indeed, the bullets were going thick enough. I told him we had nothing for it but going down upon them sword in hand, before they had time to charge again. I immediately drew my sword and cried, 'CLAYMORE.' CLUNY did the same; and we ran down to the bottom ditch, clearing the diagonal hedges as we went. There were a good many of the enemy killed at the bottom ditch, and the rest took to their heels, but received the fire of the GLENGARY regiment. Most of ARDSHIELS' men, being next the lane, did not meet with so much opposition. I had given orders that our men should not pass the bottom ditch to go up the muir, for they would have been exposed to the fire of the Glengary regiment, that could not distinguish them from the enemy. We had no more firing after this; so we returned to our first post. We had now done what we proposed; and, being sure of no more trouble from the enemy, I ordered the retreat: first, ROY STEWART's; then APPIN, CLUNY, and the Glengary men; and it was half-an-hour after the skirmish before we went off. The Atholl brigade had come the length of a bridge, within half a mile of Clifton, hearing of my being in sight of the enemy, and there waited for orders. Had the rest of the army come out, and followed the plan that was proposed, they would have been upon the flank of the dragoons that were on horseback by the time we attacked the others." * * * * * * "It was lucky I made that stand at Clifton, for otherwise the enemy would have been at our heels, and come straight to Penrith; where, after refreshing two or three hours, they might have come up with us before we got to Carlisle. I am persuaded, that night and next morning, when the van entered Carlisle, there was above eight miles from our van to our rear; and mostly an open country, full of commons."

This account is so circumstantial, and so accurate in its local detail, that it has great weight. It candidly puts the affair as an attack by the rear of the Highlanders, 1000 strong, upon 500 of the Duke's dismounted dragoons pushed forward into the Clifton inclosures; and claims no glory for having expelled them, but simply takes credit for having withstood in the outset a movement which, if permited to have been effected, would in all probability have let in the whole body of the dragoons upon the retreating Highlanders. And it receives confirmation from the fact that it stopped the pursuit. If it had been true that at Clifton the Duke of CUMBERLAND with a large body of Cavalry had beaten the Highlanders from a strong and defensible position, how came it that neither that night, nor even next day when they were retreating across the open wastes of Inglewood Forest, was any further attempt made upon them? As to the loss of the two parties it is a matter impossible to be ascertained. The first account on the morning of the 19th was that the Dragoons lost 40 men killed, six wounded, and four officers wounded, and that the Rebels having carried off their killed and wounded, the number could not be ascertained, but the *Gazette* account subsequently reduces the Duke's loss to a dozen men. In the Clifton parish register of burials is the following entry:—

"The 19th day of December, 1745, ten dragoons, to wit, six of Bland's, three of Cobham's, and one of Mark Kerr's regiment, who were killed ye. evening before by the Rebels in ye. skirmish between the Duke of Cumberland's army and them at ye. end of Clifton Moor next ye. Toun,—buried."

And on the 8th of January following another of General BLAND's was buried, who probably had been wounded and left there.

This, therefore, would seem to be the foundation of the Gazette's account. What the Rebels did with their killed which they are alleged to have carried off, it has not been explained. The story told of their having thrown 40 or 50 into the river, *to conceal them*, will scarcely bear examination.

The Highlanders continued their retreat that night. When Lord GEORGE MURRAY reached Penrith, he found the Prince just taking horse: and after a brief stay for refreshment of his wearied men, he also resumed his march. On the 19th the Prince reached Carlisle, and remained there over the 20th: the Dukc of CUMBERLAND with his army being that day at Penrith. Some parties of the Highlanders, however, with part of the baggage, appear to have gone by a route eastward of Carlisle, and to have crossed the Eden at Warwick Bridge, and so proceeded north without entering Carlisle. It is related that one of their baggage waggons 'mired' at the ford across the little river Cairn below the mill at Warwick Bridge, and was abandoned—that the miller, after they had passed on, succeeded in extricating it,—and that subsequently it was observed money became plentiful with him. This route was perhaps chosen in the hopes of being enabled to get the baggage, &c., across the Esk, by Cannoby or

Langholm, there being at that time no bridge at Longtown, and the river being swollen.

It was Lord GEORGE MURRAY's opinion that Carlisle should be evacuated—the Castle blown up,—and such of the stores as could not be carried off thrown into the river, He was aware that it was not tenable against artillery; and that altho' the Duke of CUMBERLAND had no artillery with him, yet he could in no long time procure it. It would have been happier had his opinion been acted on—but it was over-ruled; and determined that a garrison should be left. There was at the time a gloomy anticipation of the fate of those that should remain; yet none hesitated to make the almost certain sacrifice; nay we are told that Mr. TOWNLEY, Colonel of the Manchester regiment, volunteered. Accordingly he was appointed to be Governor of the City,—HAMILTON remaining Commandant of the Castle: and the Manchester regiment, about 120 strong, with 270 of the Highlanders and Lowland Scots, four French officers, and a few privates of LALLY's regiment, were at length selected to form the garrison. Lord GEORGE MURRAY, with the rest of the troops, waited for some time on the north side of the Bridge, whilst the Prince concluded this melancholy arrangement in the Town. The devoted men were drawn up to receive his parting address. He thanked them for what they had done and suffered in his cause, and cheered them with assurances of his speedy return with augmented forces to relieve them before the enemy could reduce the place. He then bade them adieu, and on the 21st of December, 1745, quitted Carlisle, never to return. Happy it had been for them if they had been permitted to follow his fortunes and to seek an honorable death in the field, in place of the cruel and ignominious fate to which they were subjected by remaining in Carlisle.

The Highlanders crossed the Esk at Longtown, an hundred men a-breast—the river was swollen and took them nearly breast high. There were at once two thousand of them in the river, and nothing of them to be seen but their heads and shoulders. Holding one another by the neck of the coat they stemmed the force of the stream, and lost not a man in the passage. The moment they reached the opposite side, the pipes struck up, and they danced reels till they were dry again. Two thousand of them with Lord GEORGE MURRAY, the Marquis of TULLIBARDINE, Lord OGILVY, and Lord NAIRN marched thence northwards by Ecclefechan: the remainder, about 4000, with the Prince, the Duke of PERTH, Lord ELCHO, Lord PITSLIGO, LOCHIEL, and KEPPOCK, took a more westerly route by Dumfries.

On the morning of the 21st December the Duke of CUMBERLAND'S whole force marched from Penrith in three columns towards Carlisle. The Duke with the centre column, consisting of the infantry, took the road by Hesket—the right column, of horse, that by Armathwaite—the left column, also horse, that by Hutton Hall. The whole reunited on Carlton Moor, about four miles short of Carlisle, where the Duke learnt the retreat of the Prince, leaving a garrison in the city. He immediately proceeded to invest and summon it. General BLAND, with ST. GEORGE'S dragoons and 300 men of BLIGH'S regiment, took up a position at Stanwix, on the north side, to close the passage of the river Eden, by the Bridges: Major ADAMS, with 200 infantry, was posted on the south side, to check any attempt from the English gate: Major MEIRAC, in like manner, was stationed over against the Irish Gate: and Sir ANDREW AGNEW, with 300 men, over against the Sallyport. The remainder of the Duke's forces were cantoned around the town within the distance of a mile and a half—so that no possibility of escape remained for the devoted garrison within it.

The Duke fixed his head-quarters at Blackhall—and occupied the house and apartments in which CHARLES EDWARD had passed the night of the 10th November, previously to his march to Brampton.

Five of Sir JOHN COPE's dragoons, who, after the defeat at Preston Pans had joined the Prince's army, and had been taken in the retreat from Derby, were here tried and condemned by martial law—and were hanged in Carlisle field on Christmas Day.

Colonel FRANCIS TOWNLEY, the Governor of the City, appears to have been resolved to defend it to the last extremity. He was the fifth son of CHARLES TOWNLEY, Esquire, of Townley, in Lancashire, who was implicated and tried for his participation in the rebellion of 1715, but acquitted. In his twenty-third year Col. TOWNLEY had retired to France, and held a commission in the French army for some years. At the siege of Philipsbourg, where he served under the Duke of BERWICK, he distinguished himself by his courage and conduct. In 1742 he returned to England; and on the breaking out of the rebellion in 1745, he received from the King of France a Colonel's Commission, to enable him to raise men for the service of CHARLES EDWARD. In consequence he raised, and was appointed to the command of, the Manchester regiment. His knowledge of military tactics made him a valuable acquisition; and his voluntary offer to remain with his regiment in garrison at Carlisle must have tended to reconcile others to that duty, who had looked on it with apprehensions, which proved in the sequel to have been well founded.

Whether it was that Colonel TOWNLEY calculated on the Duke's having no cannon, and on his being thereby necessitated to leave Carlisle merely in check by a portion of his troops, whilst he himself with the main body should follow the Prince into Scotland; or that he had made up his mind to defend the place at all hazards, and to die there sword in hand, if necessary, as the last extremity, it cannot now be known. The expression proved against him at his trial, viz., that he, being in a great passion with Hamilton, the Commandant of the Castle, for surrendering and not making a defence to the last, declared "*that it was better to die by the sword than fall into the hands of those damned Hanoverians*," favours the latter supposition.

The garrison had made such preparations as they could for defence. They had the cannon which Col. DURAND had left in the Castle, and some smaller guns which the Prince had not been able to carry off. They had put the walls into as serviceable condition as possible, by means of sand-bags and earthen-work to supply the defective rampart; and had fixed *chevaux de frize* at the gates to keep off the dragoons. Yet it could scarcely have been disguised from those amongst them that knew anything of military engineering, if such there were, that no precautions in their power could possibly avail them long against battering artillery.

The Duke of CUMBERLAND, on his first viewing the Castle, is reported to have termed it "*An old hen-coop*, which he would speedily bring down about their ears, when he should have got artillery." At the same time he expressed great indignation against those who had previously surrendered it to the Rebels; which, it may be said, would have been more justly directed against those who had neglected to place an effective garrison in it. He immediately despatched orders to Whitehaven to procure cannon from the merchants there, and surveyed the high grounds over against the Castle for the purpose of raising batteries against it. On the range of Primrose Bank, opposite to the western face of the Castle wall, where the Canal Basin and yards now are, he marked out the site of two batteries; and whilst engaged in doing that he was fired on from the Castle, and narrowly escaped the shot, which passed between him and the engineer. Meantime a reinforcement of Dutch troops from WADE's army arrived, and threw up some works at Stanwix, on the north side. The garrison fired incessantly from the Castle, but were not able to impede the progress of the works; their gunnery was not, from all accounts, effective.

On the 26th the Duke visited the troops at Stanwix, and inspected the works there—no cannon had as yet arrived. The same day the garrison having intimation that some of their friends in the country would drive a flock of sheep down the holms into the race course, nearly between the city and Stanwix, pushed out a party of 80 men with a cannon from the Scotch gate, and advanced upon the bridge, under cover of which the sheep were driven down and carried into the town.

In fact, there appears to have been a scarcity of provisions, no stores of any considerable amount having been provided, and the Duke took measures to bring famine as well as artillery to bear upon them. Learning that they had got some supplies of flour from the city mills which stand close under the walls, he caused the mill-races at Denton Holme head, by which the mills are watered, to be cut, so as to stop them all from working,

CARLISLE, FROM THE DUKE OF CUMBERLAND'S BATTERIES, IN 1745

Near the English gate of the city some of the Duke's troops having effected a lodgment in a house outside the wall, and Colonel Townley apprehending it might prove a dangerous annoyance to his men if permitted to be established, he fired on it with the citadel guns, and reduced it to ashes.

On Friday, the 27th, by dint of great exertions on the part of the country people, six 18 pounders were brought up from Whitehaven, and were placed on the batteries at Primrose Bank that night.

On the morning of Saturday, the 28th, by day-break, three guns began to play against the four-gun battery of the Castle, and three against the angle battery. The rampart of the four-gun battery being very low and affording no protection to the gunners, an earthen work had been raised upon it to remedy the defect; but the Duke's cannon speedily demolished this, and by noon day not a man could stand there. The Duke's fire continued unabated the whole of that day, and the Dutch troops also threw some shells from the works on the Stanwix side.

During the night of the 28th, the garrison made good again the earthen work on the four-gun battery; and on the morning of Sunday, the 29th, their fire from it recommenced. The fire of the Duke's batteries slackened for want of ball; but by two o'clock in the afternoon a supply arriving, the fire became more vigorous, and that night the wall was observed to totter.

The garrison now lost heart; one of the Mayor's serjeants was sent out with two letters, one addressed by the Governor Hamilton to the Duke, offering the surrender of the place on condition of the garrison being allowed the privileges of prisoners of war; the other addressed to the commander of the Dutch troops by the French officer in the town, summoning the Dutch commander to retire with his troops from the English army in accordance with the terms of the capitulation of Tournay. No attention was paid to these letters; the unlucky bearer of them was pinioned and committed to close custody.

More cannon having arrived from Whitehaven on the evening of the 29th, that night was passed in raising a new battery of three 18-pounders, which was completed by the morning of the 30th, at day break. The garrison on sight of this felt that their fate was sealed. They did not await the opening of it. On the first platoon of the old battery firing they hung out the white flag, and called over the walls that they had hostages ready to be delivered at the English gate.

Upon this the Duke sent Colonel Conway and Lord Bury with the following messages:—

1. " His Royal Highness will make no exchange of hostages with Rebels; and desires they will let him know what they mean by hanging out the white flag.

"2. To let the French officer know if there is one in the Town, that there are no Dutch troops here, but enough of the King's to chastise the Rebels, and those who dare to give them any assistance.

" Signed, Colonel CONWAY,

" Aid-de-Camp to his R. Highness the Duke."

It may be noticed that this message contains a denial very unworthy of the Duke—viz., that there were Dutch troops—it being a notorious fact that although there might be none at his quarters, nor yet in the army which he had brought with him, yet 1,000 Dutch had arrived from Wade's army, and were actually shelling the town from their works at Stanwix Bank, which the Duke had visited and inspected on the 26th, four days before. It mattered little, indeed, whether the Dutch had retired or not—for without them, as the Duke observed, there were forces enough of the King to reduce the town—which makes it the more strange that he should have denied the fact of the Dutch being there.

In the course of about two hours the following answer was returned:—

"In answer to the short note sent by his R. Highness Prince William Duke of Cumberland, the Governor, in name of himself, and all the officers and soldiers, gunners and others belonging to the garrison, desire to know what terms his R. Highness will be pleased to give them, upon surrender of the city and castle of Carlisle; and which known, his R. Highness shall be duly acquainted with the Governor and garrison's last or ultimate resolution; the white flag being hung out on purpose to obtain a cessation of arms for concluding such a capitulation. This is to be given to his R. Highness's Aid de Camp.

"*Signed*, JOHN HAMILTON."

Whereupon Col. Conway and Lord Bury were sent back with the following terms:—

"All the terms his R. Highness will or can grant to the rebel garrison of Carlisle, are, That they shall not be put to the sword, but be reserved for the King's pleasure.

"If they consent to these conditions, the Governor and principal officers are to deliver themselves up immediately; and the castle, citadel, and all the gates of the town, are to be taken possession of forthwith by the King's troops. All the small arms are to be lodged in the town guard-room; and the rest of the garrison are to retire to the cathedral; where a guard is to be placed over them. No damage is to be done to the artillery, arms, or ammunition, *Head-quarters, at Blackhall, Dec. 30, half an hour past two in the afternoon.*

"By his R. Highness's command,

"*Signed*,

"RICHMOND, LENOX, *and* AUBIGNY,

"*Lieutenant-General of his Majesty's Forces.*"

About four o'clock they returned with the following paper:—

"The Governor of Carlisle, and haill officers composing the garrison, agree to the terms of capitulation given in, and subscribed, by order of his R. Highness, by his Grace the Duke of *Richmond, Lennox,* and *Aubigny,* Lieutenant-General of his Majesty's forces; recommending themselves to his R. Highness's clemency, and that his R. Highness will be pleased to interpose for them with his majesty; and that the officers cloaths and baggage may be safe, with a competent time to be allowed to the citizens of Carlisle to remove their beds, bed-cloaths, and other houshold furniture impressed from them for the use of the garrison in the castle. *The 30th of December,* 1745, *at three o'clock in the afternoon.*

"*Signed,* JOHN HAMILTON."

On which Brig. BLIGH was ordered immediately to take possession of the town, and to have there that night 400 foot-guards, and 700 marching foot, with 120 horse to patrol in the streets.

The following is an account of the officers and soldiers, together with their artillery, taken in the place, viz.:—

"ENGLISH. 1 Colonel, Francis Townley, of Lancashire.—5 Captains: John Saunderson, of Northumberland; Peter Moss, James Dawson, and George Fletcher, all of Lancashire; and Andrew Blood, of Yorkshire.—6 Lieutenants: Thomas Deacon, John Berwick, Robert Deacon, and John Holker, all of Lancashire; Thomas Chadwick, of Staffordshire; and Thomas Furnival of Cheshire.—7 Ensigns: Charles Deacon, and Charles Gaylor, both of Lancashire; John Hurter, of Northumberland; James Wilding, John Betts, and William Bradshaw, all of Lancashire; and Samuel Maddock, of Cheshire.—1 Adjutant: Thomas Syddell, of Lancashire.—All of the Manchester regiment.—93 non-commission officers, drummers, and private men.—James Cappock, of Lancashire, made by the Pretender Bishop of Carlisle.

"SCOTS. The Governor, John Hamilton, Aberdeenshire.—6 Captains; Robert Forbes, Aberdeenshire, of Ld. Lewis Gordon's regiment; John Burnet, Aberdeenshire, of Col. Grant's; George Abernethy, Banffshire, of Ld. Ogilvy's; Alexander Abernethy, Banffshire, of the Duke of Perth's; Donald Macdonald, Inverness-shire, of Keppoch's: and John Comerie, Braes of Athol, of the Duke of Athol's.—

7 Lieutenants: Charles Gordon, Aberdeenshire, of Ld Ogilvy's regiment; James Gordon, Aberdeenshire, of Col. Grant's; Walter Ogilvy, Banffshire, of Ld. Lewis Gordon's; William Stuart, Banffshire, of Col. Roy Stuart's; two Alexander Macgrouthers, Perththire, and James Nicolson, all of the Duke of Perth's.—3 Ensigns: Walter Mitchel, and George Ramsay, both of Aberdeenshire, and of the Duke of Perth's regiment; and James Menzies, St. German's, France, of Col. Roy Stuart's.—1 surgeon, James Stratton, Berwickshire.—256 non-commission officers, drummers, and private men.

"French. Sir Francis Geoghegan, a captain of Lally's regiment; Col. Strickland, of no regiment; and Sir John Arbuthnot, a captain of Ld. John Drummond's; all of Tholouse.—1 Serjeant: Pierre La Loche, of Dieppe, of Lally's regiment.—4 private men, all of Lally's regiment; Fra. Carpenter, of Dieppe; Pierre Bourgogne, of Tourrat; Jean Poussin, and Pierre Vickman. both of Dieppe.

"Artillery: 6 one and a half pounder brass guns, 1 brass octagon, 3 brass four pounder guns, all with carriages, 4 brass cohorns, and 2 royals."

CHAPTER·IV.

The Duke of Cumberland entered Carlisle on the 31st December, 1745, and immediately ordered into custody the Mayor, Mr. Backhouse, and the Town Clerk, Mr. Pearson, whom he sent off to London.

He also ordered into custody Major Farrer, Dr. Douglas, Mr. Graham, apothecary, Mr. Davison, grocer, Francis Hewitt, merchant, John Creighton, (the person accused of having betrayed the design of the Townsmen to have seized the Castle,) Andrew Simpson, butcher, and Mr. Salkeld, of Whitehall.

The garrison were put into the Cathedral for safe custody, much to the dissatisfaction of the clergy; and a demand appears to have been made, by the commandant of the Duke's Artillery, of the cathedral bells, as being his perquisite on the capture of the town. In fact the joy of the inhabitants at their deliverance from the Rebels very speedily subsided into something like disgust with the treatment they experienced at the hands of their deliverers. Very little damage appears to have been done to the town by the fire of the besiegers; which, indeed, was directed wholly against the Castle, nor do we hear of any of the inhabitants having been killed or wounded.

The Duke took up his quarters at Mr. Highmore's house, where the Prince had lodged. During his stay at Carlisle, he received a deputation from Edinburgh, inviting him to visit the Scottish capital; but, leaving General HAWLEY in command of the army to follow the Prince into Scotland, he returned to London. General Sir CHARLES HOWARD was appointed to the command at Carlisle, in which a considerable garrison was left. He arrived there early in January, and his first care was to get the prisoners sent off to Lancaster and Chester.

On the 10th January these unfortunate men left Carlisle. The officers were placed on horse-back, their legs tied under the bellies of their horses, their arms pinioned so as to afford them barely the power of holding the bridle, each horse was tied to the tail of one before it. The privates were on foot—each man's arms tied—the whole marching two a-breast fastened to a rope ranging between them. The Governor, HAMILTON, went first, his horse led by a Dragoon with drawn sword; then followed the officers, and Dragoons in the rear. The foot were preceded by two Dragoons, one of whom held the rope to which the prisoners were attached, the whole were followed up by a body of Dragoons. In the melancholy procession which thus filed thro' the ancient archway of the English gate were many who but six short weeks before that had marched out of it flushed with victory and inspired by the highest hopes. Miserable as their present condition was, the retrospect must have aggravated their misery by awakening the most appalling anticipations of the future. They were now in the hands of the Government, alarmed and incensed by their former temporary success. Disarmed and manacled, they had no longer the alternative of a soldier's death: they were delivered over to the law, that terrible law which awards to the murderer a less bloody doom than it deals to the traitor.

Some of them were destined,—but they knew it not, and hope would flatter each that he was not one —to revisit Carlisle, only to suffer that horrid doom; some were fated to undergo it elsewhere, and their mutilated, senseless heads alone to be returned, to bleach and waste away on the turrets of that old gateway, for the edification of the citizens of Carlisle.

During the events that have been detailed, Dr. WAUGH and his family remained quietly at York, and were informed of what was passing at Carlisle, by the letters of Mr. NICOLSON, Mr. WARDALE, and others, from which the following are selected:—

"*Mr. Nicolson to Dr. Waugh*,

"Hond. Sir,—

"As I told you in my last, the main body of the Highlanders continued their march into Scotland, and got safe over Esk, except about six or seven that perished there; but left a garrison of about 300 or 400 men at Carlisle, who yet hold out the town in defiance of the Duke and his brave army, who yesterday surrounded the town. The Rebels have fired a great many cannon since yesterday about noon, when they began that dreadful work. The Duke, its said, is extremely exasperated, has sent for some of Wade's Artillery (for he has none along with him), and some 18 lb. from Whitehaven, which are expected to be up to-morrow, and many fear the whole town will be laid in ashes. My mother and sister Eliotson are here, but I cannot hear where honest Mr. Wardale is, wch. gives me great concern. Mr. Cook and his wife are at Dalston and expect nothing but irreparable ruin, as well as many more; but I trust things will yet turn out better than expected, and that the poor city will once more be given up without much blood. I am to go with the Bishop's duty to the Duke in the morning, and if anything extraordinery happens will endeavour to apprise you thereof. His Lordship does not yet get rid of cold, tho' I hope he's better, and the little complaint he had in his ankle is quite gone off. I hear nothing out of Scotland now, and am, &c.,

"J. N.

"*22nd Dec.*, 1745, 8 *at night*.—I hear the Duke expresses prodigious wrath at giving up Carlisle to the Rebels.

"*23rd, 4 o'clock in the afternoon.*—I have been with the Duke but nothing new. The cannon still firing from Carlisle, and the King's people hope to begin the same work in the morning. The Whitehaven guns were at Wigton last night."

"*Mr. Petrie to Mr. Nicolson.*

"Dear Sir,—

"I have got here to see an old friend after seeing the Duke: would have been at Hawkesdale, but must return; wth. this paper and pen (all the officer my friend has) I offer my respects to Mrs. Nicolson. No news from Scotland, but that ye. Rebels point to Sterling. It is expected they'll be repulsed, and that the affair will soon come to nothing. The cannon here will not be ready to play till Friday morning.

"R. PETRIE.

"Low Cummersdale, Wednesday, 5 at night."

"*Prebendary Wilson to Dr. Waugh.*

"Richmond, Sunday night.

"Revd. Sir,—

"A servant of Mr. Masterman's, one of the Royal Hunters, just now come in here, gives the following account,—that the Rebels, except five hundred, had left Carlisle and are scampering home; unusual for people of that kingdom to do that have once been in England. The Esk, I imagine, is too big to suffer them to ford it on foot; if so, Genl. Oglethorp will have an opportunity to ask ym. what business they had in Cumberland. This servant left his master with the Hunters yesterday noon at Kingmoor, and passed the Duke in the afternoon betwixt Harraby and Hesket. Three hundred of Wade's and Montague's horse march'd from this place this morning to Barnard Castle.

"My wife joins with me in humble service to yourself, Mrs. Waugh, and Misses.

"I am, Revd. Sir,

"Your most obedient humble Servant,

"THO. WILSON."

"Extract of an express from Ld. Lonsdale's Steward to his Lsp. at Byrom, on Xmas day.

"That the D. was before Carlisle with his whole army, and was joined by a thousand of Marshall Wade : the main boddy of ye. Rebels being gone forward, having left a garrison at Carlisle of about 4 or 500 men, they fired on ye. Duke's forces as they approached, but soon ceased, and sent out the next day to capitulate with the Duke: his answer was, that he would give no ear to them upon any terms whatever, and if they fired anr. shot he would put every man to the sword. Notwithstanding, they fired a single shot, levd. at the Duke, as it is supposed; it missed him narrowly, but went between him and his engineer, as they were marking out ground for ye. batterys."

"Mr. Nicolson to Dr. Waugh.

"About 3 or 400 Rebels (as they are suppos'd) still keep possession of poor miserable Carlisle, and fire away almost incessantly. The Duke's army has now (this evening only) with the help of the Bishop's coach horses, and the whole country besides, got six cannon ready for the batteries, and hope to begin to play to-morrow morning, many hands being at work night and day in making trenches, fascines, &c. God send a happy and ready aid; for, otherwise, it's to be feared many of the inhabitants will be starved as well as ruined in their fortunes. Mr. Birket and Mr. Wardale are both in Town, as well as many more of our friends. Jenny Nevinson has lost her eldest son Thommy, which is some addition to the uneasiness of this house, tho' he died at Blackell-wood. I have heard nothing from Scotland since my last; nor have I, I think, any thing to add, but Gardiner got safe home with the little mare last Friday.

"J. N."

"Mr. Hutchinson to Dr. Waugh.

"Barnard Castle, 26th Dec., 1745.

"Sir,—

"I received your obliging favour the 23rd instant. The last accounts from Carlisle, the Duke has got cannon from Whitehaven; it is said ther's four or five hundred in the garrison, most of them enlisted men about Lancaster and Manchester,—they proposed terms of capitulation to his Highness which were rejected, insisting they should be prisoners of war. It is expected the cannon will play upon the town this day. Sixty Rebel prisoners passed Bowes yesterday for York Gaol. Amongst ym. one Mr. Hamilton, said to be Captain of the Hussars, and whom I see by a letter from Sir Everard Fawkenor to Mr. Carlton, is distinguished as a person of some account, and recommended by his Royal Highness to be used with as much regard as may be consistent with his being kept with the utmost safety. It is said he has made great discoveries to his Highness, and amongst the rest that 6,000 of the French best troops are landed in Scotland, which I can scarcely believe,—a little time will show that. I am credibly informed ther's near 300 of the Rebels brought to the Duke's army since they passed Carlisle, and all taken by the country people, stragling in the country without any arms. A great many are certainly drowned in passing the Esk; it was so deep they passed chin high in the water. I am advised the town and Castle is to be played against by the cannon from the high ground on the Irishgate, where six cannon were mounted on Tuesday night.

"We have above 150 of Wade's horse here; they came on Sunday, and rest here till further orders. If they stay any time, hay and straw will be scarce and dear. Mr. Jackson and sister left us this morning expecting his Highness will be in possession of the town and Castle before they reach home. I wish it may be so. Mr. Tully talks not of moving yet. Your son went up to Mr. Emmerson of Midleton on Tuesday, he sent a servant and horse for him, he was very well.

"An account is come this day (by a gentleman in this neighbourhood that went to the army under the Duke), that the Rebels had set fire to the town at the Scotch Gate, and that his Highness by his cannon had done the same at the Irish Gate,—that the engineer had given his Highness assurance that he would be master of the town and Castle in 48 hours. Mr. Hamilton, the prisoner, in his passing through Bowes, told a certain person, that the retreat of the Prince as they call him was solely owing to Lord Perth; for that in general the rest of the chiefs were against it and advised giving his Highness battle; and was very positive they would have defeated the Duke. This was told me by our apothecary that dressed his wounds at Bowes, to whom he spoke it; but it must be only bounce. I shall not finish my letter till the west post comes, and then give you what further news comes.

"What I mentioned of the town being on fire, proves an idle report, and what gave it most credit, because it came from one Mr. Aislabie, a gentleman of good fortune, but suppose he excuseth himself that he had got drunk, and had taken it from a loose hand. I see a letter to day from Appleby that the cannon had ceased firing for some hours this morning, from which they presumed the garrison had surrendered. The garrison consists mostly of Manchester and Lancashire men, with some few Scotch that were deluded into the garrison. My cousin Blanchard desires me to give my compliments to Mrs. Waugh; and am,

"Dear Sir,

"Your most obedient Servant,

"W. HUTCHINSON.

"I see a letter this moment that the Rebels burnt Butcher-street; and on Saturday sallyed out of the Castle and plundered all they could carry in, and believed they'le hold out to the last."

"Mr. Petrie to Mr. Nicolson.

"Dear Sir,

"It was much against my inclination that I returned home, when I was so near you, without paying my respects to you and Mrs. Nicolson. I would have, indeed, made a stretch for myself (however inconvenient it would have been for me) to introduce my friend Lieut. Johnstone, a brother of Sir James's, to your family; but he was upon duty, and so could go no whither. I was but a few hours at home yesternight when notice was sent me from Longtown that a party of dragoons was coming from thence to plunder my house. As I thought their own safety obliged them to murder as well as plunder, I fled with my wife at twelve at night, as far as we could from the neighbourhood. This morning I wrote to your nephew at Netherby,* intreating him to go immediately to Longtown and represent to the commanding officer there, that I was astonished to the last degree to understand such a design had been form'd by the dragoons against me; who had done my utmost in the discharge of my office to show my loyalty to his present Majesty King George,

---

* Mr Nicholson appears to have had, at this period, the superintendence of the Netherby estate; then in the possession of Catherine Lady Widdrington, widow of William Lord Widdrington, and her sister, the Honourable Mary Graham. Both these ladies by descent, and Lady W. by marriage, were naturally attached to the Stuarts. Their ancestor, Lord Preston, forfeited his title in 1690, in an attempt to restore King James 2nd.—And William Lord Widdrington being taken in arms at Preston in 1715, was tried for high treason and condemned, but his life spared, his honours and estate being forfeited. He died in 1743, and the same year Lady W. and her sister inherited the Netherby estates, but appear not to have been there in 1745.

and had also used all possible diligence in giving, upon every occasion, intelligence to the Chancellor, of the motions of the Rebels while they were in Scotland, and to his Majesty's solicitor, at Edinr., after they march'd into England: that I had but just come from the Duke of Cumberland's Secretary, Sir Everard Falconer, upon that business; that there was such a resolution taken I was well assured; but for what cause I could not possibly conjecture, if it was not that that vile fellow, Caruthers, had laid this plot to do me a mischief, because he thought—(which I really never did)—complain of him for insulting me in my own house: that I might have expected another kind of reward than to be used as a Rebel and traitor: that upon the above information, I was resolved this morning to have gone directly to his Royal Highness, and laid the matter before him; but upon second thoughts, had chused rather to represent it to him (the officer) that I might take my measures according to his answer. Your nephew wrote me back, that at my desire he had gone immediately to Longtown, but that all the dragoons had return'd to Carlisle.

"The person who gave me the information last night at eleven would not tell me who he was, only that he expected they were just at his heels. But I have learned since that he had over-heard Caruthers, with some Dragoons, lay the scheme in Caruthers's house, which was to have been put immediately in execution; however, by a good providence for me they fell upon another quarry, and so I have escaped for one night, or till they return to Longtown. But in my apprehension my danger is far from being over; these gentlemen may probably execute their purpose at their return, or Caruthers may find others as ready to fall in with his views; or they may tell in the regiment, and it may spread in the army, that I am disaffected, (for though I have not heard it, I presume this must be the engine he has wrought with) and even in this country and in every place where I am known my character must suffer irreparably; for in the hurry we were in putting things out of the way, and my wife and I flying away at midnight, and after wandering long in the woods taking a bed in a small country house, the affair must spread immediately, and every body must say that I was to have been taken up as a rebel or a suspected person; and whatever part I had acted before the world, yet that the government knew other things of me, (for few in comparison will know that rascal Caruthers's private quarrel.) In this woeful situation to which I am most surprisingly reduced, dear sir, what shall I do, both for my safety and the vindication of my character? I was thinking to apply by Mr. Gilpin to Sir E. Falconer who introduced me to him; but I have no close connection with the Recorder; and besides what can he do for me? Unable so much as to tell what I would have, you are the only person I can have recourse to, and I leave it to you to manage as you think proper. Am, with my sincere good wishes to Mrs. Nicolson, to whom I return my hearty thanks for her good ale, which procured me a sound sleep in a hen roost among a litter of stinking old straw with my friend the officer,

"Dear Sir,

"Your most obliged humble servant,

"ROBT. PETRIE.*

"Can., Dec. 27, 1745."

"*Mr. Nicolson to Dr. Waugh.*

(Written at foot of the last.)

"I send you this letter only to explain the beginning of the other, and at Mr. Petrie's request went to the Duke's head quarters at Blackell, to represent his case to Sr. Everd. Falr., which I got done, and all possible assurances that there was no danger. I was also there on Friday with a letter from the Bp. to his Royal Highness in favour of the inhabitants of Carlisle, and his Highness has promised that the town shall be protected as far as the nature of the thing will admit.

"We continue your's, &c.,

"J. N."

"*Dr. Waugh to the Dean of the Arches.*

"Good Mr. Dean.

"The return of the Rebels, notwithstanding the Duke's close pursuit, is as strange as their march to the south; I doubt they are mostly got safe back to Scotland, and may do much mischief before any army of the King's can now overtake them. They will be able, I fear, soon to join their companions, and God only knows what will be the consequences. The brave Duke of Cumberland saved our country. Penrith has suffered much by robbery and plunder; that, and the remains of Lowther Hall would have been burnt had not his R. Highness come up as he did; what will come of Carlisle we know not. I am in great pain for a wortyh gentleman who has been my curate, and lived with me ever since I

* Mr. Petrie was the minister of the Scotch Church at Cannoby.

came into the country, and staid in my house with two of my women servants to protect my effects, and has managed so well that when I last heard from him, not only little loss, except in provisions, had fallen on me, but he had contrived to get out the most valuable part of my papers, and the best of my house linen, and my wife and family's clothes, linen, and what they thought most valuable that could be brought off. I have yet a great deal in the town to loose, but my family are all safe; and if I could hear those I have persuaded to stay on my account were so I sho'd be pretty easie, and submit to the loss of the rest with less regret. The post comes in here, so that there is no time to send forward the same day what we receive. On the other side I give you a copy of a letter I received from Mr. Nicolson last post. We have no account since, tho' we have hourly expected an express. If I can get in a line what I hear to-morrow, I certainly shall. I am,

"Good Mr. Dean,

"Your most obedient servant,

"JOHN WAUGH.

"York, Dec. 27, 1745.

"P.S.—My family are all, but my son who is with his uncle, placed conveniently here in a cheap and good town, I hope as safe as any place. I intend to leave them a little and see my friends in town, now I am near half way."

(On the envelope.)—"Carlisle yet holds out against the Duke. The cannon to play about Friday morning."

"*Mr. Hutchinson to Dr. Waugh.*

"Barnard Castle, 29th Dec., 1745.

"Sir,

"I have your acceptable favour the 28th inst. Tho' I am not so well situated for giving you so perfect an account of affairs at Carlisle as you may have from that quarter, yet I cannot but take part with you in your sufferings amongst such a parcel that seem to be the collected scum of the country they have passed thro'. I see a letter this day from Mr. Jackson to Mr. Tully from Penrith, who left this town Thursday last, in hopes to have the liberty of his own house by the time he could reach Carlisle; but, poor gentleman, he is disappointed. He makes the number of Rebels left at Carlisle from 500 to 1000, and says they have good engineers in the Castle from the firing that came from them. His Highness, he says, has made a breach in the Castle Wall that a dog may creep in at; and I see another letter from a gentleman, dated the last night, that it is hoped the Town and Castle will be in his Highness's hands by to-morrow; for two Mortars from Newcastle would be employed against the Castle yesterday, and this day. We have quartered here half the Regiment of Marshall Wade's horse. Collonel Whitworth, who commands, was at my house this afternoon, and tells me he expects as many Dragoons to take quarters here also; and modestly tells me if the public houses cannot afford them quarters they must make free with private houses; and to that purpose he desired me to recommend the Constables to go about the town to offer it to the private houses, and to know what number they would take if there was occasion for it. I don't see any likelyhood of their moving while the Army rests at Newcastle; tho' I see by the Newcastle papers this day that a thousand foot and some Dragoons are to join the Duke from thence, and four Regiments more of foot are marching from Newcastle to the North. The young gentleman, your son, has been for some dayes with Mr. Emerson, at Middleton; he came down on Friday from a message from Mr. Tully that he had thoughts of leaving this town yesterday, but the account from Carlisle that day changed his thoughts: and indeed I think him much in the right not to stir till the Town and Castle is actually in the hands of the King's Forces; tho' I must own his present situation is very uncomfortable. Your son, my young man tells me, is much delighted with hunting, and give broad hints of what they would be at; but as I cannot conveniently leave the town at this juncture, and think not propper they be at Egleston alone, I suffer them to take their pleasure of hunting at home, tho' seems not so agreeable as with your son. My kinswoman desires me return her thanks and compliments to you, Mrs. Waugh, and Miss W.: to whom pray join mine, and am

"Sir, your most obedient humble servant,

"WM. HUTCHINSON."

"Mr. Nicolson to Dr. Waugh.

"Honoured Sir,

"Poor miserable Carlisle continues in the same situation I wrote in my last, 26th inst.; only the Duke's people got one battery of six 18-pounders, completed on Primrose Bank, (a little above George Blamire's,) on Friday night, and played upon the

Castle most furiously on Saturday; and, as it's said, dismounted seven of the Rebels' cannon, and made some small breaches in the walls. Yesterday there was a sort of cessation occasioned, as I hear, by our want of ball; but last night they got a very ample supply with two more 18-pounders and four 24's., and will renew the attack this day with the utmost vigour; and I am told by a messenger from Cummersdale this morning that the officers say that they hope to be in the town to-morrow night; but I am greatly afraid the work will not be so soon done. Mr. Wardale, Mr. Birket, and his whole family are still in town; but in what condition God knows, tho' I hear that a servant of Major Farrar's got out yesterday, and saies that he thinks the towns-people are all pretty well yet. You have inclosed all the news I have had from Scotland since last,—only that the Rebels went by Dumfries, got £1100; and took some hostages away with them for the payment of £900 more.

"They also got all the shoes they could meet with, and goods of several other sorts to a pretty great value. The affair of the Martinico fleet is, I hear, confirmed: I wish that of the French Transports may be so too; but our worthy Postmaster will not yet let us have either news or letter here; only Mr. Brown brought your's of the 23rd to Rose as an express from Lord Lonsdale; and Pattenson's son (who used to manage the office,) gave me another for the Bishop at Blakell on Friday evening, which he said somebody gave to him—so that we are not to know where the bagg now comes, and yet he discharges the Postmaster at Penrith from opening any of the Carlisle baggs; and I am apprehensive that tho' letters are directed to Penrith, yet most of them are forwarded to Carlisle, for numbers of letters are sent us which never come to hand. I have wrote to you every post since this day fortnight except Saturday, and one post (Thursday was s'night,) twice, whether you get them or not. Mr. Wilson is now at Rose, as also Messrs. Dacre and Senhouse, and in great concern about their behaviour at Carlisle; for its apprehended a very strict enquiry will be made into the giving up of the place. I wish justice may be done to all people, which I hope the cry of the country will in some measure effect; tho' great pains will be taken to screen the Militia Captains.

"I am, your most obedient servant.

"30th Dec., 1745."

"*To Dr. Waugh, at York.*

"Barnard Castle, New Year's Eve, 1745.

"Dear Sir,

"I have an account this day from my brother Carleton, dated at his Highness' head quarters at Blackhill, yesterday, 12 o'clock, that the Rebels hung out the white flagg on Sunday night, that a Collonell went from his Highness to know their terms, who had returned and gone again to the city and said, '*no quarter*.' Mr. Salkeld is in the town with his chaise and four. Major Farrer's servant is in the Duke's custody. Brother Carleton writes me he headed 3,000 men from the bottom of Westmoreland with axes, spades, &c. He tells me the Rebels fired several times on Sunday with powder only, and pretty certain they have no ball, but plenty of grape-shot. They have given for answer they are willing to submit to the laws, and that our troops are at liberty to enter the town at pleasure; how it will terminate we shall soon hear, but I doubt their shot will make great havock amongst our troops, if they don't surrender prisoners of war, for no other terms his Highness will give them. I have it from a good hand, there's about 40 well dressed and of good figure in the town, some will have it there's some of the chiefs; and one would think from Mr. Salkeld's being in the town, there must be some of a better sort, and I wish may be.

"Mr. Tully and his Lady are at my house this evening, and have a slip to finish.

"We are drinking your healths. Please to excuse further than compliments of the season from us; and am,

"Dear Sir,

"Your most obedient servant,

"W. HUTCHINSON."

"*The Earl of Carlisle to Dr. Waugh.*

"Dec. 31st.

"Sir,

"I received your's last night. I am heartily sorry for the poor people of Carlisle, who, I am afraid, will be great sufferers. I have been considering what may be best for your service, and I really think the sooner you come to town the better, for I would not let the Duke of Newcastle cool too long upon it, not that I think a few days either one way or other can signify anything. My brother, I hear, is ordered from Newcastle to Carlisle to consider what works may be necessary to be made there, and then to come to London. This I look upon only as a pretence to send him from Wade's army, because he is an older officer than Husk, for whom they intend the command in Scotland, as soon as this rebellion is over;

therefore I think my brother will not be in very good humour, for to be sure Carlisle must be a very disagreeable place to him in the situation he will find it. My Lady Carlisle still holds out, but I expect every day she will be confined to her bed.

"I am, Sir,

"Your most faithful humble Servant,

"CARLISLE."

"*Mr. Wardale to Dr. Waugh.*

"Carlisle, January 1.

"Revd. Sir,

"I have just time to tell you that you have suffered a good deal; but considering circumstances not so much, I believe, as you may have heard, or perhaps might expect. I have luckily preserved your vault; the cellar in the house was plundered; the bed and bolster which were taken out of Mrs. Waugh's dressing room, I shall recover, as I have found out where they are. A pair of coarse sheets, some blankets, and some coarse napkins are lost, I can scarce tell what; you shall have a further account soon. We have had but a dismal time this last seige, and very few people left in town, which made it more so; but thank God the good Duke of Cumberland has set us free at last. We have six officers and servants quartered here, who are gentlemen which behave with the greatest civility and goodness, and I dare say you'll sustain as little damage as can be imagined from them. I could have wished in my own mind you had been here to wait on the Duke, as they say he seems to wonder no more gentlemen wait upon him on this occasion; the report is that T. P. has cleared himself, not without laying some blame on you; but I beg pardon for speaking my opinion where you must have better reasons than I can know; I doubt not but the truth will prevail at last, which I am sure will be in your favour. I am, Rev. Sir, with my best compliments to good Mrs. Waugh, your most dutiful and obliged humble servant,

"R. WARDALE."

"*The case of Wm. James, one of ye. Sergts. at Mace to the Mayor of the city of Carlisle and county of Cumberland.*

"At ye. time when ye. Militia and others was endeavouring to keep out ye. Rebel army of ye. said city, he always showed himself ready and willing to do every thing that was in his power to serve his Majesty King George, or Government, as is very well known to all the gentlemen in the city and county aforesaid.

"It being our misfortunes to have been overcome by the Rebel army, and commanded by a Rebel garrison; but when this city was summoned by his Highness ye. Duke's army, in order to retake the city, the Rebels, after a little resistance, thought it impossible to keep it; therefore they thought proper to surrender themselves to his Majesty's mercy. So they writ something which they called a capitulation; so most of ye. men belonging to ye. city being out of it, they, therefore, insisted of his going with this writing and deliver it to the Duke, or some other of ye. commanding officers, which he refused to do; but ye. more he refused ye. more they insisted of his going; so in order to excuse himself of the messuage, he told them he would wait of them immediately, and instead of going to them, he concealed himself; but as he did not appear at ye. time appointed, they made diligent search, and at last found him, and threatened him with taking his life, if he did not go directly. So there being no magistrates in ye. city to advise him, and not in ye. least suspecting his Highness the Duke would think it a crime, therefore he took courage and went; and when he came to his Highness' army, he was taken as a spye, and would not approve of such a messuage, upon which his Highness has ordered him to be confined; so he hopes as he was brought into this by force and innocence, he may by his Highness's permission be ye. sooner released from his confinement. This is his real case, for and against the sd.

"WM. JAMES."

"Barnard Castle, the 5th January, 1745-6.

"Sir,

"I received your obliging favour, date the 2d inst., for which I return you my hearty thanks. We have about 600 of the Foot Guards come in this afternoon, on their march to the South; they attended the Duke into the North as his Highness's body-guard, and are now returning after him. I have nothing of news to send you from the North, being assured the Newcastle prints, and the expresses that go daily from the North, give you more truth than we have here; but should any thing happen that I have the least reason to believe may be worth troubling you with, you shall certainly have it. Mr. Tully, his lady, and your son, left this town yesterday morn', and propose reaching Carlisle to-morrow to dine. I hope they'll have the weather favourable and a pleasant journey, and their own and your house very little damaged, which, from the thorough behaviour of these villains, one could scarce hope for. Lord J. Drummond acts in the most arbitrary manner, which surely cannot go down with even these in his country that may be otherwise well inclined to his party. I hope it will have a quite different effect than he expects from them, and rather set their heads against his p—r than otherwise. A report, and ment'd in the Newcastle prints, that the Prince (as the Rebels call him) is dead. I fancy it ariseth from their finding in Carlisle a coat with a stain on it, but it's suggested that he had left it, and went away disguised from Carlisle. A body of them, it is said, have passed the Frith, where they came over at their leaving Scotland. It is doubtful they'll join the Northern Rebells, and make some attempt on Edinr.

"I am, Sir,

"Your most obedient humble servant,

"WM. HUTCHINSON.

"P.S.—Cous. Blanchard desires me join her compliments to you, your lady, and Miss Waugh. I could not persuade Master Waugh to stay here till the school was opened, he wanted so much to see how things were at Carlisle."

"*Mr. Nicolson to Dr. Waugh.*

"Hon. Sir,

"You would hear, by the last post, that General Howard was come to take the command here and, as its said, is to have two regiments in garrison together with 50 gunners now upon their march to Chester. You would also find both by Mr. Wardale's letter and mine by the last post that a report prevails here that Thos. P. had thrown a good deal of odium upon you in relation to the capitulation which I mentioned this morning to the General who tells me that he apprehends all's very well in that respect with the Duke, which I was not a little glad to hear. The General is in prodigious concern at his being ordered here, complains grievously for want of magistrates to assist him; and particularly that you should now be absent. I mentioned your London journey with what I apprehended were the reasons of your resolution, which he seemed to like very well; but notwithstanding that he wished much to see you here, and desired me to write to you accordingly. The people mentioned in my last are still in custody except Will and his wife, who are discharged, but are so much plundered that I doubt they'll hardly be able to stand it, though the General is so good as to order a dinner to be here every day, which if it could be right managed might do great things. The General has been with me again, and is extremely pressing you should return to Carlisle immediately."

"*The Earl of Carlisle to Dr. Waugh.*

"Sir,

"I received your's to-day, the post not coming last night, which makes me afraid the roads are very bad for your journey. I do not know what ill offices Pattinson may have done you; I am sure he will do you no good ones. Therefore I think the sooner you come to town the better. And I am sure Mr. Cope will excuse you as it is upon business. It is thought the Duke will go very soon to Scotland, which is a reason for your making what haste you can. I am sorry to see Will Addison in the list. The Baron must take care of him. I do not know how long my brother is to stay at Carlisle; but I believe he will be in town soon.

"Your most faithful humble servant,

"CARLISLE.

"January 7th."

"*General Howard to Dr. Waugh.*

"Sir,

"I have only just time to tell you I am going into your house this moment to relieve Mr. Tullie, who is come to town; I live the most miserable life yts. possible as you may easily imagine, and declare I had rather have gone to Scotland than stay here; such is our fate; I wish you was at home, I am perswaded it would have contributed to my assistance much, but since that is not the case I wish you all success, and ye. sooner I see you the better, and am

"Dear Sir, most faithfully your's,

"CHA. HOWARD.

"Carlisle, Jan. ye. 9th."

"*Colonel Durand to Dr. Waugh.*

"London, January 9th, 1745.

"Dear Sir,

"Since his Royal Highness the Duke of Cumberland's arrival at London, I have done myself the honour of waiting on him, and have been graciously received; but it being thought necessary, for my own sake, that some inquiry should be made, you may be sure I did not decline it. And as you mentioned to me in your obliging letter, your design of being in London soon after the holidays; as you are one of my chief evidences, I should take it as a particular favour if you would come up to town forthwith, as you was so good as to promise; and you will infinitely oblige,

"Dear Sir,

"Your most faithful friend and humble Servant,

"J. DURAND."

"*Prebendary Wilson to Dr. Waugh.*

"Carlisle, January 9th, 1745.

"Revd. Sir,

"I propos'd writing to you as soon as I got into Carlisle, but Mr. Birket and Mr. Wardale were of opinion that you would be upon the road hither before a letter could reach York. I am sorry it proved otherwise. The conduct of this place has been strangely misrepresented, and the people now in it are not lookd upon as faithful and good subjects. I'm persuaded when truth comes out and circumstances are fairly stated, Carlisle will be pitied, and allowed to have suffered on all hands. A demand made by Major Belfour, in the Duke's name, of the bells of our Cathedral, as a perquisite to the train of artillery, was a surprise upon the members of the Chapter here, and very ill relished by them. Mr. Birket, Mr. Head, and myself waited on the Duke to desire his protection, alledging that the bells were the property of the Dean and Chapter, and given to them in their Charter; that the Chapter was not conscious of any behaviour in themselves but such as became dutiful and loyal subjects; and that the town had not any right in them. The answer given us was that the Duke would not interfere in it: that if it was a perquisite to a train we could say nothing against it. A moderate composition, I believe, would pacify the claimant; but I'm firmly resolved at present, as are my two brethren, not to submit to any. Is this the reward for all our toil? If the Major takes them down, which he still threatens, I doubt not the Lord Chief Justice will oblige him to replace them. The Dean has been wrote to, as would you have been by the same post, but for the reason given in the beginning of my letter. The Chapter here wod. be glad to have your sentiments in this affair.

"I am, Revd. Sir,

"Your most obedient, faithful, humble servant,

"THOS. WILSON."

"*Mr. Wardale to Dr. Waugh.*

"Carlisle, Jany. 9th, 1745.

"Revd. Sir,

"I have just time to tell you that Genl. Howard is removed to your house, and therefore my care is in a good measure over. I shall now get out into the country, I think, for a week, as I can be of little more service; and the town in great confusion. All that I can yet hear of ——— is, that he said in the country that you were the first that mentd. a ——— to him, and that when he declar'd against it you turn'd short on your heel, and said to somebody, 'what signifies talking to that hot-headed crasy rascal,' or some such thing. But, after all, as far as I find, he had no great countenance from our good deliverer, the Duke.

"I am, in great haste,

"Your most dutiful and obliged humble Servant,

R. W."

"*Mr. Jackson to Dr. Waugh.*

"Dear Sir,

"I was much pleased with your kind letter, especially with your account of your reception at court; and don't doubt of your doing justice and being of service to this poor insulted place. You would undoubtedly have been of great service to our governour and the town's people had you been here; but I hope your being where you are will turn much more to your advantage, which will be a pleasure to your friends. We have appointed a court of probate at Wigton to-morrow fortnight, and the week after at Ap. and Penrith if you have no objection to it; business is pretty brisk at the office.

"I have nothing worth your notice from this town, but have sent you the underwritten copy of a letter from Provost Johnston this morning, and am your most

"Obedient and obliged humble servant,

"THO. JACKSON.

"Carlisle, January ye. 10th, 1745."

"*Mr. Goldie to Dr. Waugh.*

"Revd. Sir,

"I had the pleasure of your's informing that you were setting out for London when I had reason to think, by accounts from Carlisle, that you were coming northward; but since you were not there when it surrendered I humbly think you have taken the route you ought to have done, considering how easily measures that (in the situation things were in) could not be avoided, have been censured. You and Col. D——d, as I hear, have your share; tho' I am quite satisfied that, but for the prudent address of you two, the ungovernable Militia would have separated long before the Rebels came before the town; and after the mutiny I saw, it was no surprise to me to hear they had acted the part they did. I beseech you remember me to the Col. I make no doubt but both of you can give a good acct. of your conduct. It is hard for a commander to acquire a reputation without an army.

"I know I shall hear from you as frequently as your leisure will admit, and on my part you may depend on my giving you an acct. of every occurrence worthy your knowledge that I hear of. I shall, as you desire, forward my letters under cover to the Archbishop. I am sensible that I am very uncapable to entertain a person of his rank and uncommon abilities; but as I have the greatest regard for that venerable prelate, who has made so noble a stand for our rights and libertys, it would ill become me to decline anything that may be agreeable to him; and, therefore, I shall write to you in my usual open way, trusting to his Grace's indulgence. At present I can give you very little materiall. The Highlanders are about Stirling,—some of them in that town, oyrs. at Linlithgow, within 12 miles of Edinr. The main body, it is said, are encamping themselves at Torwood, within 3 miles of Stirling, We are told that Lord John Drummond has joined them with 1000 or 1200 men from Perth, that their heavy artillery is to be brought over Forth on a Bridge of Boats, and that they are to besiege Stirling; these things are wrote to us, but I cannot bid you depend on them. A Gentl. who left Edinr. on Tuesday says, that only four regts. of Hawley's Army were then arrived, but that a second division was expected that day, or on Wednesday. I wish it were possible for them to make more haste, and that we had the Hessians, and then, I think, we might hope for something decisive; at least the Rebels would cross the Forth. I am, with great regard,

"Dear Sir,

"Your's, &c.,

"J. G.

"Dumfries, 10th January, 1745-6."

"*Mr. Wardale to Mrs. Waugh.*

"Madam,

"As Mr. Chancellor, I imagine, by this time is gone to London, and you must be desirous to know how affairs go at your house, I thought it my duty to give you this short and indeed imperfect account of our situation. I think I gave Mr. Chancellor an account of most of the things we had lost by the Rebels, at least of what we can discover. The officers who I told him were billeted upon us are removed, and Gen. Howard has made your house his lodgings, which I am very glad of; not so much upon my own account, (tho' it eases me of a great deal of care and solicitude) as upon your's—because while he is here we need fear no burden from other billets.

"The General keeps his own table, and maintains his own servants, and troubles the house for almost nothing, the two maids indeed find their own victuals, which perhaps the General does not design; but I do not care to take upon me to mention such a thing to him. The officers that lodged here paid indeed for their victuals &c., but far short of what it cost you. I got for victuals and hay about £2 5s. 3d. the maids have had of me in all £5 5s. which in the whole since you left us, will be near three pounds difference in balance. One thing added to another must make Mr. Chancellor a great loser, but I assure you I did all in my power, I believe more than I should have done for myself.

"One thing happened since our people got possession of the town which gave me much uneasiness and still does. A dragoon, who lodged in the servts. rooms, had forced open the closet door over the pantry and stole all the china out of a small box, which was corded up there, and which I knew nothing of, or else I would, I think, have had it remov'd or better secured. I found out the fellow, and had him severely whipped and drumm'd out of the regiment. But what satisfaction is that? We have recovd. most part of the new set of china and coffee kans, except the teapot and some old ones, and perhaps we may recover something more. I wish I knew what was in it; but that, to be sure, you cannot recollect.

"The larger box is safe, but I have not examined what is in it. The Genl.'s coming to the house has made me, I think, pretty useless in it; and therefore I believe I shall go over to-morrow to stay 4 or 5 days with Mr. and Mrs. Nicolson, at Netherby, to get a little fresh air, which I much wanted, having lost most of the little flesh I had during our troubles. This town is still very unsettled and uneasy, and most private houses a good deal burden'd; but I trust most people bear it with patience, as they are our deliverers; and, indeed, considering their numbers, they behave, in general, exceeding well and quietly. Master Waugh is with me, in perfect health and spirits. He goes for Appleby to-morrow, and tenders his duty to you and love to his sisters. I have descended to several minute particulars which, I hope, tho' perhaps unnecessary, will not be altogether disagreeable at present. I hope we shall, in a short time, all meet in peace, and if we do not forget, shall be able at least to recollect, not without some satisfactions, even the losses and uneasiness which you and we all, in some little measure, have suffered. I am in no fear but truth will prevail, and Mr. Chancellor's conduct thro' the whole affair appear in a proper light, which is all it can want, and amply sufficient. I heartily wish you and your family the compliments of the season, and am, madam,

"Your most obedient humble servant,

"ROBT. WARDALE.

"Carlisle, Jan. 12th, 1745–6."

"*Mr. Wardale to Dr. Waugh.*

"Rev. Sir,—

"I wrote last post a pretty long letter to Mrs. Waugh to acquaint her with the situation of affairs at your house and what things we had lost during the troubles. I let her know that we had the misfortune to have all the china stole out of the little corded box since our own people got the town; but I think now we have recover'd most part of it, at least the new set of china, with coffee kans, is pretty compleat, unless the teapot was in that box; as to other things we can yet discover nothing more missing than what I mentioned before.

"I think myself now so far exonerated of the care of your house since Genl. Howard came there that I am taking my diversion four or five days at Netherby, with Mr. and Mrs. Nicolson; a little freedom and fresh air was what I much long'd for, and I think wanted; for indeed (tho' I know you'll laugh) I had lost a great deal of flesh. I am persuaded it would be a great deal better for the Genl. if you were in Carlisle, for he seems not to have that complaisance which may perhaps be necessary, or at least convenient for his interest; and there is no body here who has either weight or resolution enough to advise otherwise; I am sensible Carlisle at present will not be the pleasantest place in the world to you. But the Genl. and you will settle those things. I can get no further intelligence with regard to the affair of ——, and I cannot find that he has met with any extraordinary reception, tho' I dare venture to say full as good as his behaviour deserved. I cannot help reflecting very often how great an advantage these cunning designing men of no principle have over those that act openly and upon a good principle, especially in these times whenever common fame is apt to make people appear culpable till things are thoroughly examined. I am very sensible that whenever that shall happen (and I am persuaded truth will some time prevail), your conduct throughout this whole affair can need no other encomium. But I find I shall grow grave, alias dull and tedious. Mr. and Mrs. N. desire their compliments to you, and are very well.

"I am, Revd. Sir, your most dutiful and

"Obedient humble Servant,

"ROBT. WARDALE."

"*Mr. Nicolson to Dr. Waugh.*

"Mr. Smith sent me the enclosed the other day and desired your directions concerning your rents due there at Candlemas next and Mr. Wardale (who had begun to write) sais Mr. Tullie is in want of his plate, and designs to look after very soon, but would be glad to know first what you would have done with yours, &c. On Tuesday last I sent an express to Edinr. which promised to be back as last night but does not yet appear, tho' its now almost noon, and therefore dare not wait longer for fear of losing the post; but if there comes anything extraordinary you shall certainly have it by the next. I have wrote twice to York since I had your orders, and fully designed a repetition to day had my messenger returned in time. The General, I am much afraid, does not increase his interest at Carlisle, as indeed I always expected. General Bland is returned there; and it's said a line of horse is to be stationed along the Borders, which I think will be of little use, but great inconvenience to both them and the inhabitants. I also hear that Lord Hallifax's regt. is come to stay at Carlisle, and that the Duke of Montague's is soon expected on the same errand. Capt. Gilpin and the rest of the invalid officers that were at C—— are sent for up to London, and the former was to begin his journey this day.

"I am, &c.,

"JOS. NICOLSON.

"Netherby, Tuesy. 18, 1745-6."

"*Mr. Hylton to Dr. Waugh.*

"Hylton Castle, 19th Jany., 1745-6.

"Dear Sir,—

"It is needless to make use of words on your late mellancholly situation, but to assure you I have greatly shar'd with you in all your troubles, and should not been backward in making all inquiry after you and yours, had I known where to found you. But hope you or your family has not suffer'd in your healths, and that you have once more the comfortable prospect under our worthy friend the Governour being restored to peace, quietness, and heartily congratulate you and our friends of a ridance of the villianous crew who, I hope, will have their fate in due time. I beg my complimts. to the general; and if either he or you have any commands in town I shall be glad to receive them, I purpose being there beginning next month, and am with all respect to Mr. and Mrs. Tullie, and your good consort and all friends,

"Dear Sir,

"Your most obt. and affect. humble servant,

"J. HYLTON."

"P.S.—Mr. Graham, of York has wrote to me in behalf of his cousin, John Graham, of Lake, to have him bail'd, a thing not to be done hear tho' in Newcastle *joal*, but by Mr. Hudleston and Mr. Gascoigne, your Justices who committed him, he has several bondsmen about you if the thing can be done.

"Tell Rebbell Will. Addison I have had my house fill'd with nothing but tears for him.*

"[And who would thought?]"

"*Dr. Waugh to Prebendary Wilson.*

"Revd. Sir,—

"Yr. favour of last night's post surprised me not a little; I had heard of the demand of the bells, but would not believe it was so much in earnest: it surprises every person I have mentioned it to, and am fully persuaded no law of this land, nor any military law will justify Mr. Balfeur's demand; and I most heartily and readily join in the resolution of not paying one farthing for a composition. I dined this day in compy. with an old Lieut.-Gen. of great reputation (and others in that way of great consideration) who was out of patience at the mention of it. I shall take all opportunities of enquiring farther about it, and let you know what I learn. To-night I have not time to say more than that,

"I am, to you and your brethern,

"An affectionate brother,

"And faithful servant,

"JOHN WAUGH.

"Chancery-lane, Jan. 19th, 1745-6.

"Let me hear from you, directed as before."

"*Prebendary Wilson to Dr. Waugh.*

"Carlisle, Jan. 20th, 1745-6.

"Revd. Sir,—

"Your letter was agreeable to those I have recd. and seen upon that head. The Dean assures us that the officers of

---

* "Mr. Hylton was M.P. for Carlisle along with Sir Charles Howard. *Rebel Will Addison* was the landlord of the Crown and Mitre Inn, at Carlisle; who, it would [illegible] was one of those that were too kind with the Highlanders."

the train here are made acquainted how agreeable that demand is to their superiors. Mr. Belfour has left the town without pressing the thing further. I imagine we shall hear no more from him, and that he is ashamed of the length he has gone. He has reason to be so, for it was a scandalous, unprecedented, and illegal demand; and this he ought to be made sensible of. I have no patience when I think of it. Things are settling here, and I hope in a little time we shall be better thought of, and better treated.

"It will be sometime yet before it be safe to have service in the Cathedral; proper methods I'm assur'd will be taken to have it purifyed, and I do all in my power to have them forwarded. Mr. Birket is abroad, and Mr. Head keeps his room. Mr. Tullie gives me good assistance, and the body is oblig'd to him.

"I am, Revd. Sir,

"Your most obedt. servant,

"THOS. WILSON.

"I beg my humble services to Mr. and Mrs. Robinson."

"*Mr. Wardale to Dr. Waugh.*

"Netherby, Jany. 20, 1745-6.

"Revd. Sir,—

"Mrs. Nicolson insists upon it, it is necessary to write, tho' I have nothing to write about, and I begin to think she's right, for how could you have known that, if we had not told you? The enclosed is the latest news that Mr. Nicolson has had from Edinr.; it was a little unlucky that his messenger returned just after the last post, otherwise you had had it fresher; we are in hopes soon of hearing that the Rebells are either beat or run away. Mr. Goldie wrote lately to Mr. Nicolson, pretty much to the same purpose with the enclosed, which acct. we suppose you have had, or perhaps a later from him. As to what's doing at Carlisle I can give you but little acct. at present, having been here laying in a stock of flesh and spirits for a week past. I think of staying 3 or 4 days longer, in which time I do not fear but I shall lay in a sufficient provision of both for the rest of this winter. Your sister-in-law I find is very angry with the genl., chiefly I think because he did not ask her to play at whist one night when he was there. He's represented as a mighty uncomplaisant gentn. I find by the ladies, and I am afraid the evil report will spread further than them. He is laying in great plenty of provisions at the castle against any accident that may happen; but I hope both for his and our sakes there will never be any occasion for them. The Bp. of Worcester sent Mrs. Nicolson his Majesty's good speech last post, and mentions his hearing of your being in town. I hope that all your pains and expenses and the hazards you have run will at least procure you a kind reception from every body, I am sure it must from every honest and good subject that knows the sincerity of your intentions and the service you have done. And as for those that judge rashly, or through prejudice, or by misrepresentation, time must convince them, and I trust will.

"I am, Revd. Sir,

"Your most dutiful and obliged humble servant,

"ROB. WARDALE.

"Mr. and Mrs. Nicolson join in compliments to you."

" General Howard to Dr. Waugh.

"I received two letters from you, and you will easily believe me when I tell you nobody wishes you more speedy success and a quicker return than myself. I don't doubt but you would ease me of a great deal of trouble; but the people are so poor and so given to lyes, that I think it is not in the power of any body to know how rightly to deal with them. Honest Mr. Tullie and ye. laborious Dr. has had many meetings about settling quarters and examining prisoners on suspicion. I am to provide the garrison in case of an attack—a worse country it could not happen in; people unaccustomed to it; thinking of nothing but their own interest and which way to get most; so yt. the Government will pay sufficiently, nor am I sure I can depend on their doing it in any reasonable time; this, with many other disagreeable circumstances, makes me pass my time unpleasantly, and it's hard to do the Government duty, nay impossible, and not disoblige,—the Election town is not my concern at present; I have too much publick duty to have that the least of my thoughts. Your house accommodates me very well, and I believe you are better satisfied with my being quartered there than Parson Cappock, who I sent pinioned to Lancaster Gaol, the most wicked and profligate fellow that ever was.

"I am, dear sir,

"Yours', very faithfully,

"CHAS. HOWARD.

"Carlisle, Jan. ye. 20th."

"P.S.—No Mayor acts, nor no Civil Government of any sort here, so that the people do as they have a mind. The 2 regiments here are the Duke of Montague's and Lord Hallifax's; Stanwix is with Lord Granby's, at Berwick."

"*Mr. Jackson to Dr. Waugh.*

"January 23rd, 1745–6.

"Dear Sir,—

"We got to Carlisle the eighth of this month, where we found two officers and servants wth. two dragoons, so that we had much adoe to get each a bed, and have been in much the same situation ever since. There is complaints of partiality in quartering the poor fellows, but it is to be hoped they will be better settled in a little while. I suppose it will be no news to you yt. our Govr. is to leave us shortly, and that there has been an action in Scotland, with the advanced Guard of our army under Genl. Husk. At first it was told with circumstances almost as bad as Cope's; but yesterday an officer arrived from yt. place of action, who says it was very sharp, and the runaway dragoons being put into disorder at the first, gave way and broke the Glasgow Battalion, who threw down their arms and ran away. So yt. it was looked on as a lost case, but the foot of the right wing, being old fellows, fir'd so briskly in platoons, that they drove the Rebels quite out of sight over a hill; but the storm of rain being in their faces wet their powder so as they could fire no longer, and Genl. Husk made a brave retreat and got to Falkirk, so that the Rebels got the field and plunder; we left about 500, but they above 1,000, and those supposed the best of their men—the Lord George Murray and Lockiel being slain; on our side, the brave Sir Robert Munro and Genl. Forrester. Hawley and Husk with the Hessians are now joined. So yt. we hourly expect a good acct. wh. God grant: these are troublesome times, and our market begins to be dear. Mr. Wardale is at Netherby, and as they have a good intelligence from Dumfries, you will have a better and more accurate acct. than I send. Since the office has been open we have had a pretty good run, no less than four lic. for the soldiers with their like. As, after the expiration of the last consist. court-day when there could be no adjournment, the causes all dropt; and your return may be longer than I could wish if we have not better acct. of our army; I desire you'd let me know when you would have a court appointed, and if you intend a court of correctn. and probates before you return, and when? I wish you'd enquire and give me directions about the warrants for adons wch. the St. office requires. The Rebels made a most nasty church, which will not be fit for service a long while; and left the small-pox, of which many of our soldiers have fallen down, and some dead; and to hear the blasphemy and behaviour of most of the common men and some better, is shocking. Pray God avert his judgments. Mr. Birket is gone to his living near Penrith, and I have not seen honest Jos. since I came. I hope Mrs. Waugh and the little ones were well when you heard last. And am,

"Your most sincere friend and obedient servant,

"THOS. JACKSON."

"Mr. Goldie to Dr. Waugh.

"Dear Sir,—

"I recd. your obliging letter advising of your arrival in London and promising to let me hear from you, &c. I shall make no other return to your complimts. than that I will never be wanting in showing the sincere esteem and regard I have for your person and family. You have enclosed the extracts of the most material letters that have come here since my last. As I am sensible people in high stations are often wrongfully loaded with the odium of unsuccessful events, I am not ready to believe every surmise to their prejudice. However, I will not hide from you, tho' I hope you will from every other, that Genl. Hawley's conduct is much blamed. It seems to be credited that he believed the Highlanders would retire on his approach, and expected nothing less than engagement on Friday, and consequently was not so well prepared for it as he might have been; and had fallen so much into the former error of despising those mountaineers that he gave no credit to the first intelligence he recd. of their moving towards him; and even secured the person who brought it, tho' the Rebels were then so near him that when the acct. was confirmed there was scarcely time for the army to form; but, as I observed, he may be wronged. We have had very stormy weather of late; I pray God the fleet may not have suffered by it.

"In haste, I am,

"Dear Sir,

"Yours', sincerely,

"J. G.

"Dumfries, 24 Jany., 1745-6."

"*Mr. Holme to Dr. Waugh.*

"Sir,—

"I have been in very great pain for you and the good family during those terrible times of trouble and confusion. Your old acquaintances, F. Yarde and Bill Ford, have express'd great concern, and join with me now in heartily congratulating you on your happy deliverance from such inhuman guests. It was matter of surprise to me that your city should be left defenceless, since it lays in the rout which the Scotch have generally taken when they have attempted an invasion upon England. The reason for it must be left to better judges. However, great sufferers you must have been; and if your misfortunes are such as we conceive 'em here to be, amends should be made by the public in some shape or other, and no doubt considerable contributions might be rais'd, provided it was put in practise whiles the matter is fresh in people's memories. We have no accounts at this distance, saving what the publick papers afford us, and if you would be so good as to let us know particulars you would oblige several worthy neighbours as well as myself. We cannot here be acquainted with the offence of the Mayor and Town Clerk, nor account for their being taken into custody, without we should suppose them to be creatures of the Rebels' creating. As the harvest of '44 was a bad one with you, and the last but an indifferent crop everywhere, I am afraid you must be in distress for provisions, considering the additional number of mouths among you. I should be glad to know what price grain, beef, &c., may bear with you. But I must forbear making many enquiries, for fear my affection for my native country should make me impertinent. As matters of more moment, doubtless, must employ your time, I'll desire the favour of you to prevail upon my good old friend Bob Wardale to let me know the *processus integri*. I am, with hearty wishes for the welfare of you and yours, and with great respect, Sir,

"Your most obliged Servant,

"RICHARD HOLME.

"Ottery, St. Mary, Devon,

"Jany. 25th, 1745–6.

"P.S.—I can now, upon sufficient experience, join with you in commending the holy state,—I have one lively lass about three years old, one I lost last July, but the loss is likely to be made up again this spring."

"Mr. James Hewitt to Dr. Waugh.

"Carlisle, Jan. 27th, 1746.

"Revd. Sir,—

"As I don't doubt you are acquainted of my father's being confined, and for nobody knows what, I most humbly beg that you'll assist him all that you can in getting either a hearing or to be admitted to bail, or if he continues much longer under confinement it will undoubtedly be a very great disadvantage to him. I beg pardon for giving you this trouble, but hopes when you consider our present situation and the necessity of your assistance, you'll excuse me who am,

"Revd. Sir, your most obedt.

"And most humble servt. to command,

"JAS. HEWITT."

"Prebendary Wilson to Dr. Waugh.

"Carlisle, January 27, 1746.

"Revd. Sir,—

"No further demand has been made of our Bells; and from your and other letters we are encouraged not to fear any. You may imagine better than I can describe the condition the Rebs. left the Parish Church in, for yt. was their prison: I was given to understand the damage it suffered wd. be made good, but upon enquiry no further power was given than to the cleaning and washing of it. This proves of little use, for the flags being old, spungy, and ill-laid, the earth under them is corrupted; and till that is removed the Cathedral Church will not be sweet, nor will it be safe to have service in it.

"The pews in the parish Church are most of them broke to pieces. If you can obtain a power to have this done, and the pews repair'd, you'll merit the thanks of the body.

"I am, Revd. Sir,

"Your obedt. servt.,

"THO. WILSON."

"*Mr. Nicolson to Dr. Waugh.*

"Hond. Sir,—

"I am favoured with both your's, and was exceedingly glad to hear the Duke designed for Scotland. God preserve his Royal Highness, and crown him with laurels wheresoever he goes; for he seems, under God, the support of the nation. Indeed by all accts. Genl. Husk behaved most gloriously in the late action, near Falkirk, and had it not been for him the issue would, in all probability, have been full as bad as at Preston Panns. There was a report in Carlisle yesterday that the Rebels had attempted a scalade upon Stirling Castle, and that Genl. Blackney had repulsed them with very great slaughter; it is also said, with great assurance, that the Duke would be in Edinburgh as last night, and General Bland has left Carlisle to meet his Royal Highness there, where we hear Brigadier Fleming is likewise ordered; so that we expect to keep our present commander. What I mentioned to you in a former letter is come to a much greater height than I ever expected; for all sorts of people, rich and poor, friends and foes, seem equally exasperated, and I doubt with too much reason; for no one thing is done to oblige—nay hardly (as it's said) a civil answer given to any body. All the common people most grievously oppressed with soldiers, and the large houses perhaps a single officer, in short things are all conducted in a most strange confused way; and what I am afraid will greatly add to the loss of interest is, that some of our chief friends have heard General Bland say that he could have been very easie in the command at Carlisle and made the whole town so—and this they are indiscreet enough to name in many companies, while others (under all sorts of ties to the family) say that the —— never designs to offer his services here again, but that his —— will have him elected at another place without expense or trouble.

"What can these people think, if they think at all, unless the interest is to be entirely deserted, which I never apprehended was Lord C——'s design; indeed, for my own part, I could heartily wish it was so, for if there is not a very speedy alteration I am very sure the interest will be worse than it was in 1734—a fine end of 12 years, slavery. I have waited upon Genl. Howard every time I got to Carlisle since he came there, and always met with a very civil reception; but could never get the least opportunity of mentioning particulars which I desired much. Oh, Mr. Chancellor, had you been at Carlisle, things would all have gone well; but the confusion and wrath that now appears everywhere is not to be expressed; and numbers of the lower people must be entirely ruin'd, amongst whom honest Will. Addison must inevitably be one. I was in Carlisle yesterday. Mr. Tullie was gone to Warwick, so heard nothing further about the plate, only left your letter with Mr. Wardale, who, I think, is much recruited, and quite as well as when the Highlanders came first before the city. Some of our Militia gentry are endeavouring to throw the whole blame of giving up Carlisle upon Col. Durand, by his first ordering all the men upon the walls, having no provision made for the men in the Castle, and declaring that neither one nor the other was tenable; however, all people readily allow the great service you were of, and lament your absence more and more every day. I have sent to Mr. Simpson to fix either Tuesday or Wednesday next for the rect. of your rents at Caldbeck, and shall attend accordingly. Nothing new from Edinbrugh.

"Your's, most obediently and most faithfully,

"JOS. NICOLSON.

"Hawksdale, Jany., 30th, 1745-6."

"Mr. Goldie to Dr. Waugh.

"Dear Sir,—

"You have obliged me much in adviseing me of the gracious reception you met with. I hope the time is not far distant when you shall be distinguished by some more substantial mark of favour: if my correspondence has been any way useful to you and the public, I shall have no cause to grudge my pains. Many anxious thoughts we have had since the beginning of this Rebellion; but now I hope the face of things will change under the command of the Duke, who arrived at Holyrood House betwixt the hours of three and four of Thursday morning, to the inexpressible joy of all who wish well to our happy constitution; and I doubt not but his pressence will animate the troops to do their duty. May he himself be preserved from the attempts of secret as well as declared traitors. We hear the army would march soon against the Rebels; some say on Friday. The Rebels have been unsuccessful in several attempts on the Castle of Stirling; on Sunday last they endeavoured to scale the walls, but were repulsed with great loss. They thereupon collected woolpacks under favour of which they expected to raise a battery, and it would appear they have in some measure succeeded; for we hear they have damaged some of the upper works, and made a small breach, tho' it is not doubted the castle will hold out till the army come to its relief. We are told that Genl. Blakeney has discovered four guns, 18 pounders, in a vault that has never been opened or seen since Cromwell's days, with abundance of ball and two mortars. He has made surprising improvements in the Castle, and destroyed numbers of the Rebels. We hear two French engineers have deserted to him. The Rebels are scarce of provisions and the country about Stirling is reduced to great misery. Numbers, we hear, desert from the Rebels, and several of Lord John Drummond's regiment have come into Edinbrugh. We have sent deputations from this town and country to congratulate the Duke on his arrival, and from them we shall have distinct accts. of every material occurrence, which I shall communicate to you. Upon Genl. Howard's coming to Carlisle I received a letter from Mr. Wardale, at his request desiring I might inform him of everything material, which I have readily complied with, as I know the general is your friend. Pray can nothing be done for Frank Hewitt? I dare say he is no Jacobite, but he is timorous and imprudent. The printed letters you were so good to send me give an odd notion of the author.

"I am, Revd. Sir, yours, &c.,

"2nd Feby., 1845-6. J. G."

"Mr. Nicolson to Dr. Waugh.

"Revd. Sir,—

"I most heartily thank you for the pleasure a certain letter gave me on Saturday, and hope it will be follow'd with something more substantial, which none can more ardently wish or would more rejoice at than myself. I have this moment a letter from Mr. Petrie, with an account from Edenr., dated the 30th ult., which says that the Pretender reviewed 5000 of his men at Falkirk, on Tuesday, and then returned to Stirling; that on Wednesday morning at three o'clock, the Rebells got a battery finished and began to play upon the Castle at Stirling which they continued pretty close all that day and demolished part of the parapet wall at the seven gun battery, but no part of the wall itself; that General Blakeney has abundance of materials for repairs, and its hoped will soon make the damages good; that he has fired briskly upon the trenchers and kill'd many of their men—that the Duke to the inexpressible joy of the inhabitants arrived there that morning and had recd. the compliments of the citizens, clergy, and university—that expresses were just come in from Stirling, whereupon sudden orders were given for the whole army to march next morning. God preserve the Duke and his forces and put a speedy end to this abominable Rebellion. Mr. Holmes, I find, is chiefly blamed for making informations against the Mayor, Town Clerk, &c. &c. &c. of Carlisle, and I am told that he gives it out that Col. Durand will be called to an account for making him beg pardon of the cowardly Militia officers; but this is so foolish that I should not have thought it worth mentioning, but just as a specimen of the present tattle. The General, I am told, grows rather more complaisant; but I have not seen him since my last. Pray can you possibly procure me orders from the excise office for instructing Joseph Falder into that business. They are a considerable number of freemen; and as I believe they will always be very staunch, have promised to do my utmost in this affair. They seem to chuse to be instructed in the Carlisle division.

"I am glad to hear that Lady Carlisle is again safely delivered; but a Lord Morpeth would have given far more joy to

"Your most obedient faithful humble servant,

"JOS. NICOLSON.

"Hawksdale, Feb. 3rd, 1745-6."

"*Dr. Waugh to Prebendary Wilson.*

"Revd. Sir,—

"Since I had the favour of your letter, I have made it my business to find out some method to get the church at Carlisle put in decent condition, as you say your were given to understand it should be; but cannot promise myself that I shall merit the thanks of my brethren for the success of my endeavours, tho' I shall do all I can. Yesterday I talked to the Bishop of London about it; I think from all I can learn, if the Dean and Prebends are willing, the best way is to do it effectually and speedily, and if possible to get an allowance for it afterwards; at present I fear none can be got, tho' I have one iron in the fire, that I have a little expectation from. If I fail there, I fear much we must bear the loss. I wish you had told me by whom you were given to understand that the damage should be made good. The consternation people were in here for fear of our affairs at home and abroad suffering by this rebellion, is much abated by the news yesterday, which you will have from Scotland and in this night's papers. I wish you joy on this occasion, with service to Mrs. Wilson and all friends.

"I am, &c.,

"J. W.

"Feb. 6."

"Mr. Nicolson to Dr. Waugh.

"Revd. Sir,—

"Yesterday I was at Caldbeck, and enclosed you have an account of the day's work, and if you want a bill please to let me know, and I'll endeavour to remit it by the return of post. Mr. Simpson desires to be named to you, and also to know whether the Quakers are now to be convicted, or not. He saies this is the time of the year they chuse, because they have now corn and things about them convenient for distresses, which may not be the case two or three months hence. On Tuesday night honest Mr. Wardale sent us an account that the Genl. had had an express signifying the entire dispersion of the Rebels; that as soon as the Duke came near they destroyed a good part of their arms, nailed most of their cannon, and that the young Pretender and most of the chieftains had escaped; but that numbers of the common men were drowned in the Forth, and many taken prisoners; and, in short, that this cursed rebellion had got its finishing stroke; but last night I had a letter from Mr. Goldie, which does not make the matter quite so clear, tho', in the main, I think we may safely say it will be so very soon. I expect further accounts from Edinbrugh, by the way of Mr. Petrie, before this goes to the post, which I shall send you entire. The above I only just mention, because you hear constantly from the same hands.

"Things goe on at Carlisle much as I mentd. in my last. But if your affairs made it proper to come there a little, you might, I think, oblige the whole town to the highest degree; but whether worth while or not, you only can judge. I dare hardly think on either, tho' I assure you abundance of my thoughts are employed in that way. Mrs. Waugh, however, and the children are, I believe, at York at present. Pray procure instructions for Jos. Falder if possible, for I shall have no ease till its done. The ———— is much recruited, and quite anti-ministerial; but this under the rose.

"And I am,

"Your most obedient faithful humble Servant,

"JOS. NICOLSON.

"Hawksdale, Feby. 6th, 1745-6."

"General Howard to Dr. Waugh.

"Dr. Sir,—

"I read your name with pleasure in the last news, and hope my master was as gracious to you as the news-writer mentions, and that you may soon receive the effects of it in what may be agreeable to you. The account which was sent me by express from Edinburgh last Tuesday of the Rebells abandoning Stirling and returning over the Forth, gave me and the rest of the company the greatest joy and surprise at the same time, after what had pass'd who could have conceived in the strong situation they were they would not have staid and given the Duke battle,—better much as it is—preserve his life, and I hope he will now soon put an end to this wicked crew.

"I have heard nothing of Brigadier Fleming, nor don't know whether he proposes I shall have the pleasure of his company here or not. L'd Halifax and I were yesterday at Corby, and both agreed that for Cumberland it was a very pretty place, but having been both used to the south, thus far north is great difference. I always say Carlisle for that part of the world is as pretty a town as one shall meet with, but you are very near neighbours to Scotland.

"I am, dr. Sir,

"Faithfully yours,

"CHAS. HOWARD.

"Carlisle, Feby. the 8th."

"*Dr. Waugh to Genl Howard.*

"Sir,—

"Tho' I had wrote to you before I received your last letter, I had not so long neglected writing to you, had I imagined you had left Carlisle before a letter from me could reach you. I am sorry I could not come to your assistance at Carlisle, to serve you, being always a pleasure to me: that your situation was not pleasant I could easily conceive, but I have ever found that justice might be done, and people kept in tolerable good humour at the same time, tho' it required some patience and some management to do it. The acct. you will have of the Duke's success I give you joy of; it has altered people's countenances here a great deal; now, I hope, money will be more easily raised at home, and our affairs go better abroad Mr. Wilson writes me word that he was given to understand the damage the church suffered would be made good; but that on further inquiry he finds no further power than the cleaning and washing of it, which is of little use, as the earth under the flags is all corrupted, and that it will not be safe to use the Cathedral till that is removed. That the pews, &c., are all broke to pieces; if you can give any assistance or orders about it you will much oblige me by your good offices therein. Another young lady in Soho Square—all your friends there and in Burlington Street are well. I wish you safe to London, and that my Lord Carlisle or you can do anything to help the poor people, and save his interest at Carlisle. Don't be angry that I hint so freely to you what I feel very sensibly; for to do anything that ought to incur your displeasure would be a great affliction to—Sir,

"Your most obliged and most faithful and
"Obedient Servant,
"JOHN WAUGH.

"Feb. 8th, 1745-6."

"General Howard to Dr. Waugh.

"I stop the post to thank you, Dr. Sir, for yours I received just now, in which you tell me justice may be done and people kept in tolerable good humour, with patience and management; the first part of it I can assure you has always been my view and intention to practise; the latter part, I have endeavoured to copy you as much as I could. Now, Sir, I have told you this, if there are any disobliged at my behaviour since I have had the command here, which I don't know there are, they are dirty low fellows that will never want a pretence for a quarrel, and which by experience I have learnt never to make myself uneasy about. If getting the prisoners removed in ten days by application to the Duke of Cumberland and ye. Duke of Newcastle, their expences defrayed by the publick, if quartering five companys in ye. suburbs contrary to my orders, and applying to remove six more to other places,—if applying for the Castle to be filled up, or Barracks to be built for a garrison, I suppose that will always be continued here upon ye. account of yt. neighbourhood; if these things, I say, are hurting the interest and disobliging, I am guilty of them; and since you have called upon me, which I think I did not want, I will finish with telling you, as I am a great scholar, '*Nil Conscire sibi, Nullaque Pallescere Culpa.*' Mr. Wilson never spoke to me about the Church, nor did I ever receive any orders or directions about it; but I hope its well purified and the earth wholesome, because I heard a very loyal sermon there yesterday.

"Adieu, dear Sir,
"Faithfully yours,
"CHA. HOWARD.

"Carlisle, Feby. ye. 10th."

"*Prebendary Wilson to Dr. Waugh.*

"Richmond, Feby. 14th, 1745.

"Revd. Sir,—

"A letter from the Duke of Newcastle to General Howard, purporting that the maintenance of the Rebell prisoners should not be charged to the county, gave rise to the report that nobody in the county should suffer by their being confined in the Church; and as this was mentioned by several that were about the General, (and a thing of itself so reasonable,) I could not doubt the truth of it. The burning of sulpher and tar had that effect that we had service in the Cathedral on Sunday last, which was well filled, and chiefly by the military. I am not willing of myself to undertake the repairs of the Parish Church, as I cannot yet certainly be informed whether they lay upon the Parishioners or the Dean and Prebendarys: if they do on the latter, I hope they will be effectually and handsomely done. You have my thanks for the trouble you have already had. I left Carlisle on Monday, and hope to return thither with my wife as soon as the weather is mild,—at present we have a very keen frost. Our accounts from the north continue very good, and there is a pleasing prospect that our troubles will shortly have an end. We are much surprised with the changes at Court—had they not been mentioned in the *Gazette*, I should not have credited the accts.

"I am, Revd. Sir, with my wife's service,

"Your most obedt. and faithful servt.,

"THOS. WILSON."

"*Mr. Backhouse to Dr. Waugh.*

"Uldale, Feby. 15th, 1745-6.

"Revd. Sir,—

"The many favours I have already received from you make me asham'd to beg another, was I not under the greatest concern for my poor brother, who is now in confinement at London; and if not speedily released, will be the ruin of himself and family. What his behaviour was in the time when Carlisle was besieged by the Rebells, is better known to yourself than I can inform you; but by all the enquiries I can make, and by his own protestations, what he did was by compulsion and force; and that he intentionally was, and is, as loyal a subject as any his Majesty has in his dominions. He expresses a hearty sorrow for his ever being concerned in ye. Corporation of Carlisle; and I have repeated assurances both from his own mouth, when in custody at Blackwell, and by letters from him since, yt. if his friends can get him acquitted of this unfortunate affair he is now confined for, he will never more put on the Alderman's gown; but bid adieu to the interest of those persons who have too long made a fool of him. It is, therefore, sir, the most earnest request of my mother, sisters at Caldbeck, and myself, that you will use your utmost endeavours in behalf of my brother; which favour will be acknowledged by him and the rest of our family with ye. greatest gratitude.

"I am, Revd. Sir,

"Your most faithful humble servant,

"EDW. BACKHOUSE."

"*Mr. Nicolson to Dr. Waugh.*

"Reverend Sir,—

"I was favoured with your's of the sixth instant, but as I had told you in my two former letters every thing that had then and since come to my knowledge in relation to Col. Durand, I did not write by the last post as you directed. My information was chiefly during my attendance, and often mentioned in such a manner, as I concluded it was the confirmed design of several concerned; and yesterday it happened to come again upon the carpet; and honest Gussy, amongst other things, told me that *he wou'd pray for his uncles and cousins, but never fight with them more.* I have talked with Mr. W., and hope your house at Stanwix has not suffered very much, but he saies he has given you a particular account thereof. As to your hay we will consider further about it and do the best we can; we have now a severe frost, and a pretty great likelihood of snow; and should that happen, hay must be extravagantly dear. Our Bishop is in top spirits, and much better health than he has been for many months; his Lop. has many letters from his Brother of London, to whom he has of late sent copies of all my accounts from Scotland; and his Lop. tells him they are much the best he has seen. They were, I think, all from Mr. Goldie, so you must have had the same at least a post sooner; but I suppose the chief reason of this correspondence being so common at present is a sollicitation in favour of Mr. Gilbanks, the change with Mr. Graham being intirely (as his Lop. saies) at an end. The newspapers this day have surprised us not a little; and I find it is confirmed that your Noble Lord* is first Lord of the Admiralty. God send it a happy change not only to particulars, but to the nation in general. It seems confirmed that the Rebels have taken their different routs, that Lord John Drummund is dead, and that the Duke is pursuing that party which marched towards Montrose himself, and has dispatched proper power after the rest; and the Scotch seem not a little delighted with his Royal Highness's declaring that he'll not leave the kingdom as long as any of them remain together. You say nothing about bills. I wrote some time agoe (by my wife) to acquaint Mrs. Waugh that I could easily furnish her with a London bill, but do not find she wants any. Pray let me hear from you how matters are like to goe at this critical juncture, for I am and shall be extreamly sollicitous till I hear from you. Brigr. Fleming came to town on Wednesday, and I hear the General designs to leave us on Wednesday next, and to dine at Rose on Monday. Yesterday, 7 night, I had a little conversation with his Excellency, and tooke the freedom to say that it was not only his own personal interest that would be lost, but that of the family also for ever; he replied he would not do dirty work upon any consideration. I answered that none of his friends desired any such thing, but only that he would give civil answers to people and prefer freemen and friends to other people, when all other circumstances were equal. That, he said, he was ready to do; but if the town could find any body else that would give them more money and do more for them, they might take them. I said I hope he would not talk so publickly, for nothing would be more ruinous to his interest. No, he said, he would not. I then begged pardon, and said it was my great attachment to the interest that forced me into such presumption. He was pleased to say we were even there, for he would do any thing in his power to serve me, and so we parted. You have often (with the greatest reason) mentioned my excessive bad writing, and I doubt this will exceed all, for it's wrote in the nest, and numbers of people are talking the whole time to your

"Most obedient humble servant,

"JOS. NICOLSON.

"15th February, 1745, 3 o'clock."

"*Mr. Simpson to Dr. Waugh.*

"Caldbeck, Feb. 16th, 1745-6.

"Revd. Sir,—

"I suppose Mr. Nicholson, by this time, has informed you, yt. he has received your Candlemas rents. If you

---

* The Earl of Carlisle is meant.

design to have a conviction this year, the sooner (I believe) the better, as they have their corn now ready for ye. market, which is the article the churchwardens generally go upon. I wait for your orders.

"My aunt has received a letter, desiring her to join with Mr. Backhouse, of Uldale, in asking a favour of you for his unfortunate brother: she cannot but look upon it as a very hard request from her to you, upon many accounts; yet, considering his unhappy situation at present, she hopes you will not take it amiss, if she desires you to do him any favour that lies in your power; as you were an eye witness of his loyalty and good behaviour, as long as the city was thought teneable, and must be fully convinced (I humbly presume) yt. whatever he did after the surrender, was wholly owing to terror and misguided council. My aunt begs pardon for this trouble, and hopes you'l consider his affair on the compassionate side; and does not doubt but a fair representation of his case from your mouth wou'd be of infinite service to him. My aunt joins in best respects to you, with, Sir,

"Your most obedient humble Servant,

"R. SIMPSON."

"Mr. Nicolson to Dr. Waugh.

"Reverend Sir,—

"In my hurry on Saturday, I believe I forgot to say any thing about Mr. B——, as you ordered, and indeed I am still much puzeled how to do it, for the talk is pretty diffierent, tho' in general most people, except at ————, attribute all to his natural temper; but, in short, all his friends think he was far too intimate with Sir John ————, dayly together, and when absent so much mention of him; and what occcasioned the most notice was, that gentleman's leaving his old lodgings and going to his (Mr. B——'s) house just at the time the Duke invested poor Carlisle, where he still continues with a centry over him; but Mr. Tullie told me on Saturday he would soon be permitted to walk about upon his parol; and also have his money, about £120, restored; this sum was lodged in Mr. B———'s hand, but he was discreet enough to acquaint the King's people with it at their first entering the town. I delivered your message to James Hewitt, and both he and his mother seemed very thankful. What you have heard of money being lodged with Francis was too true: he was also far too intimate with the Rebel Governor; but, poor man, more than his all was at stake, and that I dare say was the sole inducement; for I really think nobody is better affected to the present happy establishment in the illustrious house of Hanover.

"The General told me on Saturday evening that he had a letter of advice from you, which he thought he had answered pretty exactly, and mentioned some of it; and asked me if I had given the information, which I mentioned in the affirmative; which he seemed not in the least displeased with; but said he supposed so, for he thought nobody had so great a regard for the interest as me; and indeed I cannot say that I have ever heard any one body endeavour to palliate matters, but greatly the contrary, which I own, shocked me not a little. Yesterday I saw a letter from Sir James L——r, wherein he saies that there's like to be great changes at Court—much eagerness for places and great opposition. That Lord Lon——e was got to town, and he had been to wait upon his lordship to desire his assistance in getting the malicious reports which had been raised of the Mayor, Town Clerk, and the rest of their friends, removed, which he hoped would soon be now accomplished; and Clem. writes my sister Peggy that he lately heard a letter, to Mr. Spedding, read, wherein that same gentleman said he had had a great deal of talk with the King about the Rebels in this country, and that no other gentlemen who had estates in this country had given themselves any trouble in the affair; that Lord Lon——e had been very active, and done great service in Yorkshire; and all this, with abundance more of the same sort, is industriously spread all about, not only by his vile tools, but also by many irregular written letters, as formerly upon other occasions. The snow, which threatened us on Saturday, is turned to a fine thaw; but still I believe hay must be a valuable commodity. Many of the common soldiers die dayly at Carlisle, occasioned, I doubt, partly by their bad lodging and getting more drams and drink than proper victuals, tho' our markets still hold very plentiful, but prices increase. It seems to me a strange piece of management (not to give it a worse name) that the officers shou'd have lodgings gratis, and if a Major or Captain get into one of the best houses no common men are to be billeted there; whereas, had they been obliged to hire rooms, people enough in town wou'd have been glad to have taken them upon reasonable terms, and the common men might then have been much better accommodated, and none of the lower townspeople so shamefully oppressed. Indeed the General has, I believe, now got leave to quarter a part of them in other places; and he saies that he hopes in a little time only one regiment will be kept here, and conveniences fitted up for them in the Castle, which would be doing the town a most real service indeed. What news I now get from Scotland comes chiefly from Mr. Goldie, which I need not trouble you with; but whatever I can procure in any other way shall be sure to transmit it to you as quick as possible; and am,

"Your most obedient humble Servant,

"JOS. NICOLSON.

"Hawkesdale, Feb. 17, 1745."

"*Mrs. Nicolson to Mrs. Waugh.*

"Hawkesdale, Feby. 17th.

"Dear Mrs. Waugh,—

"The pleasure of your's I met with yesterday at Rose, at my return from Netherby, where I had been a few days to see a fat ox kill'd that we every day thought in jeperday, whilest Rebells were in Cumberland, having taken a fancy to that part of Esk for their passing and repassing; and Tom never expected to have had one cut at it, till the Duke once more got between us and danger; so now eats fat beef, and is thankful. The —— you enquire after (as your friend above did last letter, so good wits jump) is surprizingly well all this winter, and canty; viper broth is a restorer, so something else first I much wish for, for indeed I now have hopes somebody will be thought and found the fittest to be sett *there* when time comes. The Genll. and Lord Hallifax went to Noward on Monday for a day or two, and talks of waiting on the Bp. of Carlisle perhaps the next Monday. Brigadier Fleming is come, 'tis said, to take the command of the garrison upon him, and is at Dr. Hutchinson's. Mr. Nicolson took an opportunity to speak a few words in your hall to the Genl., tho' he had company in the parlour, so was in haste; but the little time he had allowed he made the best use of it, and told him it was not his own private intrest but that of the family was at stake; and tho' he cou'd not nor was desired by him to do *durty work*, yet a civill answer he must give, and a deal more, to all which he promised fair; this was this day se'nnight. I fancy your maids now partake of repasts that are made, for he keeps house and has often entertainments, &c. I will tell Mr. Wardale what you say about the maids. Miss Waugh's earrings had come with Jack Garnet before, but that Captain Aliburton was gone out with the key of the scritore, as Mr. Wardle told me, for I writ to him about it, so hope the next opportunity will bring all you want. I heartily thank you, dear Madam, for your kind enquiry. My mother, a miracle of her age, has her fevor again, and periodicall headacks, which I have given her bark and brandy for, and she is, I thank God, better. I cannot say but Dolly has better health and eats better, tho' much more business; she has but two soldiers now, which, indeed, one cannot help being kind to; they left their own homes with great readiness to come to banish Rebells, and seem honest country men; one of them laments his wife and five children, which he wants to see, but thanks God they have a friend which promised, if he came, to allow them 3s. 6d. a-week. This poor man has been very ill,—starved; many of them are this cold weather, with being all night upon guard, and stand many hours, nay days, together as centenals, which just kills them. Great folks will be waited on, let little ones fare how they will; a great many of them are dead in small pox and other distempers.

"We send Dolly barley bread and what things we can, that she may help them out sometimes; these finds their own meat, but she dresses and gives them what little things is wanted to make it ready with. You hear that Mr. Birkett is talked on I suppose, for Mr. Chanr. has in London, and desires to know what is laid to his charge, —'tis nothing but his constant attendance on Sr. John, and now his having him in the House, but 'twou'd have been full as discreet to have left it alone. I dare say many people wonder at your Br. and Sister for going to visit Sr. John: they got leave of the Genll. and went last week, what they have done this I know not. I think I have told you all the news I can pick up, for, except last Friday, I have never been near the town but twice going through it, and have no heart till you come to it again, and then somebody near me and I shall go with glee, thankfull we are that not the smallest blot can be laid to our dear friend's charge,—not an indiscretion; and pleasure it is to find every one you meet saying how glad they are to hear of his reception at Court. We have no accounts out of Scotland worth sending since I writ last; but the Bishop of London, who writes often to our Bishop, says, the last post, that people think the rebellion over, but for his part he cannot think so, since it is pretty certain, or some such word, that a *pretty great reinforcement was lately sent to them from Dunkirk and Callais.* Our Bp. sends him the accounts he gets, which is none at all but what he has from Mr. Nicolson, and we know our friend has it a post before. I had writ often to Mr. Maddox's lady, and sent them accounts from time to time, as the Chancellor tells us he is particularly civil and friendly to him. Indeed, I did not leave untold how much he merited to all whom I could reach by hook or by crook. Lord send him safe to us again, and something in hand to bring with him. Mr. Tireman, I fancy, will be very desirous to do any thing in the world he can for you and yours. He is a good-natured creature. He has writ to Dolly, which she beggs me to answer for her, so I will make bold to inclose a few lines. Mr. Nicolson says he will send both him and Miss Jackson a bill; she, I fancy, will want money. Her good-for-nothing br. and sister have had no trouble, and now but an officer, or some such thing, as is the case of every good house in town. Scandalous management. My paper will not do to thank you for your goodness to Clem, and many more words I may find to say. He talks of going again, and thinks to sail from London if he can. Poor fellow, I had a good letter from him, which show'd his cheerfull bearing—what his lott shou'd be. Your and our plate are yet in their safe places I hope, for I reccon your br. will not call for his without Mr. Nicolson, and till we hear of the victorious Duke's return, we will let our little sleep a while longer. This is Miss Senhouse's birthday, so must put on our *caps*, but I warrant they are far from the fashion of the caps you had in hand when you so obligingly wrote; but we will see them on ere long I hope, and I have no fear but to see Miss Waugh advanced some inches nearer the horizon than when I parted from her. I had a franck Mr. Wardle gave me directed for her, wch. he met with in the study, but I have misplaced or lost it, else wou'd have fill'd it to her. My best service waits on her and sisters. Niece desires Miss Peggy may be sent home, she wants her most sadly, and so does more folks that I cou'd name want to have her prattle. I hope pappa will not forget his *Willydown* when he returns again. I believe you will say I wou'd fain be talking; but Mr. Nicolson says I can never leave off whilest a scrap of paper remains uncovered. He and all here are most heartily at your service; and I am,

"Dear madam,

"Your truely obliged, obedient, and affectionate servant,

"E. NICOLSON.

"P.S.—*Saturday morn.*—Mr. Brown was at Rose, and says Mr. Wardale sent him word that the Duke will be at Carlisle soon, the Genll. says so; and honest Gussey says he will pray for his *uncles, aunts, and good cousins, but never fight with them more whatever happen.* There was a dinner of two courses, and coffee, tea, and a fiddler, so we danced away till seven o'clock, which was paying the pretty body a greater compliment than he ever paid her before: she is now entered her teens. Dr. Hall, of Teddington, in Surry, and some of his good neighbours, which I take Lady Blount's sister is one, have paid in fifty guineas to John Reay, to be paid here to the Bishop, to give to poor housekeepers and sufferers by the rebellion in and about Carlisle, which Mr. Nicolson is going to get lists of to day."

"*Mr. Wardale to Dr. Waugh.*

"Revd. Sir,—

"I have this day sent the three watches and some other things to York by Genl. Howard, who is the only hand I could hope for that I should have been quite easy in. The Genl., I am afraid, has rather hurt than augmented his interest by coming to Carlisle at this time; not but I believe he has mostly done right things, but the manner I doubt has given a good deal of offence to some of his friends, and a handle to his enemies. Many with doing less good would perhaps have gain'd more credit; and if he had stay'd a little longer—now things are settleing here—I fancy he would have retrieved at least all that he has lost.

"I find you have had different acccounts of Mr. Birket's behaviour in our troubles; I think, as I was an eye witness to most part of it, I ought in justice to Mr. Birket to assure you, that as far as I am capable of judging, he acted not only in a cool, open, and unblameable manner, but with the greatest steadiness and generosity. Sir J. Arburthnot was left here sick when the Rebels left Carlisle: he went to lodge with Mr. Birket, and was of a good deal of service to him, before and during the last siege, in protecting him and his house from any insults or plundering; all that he desired of Mr. Birket was to speak to some officer to come and take him prisoner, least he should be insulted and plundered by the rabble; and for fear some of ye. Foot Guards should break in upon him, he desired Mr. Birket to lay by some money for him, without any design, I am persuaded, of either of them to conceal it from proper people; as soon as the Duke got possession of the Town, Mr. Birket informed him of his being at his house, and the Duke told him he did very right in letting him know. When Col. Cary came to take him into custody Mr. Birket chanced to be step'd out; and the money being mentioned, Cary was in high dudgeon, that it should be in his custody and he not there to deliver it. Sir J. told him he had only given it to Mr. Birket least it should fall into the hands of the common soldiers; and Mr. Birket came in just then and delivered it up. I mention this particularly, because I fancy it is the only handle any body can have against him. I could say a great deal in praise of Mr. Birket with strict justice; but I know I need not to you, who from your knowledge of him are inclinable to think well of him.

"Genl. Howard, I find, has been very well pleased with Mr. Goldie's correspondence; says he's a man of sense, and gave him as clear and true accounts as any he had from Scotland, and not a day later than those he had by express directly from Edinr.

"I wish you could do any service safely for our prisoners upon suspicion, even Davison not excepted, as I really believe them innocent,—at least any further than thro' inadvertency or fear. I fancy any thing of that nature at this time would never be forgot; but this I only hint, as you must be infinitely better able to judge how far it is discreet to meddle than I. I shall venture to give orders for your house at Stanwix being repaired, without waiting for your directions, as poor Ed. James, who has been a great sufferer in his tythe hay and corn, as well as at home, is destitute at present of a place to live in.

"The Rebels have destroyed the register books of Stanwix, both old and new. I should be glad of your directions how to proceed in this particular.

"Mr. Tullie has taken up your plate and has it in his custody, where it will remain, unless I have other directions from you.

"I had several other particulars to mention, but have not time to recollect them at present, nor to write them.

"I am, rev. sir,

"Your most dutiful and obliged humble servant,

"ROBT. WARDALE.

"Carlisle, Feb. 20, 1745."

"*William Hodgson to Dr. Waugh.*

"Sir,—

"I am very sorry to give you this trouble, but hopes you'l pardon me this once.—So far as I can learn I am far the greatest sufferer of any in Carlisle, as I had laid most in for the Government's use, and paid all ready money. As soone as ye. Rebles got into ye. City they soone were informed of what I had done, and used me accordingly. My wife they tooke to ye. Main Guard, and put her in amongst the rude Highlanders, and left three small children; my goods they used at pleasure, and my bank of coals I had laid in, and design'd them all for the Castle, never doubting, nor in the least thinking, of giving them ye. City and Castle so shamefully as was done; after they got possession of my coals they used them all the while in ye. Castle and all ye. Guards during ye. time Rebells were in England till there return, and about two days before ye. Duke of Cumberland obliged them to surrender ye. City again they had laid up all the remaining part of my coals in ye. Castle, thinking to have used them if they could have held it longer very proveblеy, but thanks to Almighty God they were defeated, and my coals hapened to do a great service to our own arme when the City was keept shut up for many days least any of the Rebells escaped. Upon this I applyed to ye. Governor for this last quantity yt. was found in ye. Castle, General Howard who is Governor said if I could bring in a bill well proved of what quantity they got last he 'ould take it with him to London and get me money if it laid in his power, and accordingly he has my bill and is coming up to London. Pray, sir, be so kind as to assist him in what you can, and it will do me a great favour now under my great trouble and loss. Sir, were it not for breveity sake I could surprise you with how many dangers I went throw since I soo you for ye. cause of my king and countrey, and of which, if his Majesty were informed, I should not fear being well provided for.

"Sir, your reall friend and

"Servant to command,

"WILLIAM HODGSON.

"Carlisle, Fisher Street, Feb. 22nd, 1745-6."

"Sir, the bill Generall Howard has with him contains 120 cart-load, at 9 pecks a load, and 4½d. a peck, comes to £20 5s. 8d.: if he happens to mislay, you'l be so kind as to mind him with this, which is a true bill, and I believe he'l remember it, and, without his and your help, I can do but little for myself."

"*Dr. Waugh to Wm. Hodgson.*

"Master Hodgson,—

"Your letter of the 22d of Feb. came not to me till yesterday. As soon as Genl. Howard gets to town, I shall speak to him as you desire; you may be assured I shall represent your zeal and service as I ought, and do you all the good offices in my power. If you have any bills before for butter, &c., (which I apprehended you sent into the Castle,) send them to me to get delivered with the charges of the stores before the 1st seige, if you have not already sent them to Capt. Gilpin or Col. Durand. If I can serve you, it will give me great pleasure. Your zeal deserves assistance from all honest men; you therefore need make no appologie for writing to me.

"I am your friend and servant,

"J. W."

"March 1st, 1745-46.

"To Mr. William Hodgson,
in Fisher Street, Carlisle."

"*General Howard to Dr. Waugh.*

"Dr. Sir,—

"I believe you will not be much displeased when I tell you yesterday morning before I left Carlisle, upon being assured Aldermen Graham and Coulthard were with the Mayor at Brampton to offer the keys to the Pretender, before he entered Carlisle, that I sent for them, charged them home with it, and confined them; they did not deny their going, but said they were ignorant of the errand. I think they are fitt company for the Mayor at London, and have writt the Duke of Newcastle word so this post; and, if I judge right, they are all in a scrape they will find difficulty to get out of. This I heard by chance after living above eight weeks in Carlisle, and I verily believe near two hundred knew it. I wanted much to find out those who gave the Rebels notice every day what was doing in ye. town, and brought them back after they had left it, but in vain—great loyalty, I must confess; but I will be discreet and say no more till I meet you, and then I have a good deal to tell you, for I never knew Carlisle so much as now; and am,

"Dr. Sir, faithfully yours,

"CHAS. HOWARD.

"I propose resting myself and horses for two or three days at Castle Howard, and hope to see you in a fortnight.

"Brough, Feb. ye. 22nd."

"Mr. Wardale to Dr. Waugh.

"Carlisle, March 1, 1745.

"Revd. Sir,—

"I received your kind letter this morning, just as I was sitting down to write to you. Davison has by some means heard that an affidavit is sent up, that he went to the Mayor or G. P. and swore if they would not come into the capitulation, he &c. would go out without their consent and leave them out; he says ye. affidavit is made by T. P., and declares it absolutely false; he sent a message to me to beg that I would desire of you to represent it in a proper light to Genl. Howard, when he gets to London; who, he says, was so kind as to offer to take any memorandums with him that he could think of in his own defence.

"You have heard, I suppose, yt. Dick Coulthard and J. Graham, aldermen, were taken up just before the Genl. left us, 'tis said for carrying the keys out to Brampton to deliver to ye. Pretender. The Genl. would needs suspect me guilty of some misprision; and was sure, as I had been in town, I must have heard of it; tho' I declare I had not till just that time, and I believe no man in

England would sooner make a holyday of the best day in the year for Dick Coulthard than I.

"There is at present no body in your house but How, the Genl.'s servant, who was left in the gout. Genl. Fleming is at Dr. Hutchinson's, and I fancy, thinks not of moving. I am in some hopes they will not send any body now, but yet I am afraid; if they should do it, I will endeavour to get some officer of repute.

"Cow Willy came to me on Sunday night, to direct a letter for him to you; there is a deal of stuff in it, but I believe all he wants of you is to put Genl. Howard in mind of a bill for some coals he delivered in to him, which, considering the honest man's loyalty and zeal for the service, and the pains he took, and spirit he show'd, I believe you will readily do.

"Poor old Gulicar has been with us about a week at Carlisle; he says he came to see if he could make any thing of his soapers; but I believe to borrow a little money among his acquaintance; he asked me to lend him a guinea, which I very readily did, as I thought it a charity, that I should have been ashamed to deny him, considering the situation both he and I were in.

"Geo. Railton has promised me to repair the roof, &c., of your house at Stanwix next week, and I shall send Gardener and Brigadr. (who is come from Caldbeck hither for want of hay there) on Monday, for lime.

"I am sensible there will be things missing wch. I cannot discover, but am willing to hope they will not be things of very great value.

"We are going next week to Penrith and Appleby to hold Courts of Probates, which I must own I think there was no absolute necessity for, but I submitted to the Register; and now I find he's going to leave us to go by ourselves, but indeed he's excusable, especially if the weather is not very good.

"We have, I think, no news from the North that can be depended upon; we are told by one Kilpatrick from Dumfries, that 1800 French are landed in Scotland, but since ye. Genl. and Lord Hallifax went away I think we have no exact correspondence from Scotland, so that I hope it is not true; and if it be, I hope there can now be no great danger from them, I beg my compliments to Mr. Willm. Tullie, and am, Rev. Sir,

"Your most dutiful and

"Obliged humble servt.,

"R. WARDALE."

"Mr. Nicolson to Dr. Waugh.

"Reverend Sir,—

"As my last may make you expect to hear from me by this day's post, I think it my duty to write, tho' I've nothing now to say, but fancy all will soon be well again; at least I see no kind of reason to suppose ought else. If it shou'd be otherwise or any alteration happen, you may be sure of the earliest intelligence in my pwer; I am favoured with yours of the 24th ult., and shall write both to you and Mrs. Eliz. Tullie by the next Post,

"And am your most ob. hble. servt.,

"JOS. NICOLSON.

"Carlisle, 1st March, 1745.

"P.S.—Doctor Hales, of Teddington, some time agoe, paid in fifty guineas to be given amongst the poor sufferers here, which I got done this week, and have by this day's post sent up an acknowledgmt. thereof to Mr. Reay, to be incerted in the newspapers. The Doctor is not to be named.

"I shou'd be extremely glad to have instructions for Joe Falder now, but not at the expence of any extraordinary trouble: his friends will be very clamorous, but he may stay till the next season well enough, when I hope he'll not be disappointed.

"Mr. Backhouse to Dr. Waugh.

"Uldale, March 2, 1745-6.

"Revd. Sir,—

"Your letter to Mr. Simpson, dated the 24th of the last month, was sent to me this day, and gave me the greatest pleasure. I cannot omit the first opportunity of returning you my most hearty thanks for the many favours our family have received from you, and in particular for the last favour to my brother, which I am sure he will always most gratefully acknowledge; and shall never be forgot, if ever in my power to serve you or yours, by

"Revd. Sir,—

"Your most obliged, humble servant,

"EDW. BACKHOUSE."

"*Mr. Nicolson to Dr. Waugh.*

"Hond. Sir,—

"On Thursday last I had a letter from Mrs. Eliz. Tullie, and showed it to the gentleman concerned, who read and returned it without saying one word; but before we parted I tooke the liberty to ask if he would answer it, or what I should say, for I was very ready to serve the family in anything in my power; and if I could any how prevent a misunderstanding, much more an open breach, amongst them, it would give me great pleasure.

* * * * *

"I cannot tell what to say in the other affair; a foot is still laid up and swelling and great redness talked of, but shoes are buckled, and at times very little lameness showed; I have never seen him eat since (it is industriously avoided) which makes me think stomach is bad; but every other simptom promises length of days, as far as I am able to judge. As to the prisoners at Carlisle you have named them all, I think, except James Hewitt, of Rockliffe, (Francy's brother,) and Alderman Dick Coulthard, and his Bro. Graham, who were committed to jail just before the General left us. The General will acquaint you with the crimes laid to their respective charges much better than any of us can; I suppose there is nothing particular against any of them, but the cash found in Francy's house. I need not desire you to do them any service that lays in your way, since I dare say its what you wish to have in your power; but I should be particularly thankful for any favour showed to Davison, being well assured there is not a more loyal subject in the King's dominions; tho' at the same time time I am very sensible that few people's indiscretions have been greater.

"I am extremely glad that you have had a more satisfactory account of Mr. B. than I was able to give; and the more so as it came from so good a hand where friendship to you and general behaviour is I think not to be paralleled at Carlisle; tho' some people will tell you that he was also too great with Sir John, which I only mention to shew the difficulty of the times. Your conviction is fixed for the twentieth instant at Dalston with Mr. Brisco, &c., as usual. The poor old Brigadier is now at Carlisle, John Gardner saies they want him to lead lime to Stanwix. I told Mr. Wardale I would give him a while run out here if they would send him, for its pity the poor old creature should be knocked o' the head. I have this moment received Mr. Petrie's packet, but very little news; its said Lord London has left Inverness, and gone into Cromarty with the forces under his command, that the Rebels have taken possession of the former; that the van of the Duke's army left Montrose on Saturday was sennight, and that the Duke himself was there on Tuesday; that the ship which escaped Com. Knowles landed about

100 men at Aberdeen on Sunday, but upon finding part of the Duke's army coming up reshiped them; that it's believed in Edinr. that all the Hessians and most of the other troops now there are soon to march north. They are quite out of wafers at the office so I sent them some yesterday, and inclose you a pattern for a new supply there. I hope General Howard will yet prove the greatest benefactor that ever Carlisle saw, notwithstanding all the cavils that are still made against him, and am

"Yours, most obediently,

"JOS. NICOLSON.

"3 Mar., 1746."

"*Mr. Goldie to Dr. Waugh.*

"Revd. Sir,—

"I hope you have before this got the better of your cold, which I can hardly be sorry for as it was the cause of my being favoured with so agreeable a letter as your last. I was quite surprised with the accounts of the submission of your mayor and two aldermen at Brampton: I believe them to be fools; but cannot help thinking a certain person, whom I take to be a deceitful knave, has advised and sent them on this errand, and hope some of his tricks will be discovered. Your interposing in favour of the mayor is a strong instance of your good nature and humanity, and extremely becoming of your profession. That he was so unworthy of your care, blest be God, you did not know, and your behaviour thus must produce esteem. As for F. Hewitt, I entirely approve of your reasons for being cautious in applying for him or any other; and I the rather urge this that his son, when he came here to get certificates, and was desired by me to tell what was or could be laid to his father's charge, thought fit to conceal altogether his having the custody of Hamilton's money; tho' I think little can be said of this, all things considered, yet it creates jealousy that will determine one to act warily; and, besides, I know none of your townspeople but who, in my judgment, are somewhat wrong-headed and shallower understandings than you can meet with any where; but at the same time very self-sufficient and opinionative, as all such people are. I shall always retain the utmost regard for Coll. Durand, till better reasons be given for altering my opinion of his sense and honour than any I have yet heard. I often pitied him when I was in Carlisle, and never had any faith in your Militia, and have upon all occasion vindicated him and said what I still believe to be true, that but for you and him they would have dispersed before any enemy came near. I hope when his case comes to be considered, he will be acquitted with honour; and I think this must be the case when it is cooly thought on. I dare say you will not leave him, if you can possibly avoid it. I am extremely glad I have been able to give any satisfaction to Genl. Howard, but our intelligence since his departure is altogether failed. We are greatly surprised to hear that the Hessians are to leave us without doing any thing, and when foreign troops are stealing in to the assistance of the Rebels, and they still in a body, and perhaps more numerous than ever. The fate of war is extremely uncertain, and in the present I would have as little left to chance as possible. The Hessians may be much wanted in Flanders, and from the excellent pamphlet you have sent me, I am convinced we ought to mind the affairs on the Continent. Yet I think it is common sense to extinguish the fire at home before we run to the assistance of our neighbours. The danger is now removed to a great distance from the capital. I wish this may not make our great folks think it less than it really is. The disaffected begin to recover spirits; and we to have fears—the circumstance as to the Hessians will give them more; and who knows, if they were gone, but the Rebels may give the Duke the slip and overrun the country once more, with greater fury than ever. I expect to hear something certain to-morrow, which I shall communicate to you per next. My wife offers you her compliments and hearty thanks for your kind offer of doing anything for her; but truly this is not a time for giving commissions. I am, with great regard,

"Dear Sir,

"Your most obedient humble Servant,

"J. GOLDIE.

"Dumfries, 7 March, 1746."

"W. Hodgson to Dr. Waugh.

"Hond. Sir,—

Your's I recd. of 1st March, wherein I am confirm'd of the good opinione I always had of you when with us in Carlisle. Sir, be pleased to except of my most harty thanks for your kind letter, and desires nothing more than yt. I may be servesable to you upon any ocation. At the first surrender, I was with Genl. Wade at Newcastle; between the flags carring out and the Ribles coming in there was some space of time, in which my wife imployed all the hands she cd. get. I had then above £1000 worth of goods in the Castle. I say my wife employed all the hands she could get to bring away the goods I had laid up in the Castle to my house, but the Ribles soon seized of what was for their purposes there—there is a bill in Capton Gilpin's hands of coals, and some small things besides, yt. was used before the Ribles came, I thinke about £8 odd money, which I hope you'll remind him of if it happen you see him. Sir, I ould gladly avoid prolexity and ould as gladly let you know how I spent ye. time after I went out of ye. Saleport of the Castle of Carlisle. I nead not aquaint you how I behaved while you were with us. It was on a Saturday ye. Ribles block'd us up. I had the second gun upon ye. tenn gun battre aloted me to my care which I fired upon them with great plesure, and many times I offred to have a gibet erected and hang the first man that spake of a surrender of the Castle to the Ribles, but indeed I ever suspected the town for tow reasons, first, the week before the Ribles came some of the companys of our train bands laid down there arms for want of pay, and there Captons never show'd the reasons. I went into the mids of them and gave them money and promised them full pay out of my property if they ould stand by their arms, and further, if any one laid down his arms, I ould take it up myself by w'ch I keept them together and their own Capton never came in sight all the while. Another reason was upon Tuesday after the Ribles came about the town, I was ordred out at ye. Saleport to try what I c'd learn, and at Stanwix I met with a Highland officer, with home I engaged, and took him prisoner, and brot. him my single self in at the Saleport in sight of some hundreds of people, which gain'd me great reputation, but what followed, ye. Mayor and Aldermen indeed comited the fellow to preason, but they w'd have nothing to do with keeping of his books and papers, which contain'd the Pretender's comishion to rais men in severell countys, besides a great many letters to persons in divers places in both kingdoms, all w'ch our good Mayor and Aldermen obliged me keep, and when ye. town was given to the Ribles they were so kind to me as send there Town Sergent along w'th the Ribles, and took to sarch my house and got all his books againe, and by this peace of art they saved themselves and ruiued me. Emedeitly my wife was sent to the Main Guard, our house plunder'd, my 3 young children left to shift for themselves: this was all ye. reward I got from the Corperation of Carlisl for my indevery to save the city, which was more than all there's put together.

"I told you how I took this oficer on Teusday, and on Wedensday I dress'd myself in raged clothes, and got a cole dog and shipherd's staf, and went throw all my L'd Carlile' ground, where the Ribles were shouting sheep and plundring the poore tenents, by which I learnt they maid no difeculty in taking Carlisle. When I found this I resolved to prevent them if posable, and accord'g I set forward from Warick Brigg, where there cheef standert was fixt, about three o'clock afternoone and travled all night on foot, and early next morn'g I arived at Hexam, with torn hands and leggs, with going thorow heges and privie ways. Had it not been for my good erant, I shoud a been ashamed of my self. At Hexam I applyd to Sir Ed. Blacket, woh I found to be a vere worthy man, and Sir Wm. Middelton, member of Parlement for Northumberland, being there mounted and upon one of his best horses, and went along with me himself, express to Genarel Wade, and was exemened as to hight of our walls, our provisions and stores in the Castle, and victuals, which you know I could vere well acct. for, being mostly mine, which I p'd ready money for. After wch. he was so well pleased yt. he ordred me a hansom reward, wth. an invitation to loge at his house, wch. I did, and came along wth. him to Hexam, where we heard the sorroful news of the loss of Carlile and Castle, wch. maid me turn quite carles of my life, and maid venter upon many disperate attempts afterwards, tow tedious to mention hear. However, when the Duke of Cumberland arived my corage came againe, and I had the honour to be with him sevl. times dureing the seige, and had the honour to billet in ye. country the best officers he had, by wch. I learnt Geo. Railton, storekeeper, was discharged from the Castle of Carlisle, and I presume ye. place is becom vacent. It's now managed by some officers for the time.

"Sir, if you think I can prevail, I wod aply for this place, and wod undertak to suply the Castle with all sorts of vittles suteable for the arme, at my own charge, dureing the time ye. ware may last, wch. I presume every storekeeper wod do, and wod save the Government many thousands of pounds.

"Sir, I know vere well I've roundley trespased upon your patience, but at ye. same time knows I am writing to a real friend, that I beleve will forgive me this time. Sir, I've not discowrsed my desire to aply for this place to any man besids yourself, neither will I witht. your aprobation.

"Sir, your real friend and humble Servt. to command,

"Whilest WILLIAM HODGSON."

"Carlisle, March 10th, 1746."

"*Mr. Wardale to Dr. Waugh.*

"Carlisle, March 17, 1746.

"Revd. Sir,—

"I give you this trouble at present chiefly on Mr. Birket's account, having nothing very material to write myself, who desires you would be so kind as pay the tenths of his livings along with your own, and he will account for it at your return. I suppose the Register has given you an account of our Courts of Probates; wch. as people have not dyed, &c., according to his expectation, he thinks, I fancy, might have been let alone. Mastr. Waugh I found had been very much out of health and a good deal reduced, but when I saw him he was finely recovered, his head almost quite heal'd and his stomach and health quite restored; so that I hope it will be of service to his constitution.

"I saw Dr. Cristopherson in my return, who say he's out of all danger.

"I have got the roof, doors, &c. of your house at Stanwix repair'd; wch. will be but a trifle, I fancy the glazing of the windows will be the most: wch. I hope will be finished in two days.

"I have taken up my quarters again at your house, and we have yet none billetted upon us; I hope we may not, but at worst I think I shall scarce part with my lodgings without your directions. I at present eat at your house, wch. I was a little at a loss about, to know whether would be the best way; but as the girls must eat something, I fancy'd the difference could not be very material, whether I eat here or boarded, if frugally managed; tho' I must own I am a very bad judge in those cases: but the scheme is easily altered if either you think proper, or I should find it any great difference.

"Our officers are, to say the best of them, in general but an odd set of mortals; and the puppies among them wch. are not a few, have got into their heads that the people of Carlisle are all disaffected, and therefore cannot be too ill used. As I have little concern with them I have met with no affront, wch. I must own would be bad to bide on that subject; but I am afraid some of them will get their bones broke if they go on, tho' their discretion with regard to fighting gives me great comfort, wch. I plainly perceive they have no violent inclination to, in any shape; some of them having been sufficiently bullied by our cowardly townsmen, as we are called already. This I am satisfy'd of, that neither the townspeople, nor even the soldiers, will think they have gained any thing by the loss of Genl. Howard, as things are now carried.

"The Register has been a good deal out of health for a few days, in a great cold, and that sad distemper, the old woman; but I hope in no danger. The Dr., Mr. Nicolson tells me, is very ill, and he's affraid in a bad way, but I have not seen him; we have a great number of people die abt. Carlisle, tho' I hear of no epidemic distemper except the small-pox wch. has carried off a great number of Ld. Hallifax's men,* and several children in town, tho' I cannot find in general that they are of a very bad kind yet. Your old friend John Lowrey was buried last week, who will be found to be a great loss in several respects to the parish. I have given you the trouble of a long letter about very little, and therefore think it high time to subscribe myself,

Revd. Sir,

"Your most dutiful and obliged

"Humble servant,

"R. WARDALE."

"Mr. Nicolson to Dr. Waugh.

"Reverend Sir,—

"Yesterday I received the favour of yours, together with the order about the horned cattle, which I hope we shall never have occasion for in this country, nor consequently to enquire out the simptoms attending that frightful distemper, which have not I think ever yet been published in any of the newspapers. I read the letter to the Bishop, who seemed pleased with it, and ordered me to return his compliments to you, as I do my most humble thanks for both it and the enclosed. * * * *

"George Blamire desires you'll give the enclosed to General Howard, and promote his interest therein all you can. We have made duplicates of the estimate, and given the other to the engineer here, who expects to leave this place very soon, and will take it up with him to the Board. I wish the form may do, for I could get no directions from any body. I was also forced to do it in a very great hurry, as indeed all my business is, and must, I think, be always done. I spoke to the General to get Ben. Railton employed (as a carpenter) in the Castle, which he was pleased to give directions about immediately; but they would only allow him common journeyman's wages, which he would not accept, being, I am sure, as good a workman, and an honester man than the chief carpenter employed; and if it be in the General's power, and without much trouble, I wish he might be the man.

---

* "The mortality amongst the King's troops was very great; between the 20th January and 15th June, 1745-6, there was no less than 111 buried at St. Cuthbert's and St. Mary's Churches."

"Doctor Hutchinson recovers bravely, which Mr. Salkeld has the honour of. I wish I could say as much of the honest Register, who is, indeed, much indisposed, tho' I hope in no danger. We have not disposed of any your hay, for we cou'd never get above 3½d. per stone, and that only for small quantities; and as here is an appearance of a very growing spring, I suppose the price will now fall every day. We are pretty hearty here; but looks grow worse, tho' the coach is out every day; and I cannot help fancying a month or two may possibly make some alteration. What you said in your former letter, of having lost a friend, still gives me great uneasiness, for I own all hopes of any recompence for some body's great trouble and unlimited expence is intirely gone from me: God send that I may be greatly mistaken.

"Please to forward the inclosed to Mrs. Tullie, for

"Your most obedient and most faithful, hble. servt.,

"JOS. NICOLSON.

"Hawksdale, March 24th, 1746."

"*Mr. Wardale to Dr. Waugh.*

"Carlisle, March 27, 1746.

"Revd. Sir,—

"I doubt not but you'll have several accounts by this post of Dr. Hutchinson's death; which was a kind of surprise upon us at last. I told you in my last of his being ill, wch. then appeared to be intirely pleuritic; and about Thursday the symptoms seem'd to be got the better of; and he himself as well as others thought he was in a fine way of recovery, wch. continued till Sunday night or Monday morning, and then there suddenly appear'd some bad symptoms of the nervous kind (as the Doctors tell me), with a stupor and sleepiness; wch. bad symptoms continually increased till last night about nine o'clock, when the poor Doctr. died. It has given Mr. Tullie and all of us here very low spirits, and I doubt not but this account will give you a very sensible concern; I pity poor Peggy and Molly extreamly who are in great distress; and I am told the Doctr. has left no will, but that I am not sure of. Affairs at Carlisle are, I think, pretty much in the same situation as when I wrote last; we are told that Col. Stanwix is to come shortly to Carlisle, to see what advantage he can make of other people's mismanagement; and I know he has given it out that he will be here as soon as he can; but I cannot believe that he will be in any hurry abt. spending money so long beforehand. I find the cry is to be that tho' Genl. Howard never designs to stand for Carlisle again, yet he might have done something for the town in consideration of former favours. Dr. Christopherson tells me Mastr. Waugh is perfectly well. I beg my humble service to Mr. W. Tullie when you see him,

"And am, Revd. Sir,

"Your most dutiful and

"Obliged humble servant,

"R. WARDALE."

"*Mr. Wardale to Mrs. Waugh.*

"Carlisle, March 27th, 1746,

"Madam,—

"I have just now writ to Mr. Chancellor upon the same subject I am now writing to you, which, I am afraid, will occasion some surprise, as I fancy you have heard nothing of it before. Dr. Hutchinson, about ten days ago, was seized with a pleuritic fever, but upon proper methods being taken it seem'd to go off, and he was thought to be in a good way of recovery till Monday last, when some very bad symptoms shew'd themselves, and still increased till last night about nine o'clock, when the poor Doctr. died. It has given Mr. Tullie very low spirits, and all his acquaintance uneasiness, and I know it will give you a sensible concern; but the loss of acquaintance is a tribute we are all obliged to pay for living. I pity poor Peggy and Molly extreamly who are in great distress, both from the suddenness of the misfortune, and perhaps from the consequences of it w'th regard to them. I am told the Dr. has left no will, w'ch, if true, will be still harder upon them; but I have dwelt too long upon so melancholy a subject.

"I am glad to hear the Genl. retains his complaisance for the ladies at least, and was in good humour at York; but, indeed, if he had not, his best friends must have given him up, and there could have been no excuse left for him. I wish he had had a little of it at Carlisle, but indeed he was so excessive cross at his first coming to Carlisle, that it gave a great handle to his enemies, and scarce left room to his friends to excuse him a little. He grew a little better before he left us, and his successor has not done one kind thing to make his behaviour odious.

"We have had no body in your house since he left us, and I hope we shall keep clear, but cannot promise.

"The parchment you speak of is safe with me in the study, which I have not looked into and shall deliver to Mrs. Nicolson, whom you desired to take care of it the first opportunity.

"You gave me great pleasure in hearing your sentiments of the jumble at Court, as I was a good deal concern'd about it, but did not care to mention it in any letter to London.

"R. W."

"Mr. Wardale to Dr. Waugh.

"Revd. Sir,—

"I waited upon Brigr. Fleming on Saturday last according to your directions, who desired me to return his compliments to you and a thousand thanks for your kind offer, and to let you know that he will accept of the favour as soon as he can be removed; for at present he has got the gout pretty violently, only in his ankles, his wrist, one of his knees, his hip, and his groin; I never mentioned it before, because, I believed, he would accept of the offer, and I was in hopes to get the house kept clear, and the best of them cause some expense to the house where they are; but this is only my own private excuse for not mentioning it sooner to him; when he comes I shall let you know how we are like to go on.

"All your things are in town except your papers, in the iron chest, which is at Caldbeck. I am in hopes we shall not be plagued with those vermin, the Rebels, any more; but if that should happen I doubt not but I shall have time to send your plate, the best of your linen, &c., over to Mr. Nicolson, who will convey them further as he finds occasion. This is what I resolved till I have further directions from you; if you think of any better method I hope you'll have time enough to send me your orders. We have a talk in town of an action between the Blair of Athol and Sterling, a pass guarded by Sir A. Agnew, which they designed to surprise; but the Prince of Hesse coming in time to support Sir Andrew, they cut off and took about 1000 of the Rebels; a sergeant from Edinburgh, says he saw about 300 of the prisoners into Edinr. on Thursday; but if there is any truth in it, I doubt not but you'll have a better account of it before this comes to hand. If you are with Mr. Graham, I beg my compliments to him, and am,

"Revd. Sir,

"Your obedient, dutiful Servant,

"ROBT. WARDALE.

"Carlisle, March 31st, 1746."

"*Prebendary Wilson to Dr. Waugh.*

"Carlisle, April 3rd, 1746.

"Revd. Sir,—

"Church work at Carlisle, you know, goes slowly forward. It is but a few days since I got an estimate from workmen of the expence we must be at to put the church in the repair it was before it was made a prison. If it fall wholly upon us, we need not, I think, be much dismayed, as thirty pounds will defray all. One application, out of the number that was made to General Howard, might easily slip his memory; for certain it is that Mr. Birket apply'd to him upon our account. The behaviour of the military gentlemen to the inhabitants in and about this place has been so disrespectful and arbitrary, that I wish I had follow'd your example and fixt my family in some other county, so long as the civil power is trampled under foot, Carlisle will be no comfortable situation to me; never had it greater need of magistrates that would act with spirit and resolution. I am not oppress'd myself, but I can't be unconcern'd to see that others are that as little deserve to be. The people in general we know are honest here, and at least wish well to our happy Government. The small-pox and a fever have swept off great numbers of the soldiers; both these distempers are at present abated.

"I am, Revd. Sir,'

"With all due respect,

"Your most obedient humble servant,

"THO. WILSON.

"My wife, who is in better health than when you last saw her, desires her humble service."

"*Mr. Wardale to Dr. Waugh.*

"Carlisle, April 17, 1746.

"Revd. Sir,—

"On Tuesday Brigr. Fleming came to your house, a most terrible martyr to the gout and stone; he tells me he has not slept this forty nights. His man says he'll buy coals for his master's use; and as neither of them designs, I fancy, either to eat or drink, they'll not wear your kitchen utensils much, nor give any great trouble I think to the house. W. Gray has dressed your gardens, and I. Gardner your hedges and closes. I wish it was convenient and safe for you to be at home and see things done yourself as they should be; but I do not see that we are like to be so happy very soon. Mrs. Walker, of Kirkbride, desired me to tender her compliments to you and to put you in mind of her affair now while you are at London. I think we have nothing new here worth your hearing; we are pretty much in the same situation.

"Mr. Tullie tells me there came an order for 400 men to go directly into the Castle; but the Governor remonstrated for want of utensels—pots, kettles, plates, trenchers, &c.,—so that, as I fancy, they think the soldiers are better in town; I cannot tell when the town will be eased. I believe both the town and country are sensible of the misfortune of your being absent in these troublesome times. But Mr. Tullie has taken more pains, and exerted himself more vigorously for the good of the town than one would have almost expected from his indolent temper; but he wants not good sense, nor resolution neither, on a proper occasion; but this is telling you no news.

"I am, Revd. Sir,

"Your most dutiful and obliged humble servt.,

"ROBT. WARDALE."

CHARLES EDWARD was now approaching the termination of his career. Ever after the retreat from Derby his fortunes ebbed, as the retiring tide after it has reached its limits,—

"There is a tide in the affairs of men,
"Which, taken at the flood, leads on to fortune;
"Omitted, all the voyage of their life
"Is bound in shallows and in miseries."

The history of his enterprize is a commentary on the text of the immortal bard. There was a tide so strongly in his favour as to excite the astonishment of all observers. He missed it; and achieved not fortune, but irretrievable ruin.

At Falkirk, it is true, a transient success enlivened the deepening gloom of his prospects. There General HAWLEY, whom the Duke of CUMBERLAND had left in command of the army to pursue the Highlanders into Scotland, being possessed by an inordinate contempt of them, suffered his troops to be surprised, and yielded another laurel to the intrepid clansmen. But it was a barren victory, for want of skill to improve it. The Highlanders kept the field, many of them in ignorance that a victory was gained; whilst a vigorous and combined advance might have enabled them to convert HAWLEY'S retreat into a total rout. The opportunity was lost: one chieftain threw the blame on another; all perceiving, when it was too late, that an immense advantage had escaped them.

The Duke of CUMBERLAND was immediately directed to resume the command. He set out from London on the 25th January, 1745-6; arrived at Edinburgh early on the 30th; the same day he carefully inspected the troops; and gave orders for the march next morning.

A battle was now generally looked for. The Highlanders engaged in the siege of Stirling Castle, were not expected to raise it without risking an action. But on the 29th the Chiefs had presented to the Prince a paper advising retreat to the North. Dependent altogether on them, he had expressed his bitter disappointment, and having no alternative had acquiesced. Accordingly, on the 1st of February, instead of awaiting the Duke's approach, they hastily raised the siege of Stirling Castle, spiking and leaving behind them their heavy cannon; blew up their magazine in St. Ninian's Church; and retreated across the Forth by the fords of Frew. Then dividing into two bodies, they continued their retreat towards Inverness by different routes.

A detail of the campaign is not here intended, but simply to notice the final catastrophe. The Prince's forces engaged in a series of desultory and detached operations, their point of concentration being fixed at Inverness. The King's army continued its advance cautiously. At that early season of the year the condition of the roads and rivers precluded a rapid pursuit; and the ill success of COPE's march into the Highlands in the preceding autumn was fresh in men's recollection. The Duke of CUMBERLAND, moreover, had to restore the *morale* of his army, impaired by the incapacity of successive commanders. Plundering and insubordination, the usual consequences, which had proceeded to considerable extent, he repressed by severe examples of punishment. With improved discipline, the confidence of the troops revived. The Duke himself, far from despising the seemingly scattered forces of the Prince, adopted every precaution against their sudden concentration and irruption; aware that sooner or later the tactics of regular warfare must inevitably prevail over the impetuous but simple mode of assault of the Highlanders.

In the month of April the Duke's army marched from Aberdeen towards the river Spey. This river, deep and rapid, is fordable at a place where its northern bank rises into high and commanding ground, on which a comparatively small force might successfully contest the passage of an army. On the 12th of April, the grenadiers forming the advanced guard, with two pieces of cannon, approached the ford; on the northern bank were posted Lord JOHN DRUMMOND and the Duke of PERTH with a strong body of the best clans, by whom without doubt the passage might have been successfully opposed; yet they retreated on sight of the Duke's advance guard, without firing a shot; and the army, instead of having to force its way amid the thunder of hostile artillery, gaily breasted the stream to the music of their regimental bands, playing in derision of the once dreaded Highlanders the tune of

"Will ye play me fair play,
"Bonnie Laddie, Highland Laddie?"

The Prince's troops being not as yet fully re-assembled at Inverness, the news of the Duke's passage of the Spey came on them like a thunder clap. That strong defensible line being abandoned, they now were liable any day to the attack of a superior force in the open field.

Their conduct betokened a sinking cause, and was viewed in that light. An officer of BLYTH's regiment in the Duke's army at the time thus decribes it:—

"*Quos Deus vult perdere prius dementat*, was never so much verified as it was on Wednesday last, when our troops, led on by our brave and well-beloved General, the Duke, gain'd a most compleat victory over the Rebels on Cullodon Muir, near to this place. All their steps, from the time we left Aberdeen to the very moment they were totally routed, showed plainly that that power that had hitherto permitted their success had now forsaken them. For instead of disputing with us the passage of the Spey, which is the most defensible post I ever saw, the river being the deepest and the banks on this side the most proper for planting cannon upon to oppose the passage, Lord John Drummond, with 2,500 of the best of the clans, forsook the banks on the approach of our Grenadiers with two pieces of cannon, who that day made the advanced guard, and lett us pass and encamp on this side without mollestation; whereas, had he disputed it, the passage, at a moderate calculation, must have cost us 2 or 3000 men,—if we had at all effected it. For this they gave for reason that it was to no purpose to oppose us there; that what they wanted was to have us farther up the country; that so they might cutt us all off without hopes of retreat or mercy. A modest way of talking you'll say, considering we were 15 battalions and 9 squadrons, besides 400 Campbells, who came with a design to fight them wherever we found them, relieve our oppressed country, and wype off the stains we had received on the two former defeats they had given us. However, in pursuance of this plan and great design of theirs, they suffered us also to pass the river of Findhorn, just beyond Forres, which, next to the Spey, is among the largest in this country, and then was excessively deep and rapid. In the mid-way between Forres and Nairn, they appeared again, but went off upon the approach of our Quarter-Master General and all the horse. They repeated the same again at Nairn, and the brave Duke himself pursued them a little way, and sent the horse and dragoons after them about three miles. When we encamped there, we were told they were to fight us next day, and their number was at least 9000. They left a message to be delivered to the Duke by Lord Lyon, viz., that his Royal Highness would take care of his person; and publicly said they would next day cutt us all in minced meat."

The 15th of April being the Duke's birth-day, he halted the army at Nairn. The Highlanders, drawn up in order of battle on Drummossie Muir in the morning, in expectation of an attack, finding that he made no movement, and imagining that his troops, celebrating their general's birth-day, would be off their guard, planned a night attack, by which it was thought his camp might be surprised and his army annihilated.

This was attempted, but proved entirely abortive. The Highlanders marched at night towards Nairn in two columns—one after the other—but the night was so dark, and the line of country they took to avoid notice so wet and heavy, that it was nearly day-break before they arrived within sight of the fires in the Duke's camp. It being then evident that before they could attack, the sun would be up, they retraced their weary steps to Culloden, wet, famished, and worn out with fatigue. Many lay down to sleep on the way, others dispersed in quest of food,—never was an army in such a state of general and individual exhaustion, when about eight o'clock in the morning of the 16th they were aroused by intelligence that the Duke with his whole force was in full march to attack them. Thus were they the party taken by surprise, and under every imaginable disadvantage.

In this extremity there was no exhibition of dismay. All within reach were speedily mustered, and drawn up in two lines on the muir near Culloden

House. The Duke's army approached them also in two lines, each consisting of six regiments, with two pieces of cannon in the intervals between those of the front line—the horse and dragoons on each flank and three regiments in reserve. The battle commenced by cannonading on both sides. The Prince's artillery did little execution—the Duke's, admirably worked by Major BALFOUR, soon galled the Highlanders into ungovernable fury. The MACKINTOSHES forming the centre of their front line were the first to attack, rushing forward sword in hand. The ATHOL brigade, with the regiments of LOCHIEL, APPIN, and FRAZER, forming the right, immediately followed the example. Their charge is related by eye witnesses to have been in the highest degree imposing. Their bonnets closely pulled over their brows; their targets on the left arm covering the body; their claymores leaping like a flash of lightning, as it were, from the scabbards, and then firmly grasped, with the point inclined towards the left knee; they came down upon the Duke's line amidst a storm of fire from the front, and from WOLFE's regiment in flank, with such intrepidity and impetuosity as nothing could withstand. Warned by the example of Preston Pans and Falkirk where the Highlanders received the point of the bayonet on their targets, and cut down the soldier before he could disengage it, the Duke had instructed his soldiers not to point the bayonet at the man in front, but to thrust at the breast of the man to his left, by which it was thought the assailants would be disconcerted, and the fiery edge of their attack in some degree turned. But it availed nothing. The claymores once more prevailed over the bayonets, and broke through the Duke's first line, consisting of BURRELL's and MUNRO's regiments. It was only by the dispositions of regular modern warfare that they were now to be overcome. Whilst the broken regiments were getting out of the way, and the

Highlanders were preparing to rush upon the second line, SEMPILL's and BLYTH's regiments had steadily moved forwards some sixty paces, and coolly awaited the torrent which had swept over their comrades in front; ranged three deep, the front rank kneeling, and the second inclining so as to allow the third to fire over them, they reserved their fire till the assailants were close upon them, and then delivered it with such precision that no human force could have withstood its destructive effect. The Clansmen are said to have fallen there three deep on the ground—the survivors in a moment found themselves no longer a compact body, but shattered remnants—none ever reached the Duke's second line.

The defeat of the centre and right decided the battle. The MACDONALDS, who stood on the left, offended on being placed there, had sullenly kept their ground when the others charged, and in silence witnessed the sacrifice of their chieftain KEPPOCH, who, reproachfully exclaiming—"*Good God, have the children of my clan forsaken me*," rushed on alone, and met his fate. The Duke's cavalry sweeping in upon the flanks completed the defeat; and the total route and massacre of the clans would then and there have ensued, but for the French and Irish troops, which stemmed for a time the tide of victory, and gained an opportunity for such as remained unbroken to effect a hasty retreat.

The blow was a decisive one: for tho' a considerable number of the clans afterwards rallied at Ruthven and desired to continue the contest, CHARLES EDWARD felt, and rightly felt, that it was hopeless,—that the time and opportunity had passed away,—that the crown which he had failed to win by his daring invasion of England was not to be won by means of a guerilla warfare in the fastnesses of the Highlands. They therefore dispersed, and he became a fugitive.

Then commenced those severities, military and legal, which sullied the name of the Duke of CUMBERLAND, and betrayed a most vindictive spirit in the rulers of that period. True it is that the soldiery, ashamed and exasperated by the affronting defeats they had suffered at the hands of the Highlanders at Preston Pans and Falkirk, might be forward to revenge themselves, and difficult to be restrained. But there is reason to believe that they were rather encouraged. The country of the insurgent clans was laid desolate—so much so that famine was anticipated in the next ensuing winter, from the total cessation of all culture.

The vengeance of the law was more deliberate. Of that Carlisle was destined to witness some fearful examples, but they were deferred till the autumn of the year. The French and Irish, who surrendered themselves prisoners of war after the battle of Culloden, were sent thither in the month of May,—and the town continued to hold a considerable garrison; very much to the dissatisfaction of the inhabitants, as it appears by the correspondence of honest Mr. WARDALE, Dr. WAUGH'S curate. The Doctor wisely remained at York. To have witnessed the contumelious treatment which his townsmen experienced must have involved him in great difficulty. He would have been appealed to by the sufferers, and forced either to abandon his friends and townsmen, or to place himself in remonstrance against the dominant powers.

"*Mr. Wardale to Dr. Waugh.*

"Carlisle, April 24th, 1746.

"Revd. Sir,—

"I have enclosed with this (as you will see) a letter from Mr. Blair, of Annan, which he sent by an express. I doubt not but you'll have a more particular account before this of the action, in wch. the Duke certainly deserves immortal honour. Brigr. Fleming, who desires his complemts. of thanks to you for his good lodgings, had last night an acct. of the action from one of the Duke's Aid-de-Camps, wch. agrees in all particulars with the letter sent to you, except one or two paragraphs.

"Wm. Hodgson came to me and said Captain Hutchinson told him Genl. Howard had sign'd his bills, and he would have his money very soon; he says he would be glad, if it would not give you trouble, that you would receive it for him, and acct. when you return to Carlisle; if you think it worth while to take that trouble, I suppose you must have an order from him, wch., if you please to signify to me, I will take care to have it sent you. This battle, I hope, has put an utter end to our unhappy troubles; and will make us happy in your return, much sooner than we could have expected, wch. I am satisfy'd will be a general satisfaction to everybody here. You can scarce imagine how universal a joy your safe return will give to both town and country. I am in so great a hurry of spirits upon hearing our cannon fire upon this joyful occasion that I am sure I shall write some nonsense or other, wch. I hope you'l excuse.

"By an acct. just now receiv'd, the Duke contributed to deceive the rebels, by saying, on the 14th, in the evening, amongst a number of officers, that to-morrow was his birthday, they would all be merry one day at least; but next day gave strict orders that no notice shd. be taken, but that all should be ready for a march at a moment's warning, wch. he made them believe would be that afternoon; his former night's conversation quickly ran thro' the army and was carried to the Rebels, wch, helped to lead them into their mistake, and give him an opportunity to attack them fatigued, when his men were fresh and in spirits.

"There is another circumstance wch., if true, contributes think to ye. Duke's honour—viz., that he himself was in the front, in a common soldier's dress, with a gun and bayonet; wch. both encouraged his own men; and prevented any malicious firing at him in particular from the enemy.

"These several particulars, if true, I doubt not but you'l have them from other hands; and therefore shall trouble you no further at present, but by subscribing myself,

"Revd. Sir,

"Your most dutiful and obliged humble servant,

"ROBT. WARDALE."

"*Mr. Nicolson to Dr. Waugh.*

"Hond. Sir,—

"Tho' you must hear of the glorious Duke's compleat victory over all the cursed Rebels long before this can reach you, yet I cannot help incloseing you the accounts I have had of that joyful day, and more especially as Mr. Goldie desires me to forward his, w'ch came this morning, to you. The other Mr. Petrie sent me on Tuesday night after I was in bed; but up I got and dispatched copies to Carlisle, Rose, &c., all before day. The messenger had the gates opened before two, and numbers of the town soon left their beds; and he received many blessings from the people in every street as he passed along, for the news he carried. I sent the express first to Captain Maitland, as I thought him General Howard's chief friend amongst the military there, and as I thought it was not proper to disturb the Brigadier. I am favoured with your's of the 18th inst., but have nothing new to say upon affairs at Carlisle, since my last, by Monday's post, would acquaint you with what I met with that day. We dispatch so many letters this day that I can add no more but that I am,

"Your most obedient and most faithful hble. servt.,

"JOS. NICOLSON.

"Netherby, Apr. 24th, 1746."

"*Mr. Nicolson to Dr. Waugh.*

"Hond. Sir,—

"Yesterday, the Bishop gave me your's of the 30th ult., and you may be assured I shall, with the utmost pleasure, send for Master Waugh, and take the greatest care of him here we possibly can. Mr. Wardale had a letter from him by Saturday's post, to desire horses this day, which shall be done accordingly. Indeed, Carlisle still continues, in my opinion, a very melancholy place; numbers still dying, and both the military and civil government carried on very oddly,—none of the soldiers yet gone into the Castle, and many poor people still grievously oppressed. I send you enclosed a letter I had yesterday from Mr. Jubb, and am,

"Your most faithful hble. servt.,

"JOS. NICOLSON.

"Hawksdale, May 5th, 1746.

"P.S.—Mr. Tullie has got the gout in both feet. We have recruited here a good deal these three or four last days, and now gets out constantly on horseback.

"Geordy Blamire is greatly indisposed, tho' I hope rather upon the mending hand."

"*Mr. Goldie to Dr. Waugh.*

"Dear Sir,—

"I have either been abroad or so hurried at our assizes that I could not write; but had it been otherwise I could not have given you any particulars with respect to the late glorious victory or the consequences of it. All I can say now, and indeed it is a great deal, is, that by all accounts the Rebels are quite dispersed, and I hope shall never in our days have it in their power to disturb the public peace any more. Their cash was exhausted before the battle; one strong instance of this is that the Marquis of Tulliebardine when taken had not one shilling about him. This want of money and the disappointment of the supply they expected by the *Hazard* sloop probably determined them to give battle, which proved their ruin. Now that the danger is happily over I cannot help observing to you two things; the first is, that the Nonjurant Episcopal Clergy have had a great hand in keeping up the spirit of Jacobitism, and consequently in raising the rebellion: this is so certain and evident, that there is not almost a family which frequented their meetings, but what has either openly or covertly assisted the Rebels; so that never any government met with such ungrateful returns for lenity and toleration. When I say this, I am far from wishing liberty of conscience abridged; no man loves it more when it is not attended with hazard to the state; but when that is the case, I dare say the wisdom of the nation will take care to restrain the influence of a sett of men who, with great industry, corrupt the minds of their hearers with principles pernicious to our civil and religious liberties. The other thing is, that from the time this cursed rebellion came to any head, I still feared they would have taken up and carried away with them every person of any weight or influence they knew to be their enemy, and sent them to France to be pledges for their security in case their attempt misgave. Blest be God this did not occur to them; I never mentioned it to any before; I am with

"Great affection, dear sir, yours,

"J. G.

"Dumfries, 6th May, 1746."

"Mr. Nicolson to Dr. Waugh.

"Hond. Sir,—

"I cannot omit acquainting you that Master Waugh got well here on Tuesday at noon, and that his looks and everything else about him are as good as you can wish. Mr. Thompson came to see him yesterday on the evening, and he's to go with me to Rose to-day. The Bishop asked me the other day if there were to be no courts this year; and upon my answering in the affirmative, ask'd further if you would be down, or who was to do it for you? I told him you did not seem quite resolved, but if you could not be there yourself I believe you had some thoughts of begging the favour of the Archdeacon, which ended our discourse upon that subject. But whether he may not expect to hear from you thereupon I cannot tell; nor how far a compliment of that kind *quatenus* Bishop may be proper; but further than that I see no reason.

"I hear about seven of the French officers got to Carlisle on Tuesday, and that about 300 common men are upon the road. The new customer, I am told, has been there, and went for Whitehaven yesterday.

"Mr. and Mrs. Tullie are for Yorkshire, it's said, very soon, for the whole summer; and I am,

"Hond. Sir,

"Your most obedient hble. servt.,

"JOS. NICOLSON.

"Hawksdale, May 8th, 1746.

"P.S.—No further accounts from Scotland, only they say at Carlisle that it is certain the Marquiss of Tullybardine is taken.

"My wife is gone to Edenhall this morning, where I design to call for her in my way from Renwick to-morrow."

Mr. Goldie to Dr. Waugh.

"Dear Sir,—

"I received yours by last post, for which I thank you; I had heard before with some concern the unlucky circumstance of breaking windows*; but this was alleviated from cer-

---

* This seems to refer to the breaking of the windows in Edinburgh, on the night of the Duke of Cumberland's arrival there, which took place to such an extent that glass could not be found in the city to repair them. The mob was Hanoverian on this occasion, and the sufferers Jacobites.

tain information I had, that the cause was in no way to be laid to the charge of the D—e, whom I have the greatest reason to believe to be so well affected to the Protestant succession, and to our laws, religion, and liberties, which can only be secure under it, that I know no one whatever who wd. more readily have drawn his sword in their defence. For he, I am told, knew nothing of it. If the mob was so cool as to send the message you mention, it was more than mobs use to do. The return I wish had been less philosophical, tho', after all, among the Romans there were no rejoicings for victorys obtained during civil wars, and good reasons are assigned for this conduct in that great and wise people; but mankind must conform not only to the customs, but many times to the humours, of those they live with. I wish with all my soul there had been an universal uniformity in the present case; there was great cause to rejoice and to be thankful for our deliverance; and since the populace inclined to have illuminations (for I don't find they were appointed by any authority,) every one ought to have concurred. However, if I be not misinformed, the windows of sevl. considerable persons among the English have been broke—so that it is not peculiar to the Scots. Upon the whole, I hope that distinctions will soon be abolished; and that as our interests are the same, all will concur to promote the general good of Great Britain. It is true this wicked rebellion begun here; but I scarcely think that could have happen'd, unless strong assurances of assistance had been given by the English. However, I think nothing can be more evident than that the generality of the Scots are well affected, if it be considered how few join'd the Rebels after their extraordinary success. Give me leave to say, if these events had happen'd in England, they wd. have had a greater accession of numbers. Here they were joined by none but persons of depraved principles, desperate fortunes, or born slaves. I pray God our present success may be so improven as may secure us from any future surprise; for still I cannot help considering all that past for the last six months of the rebellion as a dream, and I can scarcely think the narrative of it will be credited by posterity.

"We all believed Lord Elcho was in France; when he was here he was very far gone in the distemper I formerly mentioned; and we were told he was gone to be cured. It now appears we were misinformed. We hear that Lovat's lurking place is discovered, and that a strong party is sent to apprehend him and others with him, I am extremely glad to find that the Duke stays till the peace of the Highlands be absolutely settled; his presence is of great consequence. I am sorry you have had so much trouble about the list of those intended to be attainted, and the heads of the bills for that purpose; had I known it would have been so difficult, I had not desired it; but my curiosity prompted me to ask the favour, though I have not the least connection with or interest in any of the Rebels,—save one who is a Roman Catholic and was my most intimate comrade, and the honestest and most rational man of that religion I ever knew. Nothing but the desperate situation of his private affairs made him a party to so foolish and desperate an attempt; but though he has the name of an estate, I know, were all scores cleared, he would not have a reversion of above £500; and yet he is a valuable person in private life.

"You, who know the power of friendship, will easily forgive my saying thus much of one who has as much of it in his temper as any man I ever knew; whether he be kill'd or alive I have not certainly learned. The general assembly of our Church should have met last Thursday, but the commission has unluckily miscarried. It is believed to have gone forward to Inverness amongst other despatches for the Duke; no doubt it will soon cast up, and all the effect that can follow, will be a longer attendance for the clergy. I thank you for your prayer,—improving the victory in this dutiful manner is the most likely way of obtaining the favour and blessing of that great God who made and governs all things.

"I ever am, dear sir, yours,

"JO. GOLDIE.

"Dumfries, 11th May, 1746."

"Mr. Wardale to Dr. Waugh.

"Revd. Sir,—

"As many apologys as I have made in my lifetime for my neglect, I can think of none at present that's fit to offer you; for my having been out of town this fourthnight,—one week at Netherby, and the other at Knarsdale—I doubt will not pass, since I ought always to have found time to answer your's; but, indeed, I depended upon Mr. Simpson's writing about the hay, &c., w'ch I suppose he has done before now, and then, of course, he must have mentioned other particulars. I sent up to Caldbeck every thing you wrote for from the cellar, except brandy, of w'ch I could find none, tho' perhaps there may be some, for there are several parcels of bottles w'ch are not mark'd; I sent four doz. of port, and but small quantities of other particulars, because I know it will be no inconvenience to take anything of that kind up from Carlisle after you are settled at Caldbeck, w'ch was the reason I did but send two or three doz. bottles of ale, tho' without orders; for if there had been no other occasion for it I think I could have made a shift to have got over now and then to drink it out myself; I think there is between 12 and 13 doz. in the cellar, for, if I remember right, there was about 13 doz. in February when it was bottled, and I have made use of no more than five or six bottles since.

"We have changed our soldiers for new ones, I think pretty near the same number; but these are all billeted on public houses, who, poor creatures, I believe, have very few of them beds left sufficient for their own families. I am surprised that most of them do not run away and leave them their houses, tho' to do these soldiers justice, I am told that they behave with extream civility towards the townspeople. We have the two regmts. of Drags. from Edinburgh, who lay under a suspicion of behaving agt. ye. Rebels not much better than ourselves, and ten or eleven additional compys. of Foot from different Regmts.,—Genl. Howard's, &c.

"The two aldermen confined when Genl. Howard was here, viz., Coulthard and Graham, are admitted to bail, on Sr. James' application as they give it out, which occasions some little triumph, and makes others whisper that your friend, ye. Genl., either does not apply heartily, or has not much interest.

"The fitting up of the Castle for some of the soldiers goes on very slowly, and, I think, may perhaps be ready to take 400, when I hope there will be little occasion for them two months hence.

"I was just going to make an apology for taking upon me to trouble you with these things, but Brigr. Fleming, who desires his complemts. to you, came in and kept talking so long that he has but just left me time to pay my respects to Mrs. Waugh and all your family, and subscribe myself,

"Revd. Sir,

"Your most dutiful and obliged humble servt.,

"ROBT. WARDALE."

"*Mr. Wardale to Dr. Waugh.*

"Carlisle, May ye. 15, 1746.

"Revd. Sir,—

"I received yours, and am very sorry to find things go on so slowly, as you are so good as inform me they do; for I am persuaded the two things you mention would have been exceedingly popular; and not only so, but also very good in themselves. Poor Carlisle is much oppressed, and little pitied; and I think both very unjustly, having merited just the contrary usage; but this is impertinence to you, who know it so well. Everything is now growing exceeding dear with us, wheat above 20s. a bushel, and I am afraid not likely to mend soon.

"I saw Mastr. Waugh yesterday. He is to stay two or three days with his uncle next week; when I design to make some inquiry about his task. He looks extreamly well, and is in good health and spirits. Mr. Tullie had but a slight fit of the gout, tho' it was very painful for three or four days, and was in both feet; but did not confine him to his bed. It left a little soreness and weakness: but he is almost quite well now.

"Brigr. Fleming (who desires his complmts. to you) is still confined, tho' I think a good deal better. He gives as little trouble, and I believe is as careful of doing any damage in the house, as is possible. He seems to be a good-natured man; not at all enterprising; but loves to have things continue just as they were left to him: a little phlegmatick; but no wonder, after a six months' fit of the gout, and not recover'd yet.

"We have a good many French prisoners already come, but as they are in numbers together in the gaol, Scotch Gate, and some houses taken on purpose, they do not incommode the town so very much. The officers (about nine already come) are at liberty to walk about the town with yr. swords, upon their parole. They speak extreamly well of the Duke, and the civil treatment they met with from him, Lord Albemarle, &c., and seem wonderfully rejoiced, officers and men, that they are in their present situation, out of Scotland and the project.

"James Jackson was buried two days ago; and Goodman, who died suddenly sitting in his chair, after drinking a glass of water, last night.

"I do not know why, but I long very much to see you, or at least Mrs. Waugh and family in the country again, and I cannot very well tell you for what reason; but methinks I am extreamly tired of being housekeeper; it is not for the trouble of it I am sure, for that is nothing; but I think people look better after their own affairs than either stewards or servants do. But I hope your staying may not be for nothing, though I think the more I wish it the more I fear it. I beg you would excuse this impertinent trouble, and am, Revd. Sir,

"Your most dutiful and obliged

"Humble Servant,

"ROBT. WARDALE."

"*Genl. Howard to Dr. Waugh.*

"Sir,—

"I writt to you last post to Carlisle, don't know whether you are yett gott thither; this is to acquaint you I received orders yesterday to go as Major-General under Sir John Ligonier for Flanders, with four regiments from hence, and three to joyn us from Scotland, mine one; these are quick transitions we military people are obliged to submit to, I can't say very agreeable, but wherever I go,

"I am Mr. Waugh's faithful humble servant,

"CHA. HOWARD.

"June ye 7th."

"*Mr. Nicolson to Dr. Waugh.*

"Reverend Sir,—

"I am favoured with yours of the 5th, and suppose the days of Visitation are fixed accordingly; for Jacky Nicolson went yesterday for that purpose to Gilsland Wells, where, we are told, the Archdeacon now is. Harry Waugh is at present riding round the diocese with an address to be signed by the clergy, and which, as I was told yesterday, was to have been sent to the Bishop of Worcester, had he been in London; and you were also to have had notice to have waited upon his majesty therewith. But both his Lordship and you being now out of town, has broke all our measures; and as there is now nobody else, it must goe to the Bishop of London by the next post at furthest, if the apparitor does not get in time for this which is expected at Rose. Master Waugh is just leaving us for Appleby: he is very well, and seems quite easie as to his task, so that I suppose he is well prepared. Mr. Wardle was to have been with us last week, but has been indisposed with something of the gravel.

"Mr. Tullie was prevented from beginning his journey on Friday by some cold which his lady had got; but we hear they are to proceed this morning. He, I still think, is in a very bad state of health, and unless more exercise, &c., be followed, which is next to impossible, cannot hold it long. You wou'd hear from Carlisle on Saturday that honest Mr. Tho. Dalton was a dying, which I suppose has come to pass ere this, tho' I have not yet heard it confirmed. Poor old George Braithwait is in a most deplorable condition; the town in general very so so; and a certain affair, which has cost much money and more pains, I think almost ruined. Sir John Arbuthnot (as called) has at last left the Abbey, to the joy of every one that wishes well there.

"I am still favoured with a constant correspondence from Mr. Goldie, and now and then am employed by him, which gives me great pleasure; but have had very little news of late; only, by his accounts, I hope there are no great numbers of the Rebels together anywhere. My other intelligence by Mr. Petrie has intirely ceased since the glorious action at Culloden. I shall be very uneasie till I hear your stomach is restored.

"And am, your most obedient, humble servant,

"JOS. NICOLSON.

"Hawksdale, June 9, 1746."

"*Mr. Wardale to Dr. Waugh.*

"Carlisle, June 23rd, 1746.

"Revd. Sir,—

"I recd. your's, and am glad to hear that you and Mrs. Waugh are got safe to Scarborough. I acquainted the people you mentioned, and they all desired me to return their thanks to you for your kindness and trouble; they have since had orders to draw for the money. We have got the visitations over at Wigton and Carlisle, and to-morrow evening we shall go to Penrith. The A'Deacon gives us a pretty discourse, by way of charge, on catechising, which, I am told, is part of something he designs to publish. We did but just save the gates at Wigton, having had, I think, near 60 seals, besides licences, w'ch the Register seems to think were more than he expected.

"The A'Deacon stayed at your house that night, but went home after the visitation at Carlisle. Brigr. Fleming desires his compliments to you. I think I had worse impressions made of him before he came hither than he deserves; now he is able to stir about a little; he seems to be a good-natured, easy, well-behaved gentleman, and lives in a pretty tho' frugal way enough; he has generally three or four persons to dine with him every day. I perhaps have a better opinion of him because he generally invites me three or four times a-week; but be that as it will, I think I ought not to take up any more of your time about it. Mrs. Harrington is recovd. and is in a hopeful way. Miss Cook is exceeding ill, but I hope not very dangerously so, as Mrs. Cook tells me she is something easier this morning. The Dean is come down and turned poor Dr. Douglas out of his house, and, I am afraid, designs he should come no more into it, but I am not sure of that. We are now flattered that none of the Scotch Rebells will be sent here, which, if true, will be very happy, I think, for the town. As to the French we now have, I look upon them to be of great service to the town, for they incommode us very little and spend a great deal of money. Corn, &c., is finely fallen in price since I mentioned it to you, and things are not excessively dear now. We long to see you in the country, but hope to hear you are quite well first. I beg, by you, to pay my complts. to Mrs. Waugh, and I am,

"Revd. Sir, your most obliged dutiful servt.,

"ROBT. WARDALE."

Mr. Goldie to Dr. Waugh.

"Dear Sir,—

"We are told that old Lovat is at last taken, and that a great many of the Clan of Cameron, with Cameron of Dungallon at their head, have submitted and surrendered their arms. But, notwithstanding all that has happened, the Jacobites still keep up their spirits. Whether they expect any thing from the Brest Fleet I know not, but I can see nothing else they can found their hopes on; their behaviour on this occasion reminds me of what old Mr. Mc.Cleran, one of the Ministers of Edinburgh, said of them above twenty years ago. He was discoursing to his audience of Faith, and blaming them for the want of it; and among other things said, your faith, though better founded, is far weaker than that of the Jacobites; for tho' all outward appearances are against them, yet they every year firmly believe that before the year's end their Jamie will have the Crown. Great care is taking to have a true state of Scotland. The officers of the Customs and Excise are ordered to send in lists of all who have been in arms, or who have aided or assisted the Rebells; and the same thing is required of all Magistrates by a Proclamation issued by the Duke. The Ministers of the Established Church are desired to send attested lists of all persons in their several parishes who have not been concerned in this wicked rebellion; one copy to the Ld. Chief Justice Clerk, the other to Sir Everard Fawkener: so that it will be difficult for the guilty to escape. I wish the Government may be directed to follow such methods as may secure us from future convulsions, and in order to this I wish we had an honourable peace.—I am, with particular regard, dear Sir,

"Your most affectionate, humble servant,

"JO. GOLDIE.

"Dumfries, 13 June, 1746."

"*Mr. Goldie to Dr. Waugh.*

"Dear Sir,—

"I received yours of the 17th from Scarbourgh, and I sincerely wish you may receive benefit from the waters. Mr. D. Argenson's letter is very curious. He might be certain it would have no other effect than keeping up the spirits of those deluded people who to their own ruin and the unspeakable loss of their country had been the Dupes of France. Mynheer Vantwy's letter is the oddest rhapsody I ever saw. I have observed that in all accounts from abroad where the young Pretender is mentioned he was still called P. Edward, which pusseled me; but I am informed that his name is Charles Edward, and that in France when one has two names the first is supprest; the name of the other is Henry Benedict, so by the same rule he has a very Catholic name. There seems to be reason to think that the Pretender is not got away; it is believed he is concealed in Long Island; the Highlands are quite destroyed,—the houses burnt,—and the cattle taken away; and though they richly deserve the severest treatment, one cannot help compassionating the women and children, many of whom must inevitably perish for want of food. I am very sensible of the importance of Cape Breton; and if we could keep it, would greatly hurt the trade and naval power of France; but I do not see we can hope for peace, or that France will yield up any of her conquests unless it be restored. I am much obliged to you for your kind invitation, which I accept of upon this special condition, that you incommode yourself in no shape on my account; any little place will serve me to sleep in, and I should be sorry if any of your friends were kept away on my score. It seems to be quite certain that Lovat is taken, which is very agreeable news to every honest man. I am advised there is to be another bill of attainder, but little can be made of the forfeiture. The Duke is not come to Edinburgh; there are great preparations making there for his reception.

"I ever am, Revd. Sir,

"Your most obt. humble Servant,

"JO. GOLDIE.

"24th June, 1746."

"*Mr. Nicolson to Dr. Waugh.*

"Reverend Sir,—

"Yesterday I was favoured with your's of the 22nd inst., which I showed to my brother Hall, who, I suppose, was well pleased therewith, tho' his innate sullenness would hardly permit him to say so; and I am extreamly glad to hear that your stomach is so much better, for being able to take victuals with pleasure is a great point gained.

"Matters go on at Carlisle much as usual, only more and more imperiousness and voraciousness if possible. I have never heard you named at all, nor has there been the least wrangling. I think with Mr. B. I, indeed, have had a pretty deal for Mrs. Nevinson, about the fee farm rent, and tho' they could not bully me out of it, yet upon looking into your records for about seventy years backwards, and so compareing every year's account till the present time, I found the money was allowed Mr. Carlile, and therefore readily gave it up.

"There was but two public days, Monday and Tuesday, on the former of which the Bishop was expected; but having only had an invitation from the Vice-Dean, and hearing nothing from the principal till that morning about nine or tenn, would not favour them so farr, which the other does not seem a little huffed at. There has also been a pretty warm dispute between the Dean and Mr. Head, about Mr. Brown's refusing to do duty in the Cathedral; but notwithstanding all those bickerings, one certain reason must prevent all open ruptures. I cannot yet certainly tell you what sort of a chapter it may be as to ffines, but I fancy a pretty good one, tho' the Chief of Befram is not yet come in for Corbridge tithes, nor is there any agreement for the renewing with Mr. Tullie; the body insisting upon a particular of the present rental, which Mr. Dobinson is to write to Kilton about by this day's post; and should that point be accômmodated, another will instantly arise not less difficult, to witt, the want of cash, for when the leases were delivered to Mr. Dobinson with orders to renew them, not one word was said how that was to be procured. Do you think of seeing Kilton this summer? I much doubt the journey would not answer in any shape; and yet something should be set about directly, for he is certainly in a most dangerous state of health.

"I wrote to you about Harrington's affair with Mr. Cornforth, just about the time you left London; but being apprehensive of that, I inclosed it to Mr. Will. Tullie, and desired the favour of him to talk to that gentleman about it; for Harrington seems to have acted a very honest part, and is very willing to refer his accounts to any indifferent knowing person, as he at first told Mr. Cornforth by Mr. Dobinson; to which no answer was ever given but what came from you. Poor man, he is again relapsed—I doubt very dangerously.

"Francy Hewitt is very sanguine that he'll yet be discharged before the Assizes, as he might have been long agoe if he had not trusted to empty professions, &c., &c. Davison is yet in jail, and I am something afraid that he'll at last add the compleat villain to his other indiscretions; for his ffather is lately dead, and at the son's instance, as supposed, settled his whole estate upon his grandson. Poor Jack Gill, the brazier, is also a dying, as are several others; amongst which Betty Cooke was thought one, but she is a good deal better. I am, ever yours, most faithfully,

"JOS. NICOLSON.

"26th June."

"*Mr. Wardale to Dr. Waugh.*

"Revd. Sir,—

"We have now finished the visitations and returned; I parted with Mr. A. Dacre at Appleby, who desired his compliments to you and Mrs. Waugh. The Register thinks the people a little uncomplaisant in this round not to die faster these troublesome times; both the other Courts of Probates, &c., scarce equalling Wigton. Master Waugh is perfectly well, and tells me had a letter from you. But what chiefly makes me give you this trouble at present is a piece of news that surprised us here a good deal. A messenger came this morning from London to take Capt. Davison thither, and they will set forward post in half-an-hour. He says he was ordered to make all the haste he possibly could, but knows nothing of the occasion of ye. sending for ye. Capt. As to people's conjectures here, they are not worth troubling you with, being mere conjectures; but the unexpectedness of the thing made me think it might not be unacceptable to you to hear it. I have been hunting to see if I could find any body that knew the occasion of it; but find that neither himself nor any body else does, which has made me have only just time to subscribe myself, with complements to good Mrs. Waugh,

"Revd. Sir,
"Your most dutiful and obliged humble Servant,
"ROBT. WARDALE.

"Carlisle, June 28th, 1746."

"*Mr. Nicolson to Dr. Waugh.*

"Hond. Sir,—

"The Chapter at Carlisle ended on Wednesday last, and the dividend amounted to £120 for each member. The righteous Dean left the town the next morning with the same character and good wishes as heretofore. His behaviour towards Mr. Birket was all along extremely civil, and pretty much so to me too. The evening before the Chapter broke up I moved for leave to appoint my nephew John my deputy; which was strongly opposed by Messrs. Head and Wilson, and as strongly seconded by the Dean; so that an order was at last made in the affirmative, during the pleasure of the body. Mr. Wilson is Vice-dean for the remaining part of the year, Mr. Birket, treasurer, and Head Recr.-general.

"Mr. Tully was forced to comply with the payment of £140 for a fine, which by his letter to Mr. Dobinson has provoked him not a little.

"The grass is all cutt in your two fields at Carlisle, and but a midling crop, and has already suffered a little by the weather which has been extremely bad all this week; but this morning looks well; and as the glass has been rising for these 24 hours last past am in great hopes of better days.

"Poor Joseph Robinson, the captain of the cruiser at Whitehaven is, I doubt, dead—or however a-dying; who are candidates for the place I do not hear, but believe there is hardly a more advantageous one in that part if properly managed.

"The public houses at Carlisle (the Bush excepted) have been grievously loaded with soldiers since the new ones came,—private houses absolutely refusing to take any, and the Castle still continuing empty,—tho' General Howard told me in his letter of the 5th of April that an order was come the Thursday preceding for taking as many men into it as the beds would hold, which would be above 400. Indeed the Foot are all marched again for Barwick, as it's said, so that there are not at present above 300 in the whole town, but we are told that great numbers are coming to us, as also many hundred Rebels. I have had nothing from Scotland of late, only that poor Sr. James Johnstone is a-dying at Edinr., his Rebel lady and daughter having broke his heart.

"I am ever your's most faithfully,

"JOS. NICOLSON.

"P.S.—I have seen your letter to Mr. Wardale, and am extreamly concerned to hear of your indisposition. Pray let not the getting here against the Assizes or anything else make you risque the getting cold before you are perfectly well again. I hope Mrs. Waugh is very well under all the fatigue which she must now undergoe. We shall all do our utmost to get your business properly dispatched; but, indeed, for my own part, my hurry is so excessively great at all times that I hardly finish aught."

"*Mr. Jackson to Dr. Waugh.*

"Dear Sir,—

"I deferred writing till I knew how our Courts turned out: they have answered beyond my expectation.

* * * * *

"This year has been a scene of troubles, but I was in hopes your endeavours would have been amply rewarded, and am concerned they are not. I am glad to hear the waters agree with you, and if it please God to give you health, you are young enough to live and see better times. We have indeed had a gloomy time here, nothing appearing like what it was, being subject to the military gentry; and now these 2 Regiments, w'ch are a wicked rabel, expect to be sent home in a short time, but in their room one whole Regt. a 1000 compleat old R.'s is to supply their place. We were pleasing ourselves yt. when these left us we should have our houses to ourselves, but we are told it will be otherwise, and whatever laws and liberties the rest of the kingdom enjoys we are to be exempted. Hard fate! the consideration of w'ch is too heavy for my sister's spirits. I was intending to have gone to W'tehaven for a month to have cheered her, and adjourned the Court to the last of Augt., but I am afraid we can't leave our house. It was once said the Castle would be fitted for 3 or 400; and Genl. Howard took a deal of pains about it, but no orders are yet come to finish that work, and without it the town can't contain 1000 private men, 60 officers, serjeants, &c., besides French prisoners. Sometimes I wish to have you here to help us, but I can't wish you so much trouble and grief of mind, w'ch I dare say our condition will give you. However, I wish and long to see you, and am, with success, and my service to Mrs. Waugh, your most oblged

"Humble Servt.,

"THOS. JACKSON.

"Carlisle, July ye. 2d, 1746."

"*Mr. Nicolson to Dr. Waugh.*

"Revd. Sir,—

"Mr. Simpson sent me the inclosed the other day, and desires your directions concerning your rents due there at Candlemas next; and Mr. Wardale (who had begun to write) saies Mr. Tullie is in want of his plate, and designs to look after it very soon, but wou'd be glad to know first what you wou'd have done with yours, &c.

"On Tuesday last, I sent an express to Edinr., which promised to be back as last night, but does not yet appear, tho' it's now almost noon, and therefore dare not wait longer for fear of losing the post; but if there comes any thing extraordinary you shall certainly have it by the next. I have wrote twice to York since I had your orders and fully designed a repetition to-day, had my messenger returned in time. The General, I am much afraid, does not increase his interest, at Carlisle, as indeed I always expected. General Bland is returned there, and it's said a line of horse is to be stationed along the Borders, which I think will be of little use, but great inconvenience to both them and the inhabitants. I also hear that Lord Hallifax's regiment is come to stay at Carlisle, and that the Duke of Montague's is soon expected upon the same errand. Captain Gilpin and the rest of the invalid officers that were at C—— are sent for up to London, and the former was to begin his journey this day.

"I am your most obedient, hble. servt.,

"JOS. NICOLSON.

"Netherby, July 18th, 1746.

"P.S.—Mr. Wardale is here: sends his compliments; and designs to change with one of our clergymen to-morrow. I shall be at Rose again before the return of the post."

"*Mr. Wardale to Dr. Waugh.*

"Revd. Sir,—

"I received your kind letter last post, and was much concerned at your acct. of your own and the poor little folks' state of health. I would not even wish to see you in the country till we can see you well; and I must own I can see no kind of necessity for your hurrying, with the least hazard to yourself, or indeed of what service it would be, any further than the satisfaction yt. the people concerned and every body would have in having you in the country at such a time; for most people think if you had been here things would some way or other have been better managed. I cannot say but they are in the right of that, but, upon the whole, I think it is as well as it is. You would have had an infinite deal of trouble, and things could not have been done as every one would have expected. I am exceedingly glad that good Mrs. Waugh keeps her health, as I hope she does, since you mention nothing to the contrary. The Brigr. is strangely distressed what to do with the Rebel prisoners when they come here; the Sherif will not part with the County Gaol; and the Corporation, whom he curses from morning till night, will lend no assistance, so that I am afraid ye. expedient of putting them again into the Church (w'h G. P. advises) will be fallen upon; but let them fight it out. Capt. Gilpin arrived here from London yesterday. I had a letter from Mr. Goldie last post, wherein he tells me the Duke played them the same trick at Edinr. he did at York. He mentioned nothing of his coming at the Assizes; but in answer I mentioned what you said, which, I suppose, was the reason of his writing. I will take care to have all things done according to your directions. Gardener says there are two carts at Caldbeck, but I shall send to Mr. Thompson to have two made as you direct. I have just been telling the Brigr. that he might bring the French prisoners out of the Gaol and put them into the Poorhouse, and then fill the Gaol with Rebel prisoners to be tryed, which, I think, he will, and says he can take 100 into the Castle, and nothing, but the last necessity, shall make him have any thoughts of making use of the Church. Dr. Douglas tells me there is a fever in town, with very bad symptoms, viz., spotted, but as the weather is now turned very cold and rainy instead of very hot, I hope it will put a stop to it. One always fears the thing will be worse than it turns out. I beg to pay my respects to Mrs. Waugh, Miss Waugh, and all the little folks, and am,

"Revd. Sir,

"Your most dutiful and obliged humble servt.,

"R. WARDALE."

On the 15th of July *Colonel Townley*, was brought to trial at the Court House at Saint Margaret's Hill, Southwark, found guilty of high treason, and condemned. At the same time, *Captains George Fletcher*, *James Dawson*, and *Andrew Blood; Lieutenants Thos. Deacon*, *John Berwick*, and *Thomas Chadwick ;* and *Adjutant Thomas Syddell*, all of the Manchester Regiment, who had been taken at Carlisle, were also tried and condemned. The principal witness against them was Samuel Maddock, an Ensign in the same regiment, who saved his own life by assisting in the conviction of his friends. On the 30th of July they suffered at Kennington Common; meeting their appalling fate with composure; and declaring, at the last moment, that they died in a just cause. The horrible detail of the punishment awarded by the law of treason was critically observed. The half-hanging, the embowelling alive, the mutilation of the senseless corpse, were all performed to the letter, before an immense concourse of spectators; and, as it might be expected, excited sympathy and pity for the sufferers, mixed with a feeling of admiration of their constancy and courage.

The heads of *Colonel Townley* and *Captains Fletcher* and *Dawson* were placed on Temple Bar.* The heads of *Captain Berwick* and *Lieutenant Chadwick* were sent to Carlisle, and there placed on the English Gate.

Hamilton, the Governor of the Castle, was also brought to trial, and suffered the like cruel death.

In the latter end of July, a number of the prisoners, taken at Carlisle on its recapture, who had then been removed to Lancaster, were sent back to Carlisle, in order to their trial at the Assizes.

On the 2nd of August, Mr. WARDALE writes to Dr. WAUGH, in anticipation of these proceedings, which naturally enough were disagreeable:—

"The town seems quite easy since the additional compys. of foot left us. The two regimts. of drags. and compy. of foot left have behaved so extremely well, that tho' they are ten or twelve at several ale houses, and cannot all get beds, yet there are no quarrels, no complaints on any side; all the town as quiet in an evening as if no-

---

* Some years afterwards, through the instrumentality of an optician, who used to let out glasses to people desirous of viewing the heads on Temple Bar, the skull of Col. Townley was obtained by his relatives, and is now in possession of one of them under a glass case.

body was in't,—at least it is much the best it ever was since our troubles first began. These dragoons are to march as soon as the regimt. of foot comes in. We had about forty prisoners brought in yesternight from Lancaster, (amongst wch. is my old friend the Bp., as he once call'd himself,) and I hope your acct. about the number we are to have here will prove true, as I hear of no more yet, except from Whitehaven and N.Castle. The fever I mentioned, I fancy, is abated, as I hear little more of it; and I do not fear but we shall get these troublesome assizes over much better than we ever expected. The Barracks in the Castle will be quite fitted up for 400 men before the latter assizes; and I begin to see some little daybreaking of hope, that Carlisle will be almost Carlisle again in a little time; but that it cannot be till you and the family come there. The King's Sollicr. came hither yesterday; and he and the Brigr. have been bullying and threatening poor T. P.*; who, like a true honest philosopher, only says that he values little what any of them can do to him; he knows he has not long to live; nothing in life signifies much to him. I have heard nothing of what you mentioned in Mr. Nicolson's letter, and I hope I shall not for some reasons I have, besides the ungratefulness of the thing itself. If he does speak to me, I shall give him all the satisfaction I can, wch. I think will not be much. I beg leave to pay my respects to Mrs. Waugh and all your family."

But Mr. Wardale's hopes as to the number of prisoners intended to be sent to Carlisle proved ill-founded. Besides the 40 from Lancaster and those from Newcastle and Whitehaven, a large body was sent from Scotland. Altogether, there arrived 382; and there is too much reason to believe that, owing to the limited means of accommodation in the Jail and Castle, they were huddled together promiscuously, in places which we now almost shudder to look into. No doubt it was impossible to find room for the safe custody of so large a number separately, and that fact alone suffices to condemn the authorities for bringing so many together; in the sequel they tacitly admitted it by allowing the prisoners to cast lots for the selection of a reduced number to stand trial, finding that to try the whole was out of the question.

---

* Pattinson, the Deputy-Mayor, seems to be meant. He died soon afterwards.

On the 12th of August, 1746, the Chief Baron PARKER, Sir THOMAS BURNET, Sir THOMAS DENNISON, and Baron CLARK, opened their Commission for trial of the prisoners at Carlisle:

The GRAND JURY consisted of:—

Sir Geo. Dalston, Bart., of Dalston Hall.
Sir Richard Musgrave, Bart., of Hayton Castle.
Henry Fletcher, Esq., of Hutton.
John Dalston, Esq., of Mellrig.
Edward Hasell, Esq., of Dalemain.
Wilfrid Lawson, Esq., of Brayton.
Henry Aglionby, Esq., the elder, of Crossfield.
John Brisco, Esq., of Crofton.
Richard Crackenthorpe, Esq., of Ousay.
Montague Farrer, Esq., of Carlisle.
Edward Stanley, Esq., of Ponsonby.
Robert Lamplugh, Esq., of Dovenby.
Fletcher Partis, Esq., of Tallentire.
Humphrey Senhouse, Esq., of Netherhall.
Richard Brisco, Esq., of Lamplugh.
Joseph Dacre, Esq., of Kirklinton.
Richard Cook, Esq., of Camerton.
Gustavus Thompson, Esq., of Arkleby.
John Benn, Esq., of Hensingham.
George Irton, Esq., of Irton.
Peter How, Esq., of Whitehaven.
Richard Huddleston, Esq., of Whitehaven.
Thomas Smith, gentleman, of Penrith.

It was immediately found that to try the whole 382 prisoners would prove too much for both Judges and Juries. It was, therefore, arranged that, with some exceptions, they should have the option of drawing lots for selection of one out of every twenty to stand trial,—the nineteen remaining to submit to transportation. Several accepted of these terms, and by these means the number for trial was reduced to 127, against whom the Grand Jury found bills of indictment, viz. :—

JAMES ANCRUM, of Boness.
ALEXR. ANDERSON.
ALEXR. BRODIE.
RICHARD BROWN.
JAS. BRAITHWAITE, of Penrith, saddler.
JAMES BRAND, Quarter-master.
EDMUND BANE.
LEWIS BARTON.
THOMAS BARTON.
FRANCIS BUCHANAN, of Arnprior.
THOS. BUCHANAN, } his brothers.
PATRICK BUCHANAN, }
JON. CAMPBELL.
THOS. CAPPOCK,—the Bishop.
JOHN CAPPOCK.
WILLIAM COOK.
JAS. CHADWICK.
THOS. COLLINGWOOD.
HUGH CAMERON.
JAS. CAMPBELL, alias Mc.GREGOR.
HARRY CLERK, Esq., of Edinburgh.
WILLIAM DUNCAN.
CHARLES DOUGLAS, titular Lord Mordington
MICHAEL DELARD.
JO. DAVIDSON.
ALEXR. DAVIDSON.
JAS. DRUMMOND.
MOLINEUX EATON.
CAPTAIN ROBERT FORBES, brother of Forbes of New.
ROGER FULTHORPE.
STEPHEN FITZGERALD.
ROBERT FINSLEY.
CAPT. JAMES FORBES.
JAMES FERGUSON, of Athole.
WILLIAM GRAY, surgeon.
CHARLES GORDON, of Dalpersey.
HUGH GRAHAM.
JOHN HENDERSON, Captain.
GEO. HARTELEY.
JOHN HAITLEY.
THOS. HATCH.
WM. HARGRAVES.
THOS. HAYES.
THOMAS HARVEY.
PHILIP HUNT.
VALENTINE HOLT.
JAS. HARVEY.
DAVID HOME.
WILLIAM HOME.
ALEXR. HUTCHESON.
CAPT. JAMES HAY.
THOS. HUTCHINSON.
COLONEL JAMES INNES.
ANDREW JOHNSTON.
PATRICK KEIR.
THOMAS LAWSON.
WILLIAM LECKIE.
SAMUEL LEE.
SIMON LUGTON.
MARK LINDSAY, writer.
DAVID LAYES.
ROBERT LYON, Episcopal Minister at Perth.
PETER LINDSAY.
JOHN MACNEIL.
NEIL MACLAREN.
DONALD MACKENZIE.
BARNABAS MATHEW.
JAS. MELLON.
JOS. MACKENZIE.
MAJOR DONALD MACDONALD, of Tyendrish.
DONALD MACDONALD, of the City Guard.
RONALD MACDONALD.
RICHD. MORRISON, the Prince's valet.
ROBERT MAXWELL, writer.
DONALD MAIBORMEG.
ARCHIBALD MACFARLANE.
DONALD MACDONALD, of Kinlock Moidart.
ROBERT MURRAY, writer.
JAS. MURRAY, surgeon.
PATRICK MURRAY, goldsmith, Stirling.
JOHN MARTIN.
JOHN MACNAUGHTON.
PATRICK MACGREGOR.
DUNCAN MACGREGOR.
JAS. MITCHELL.
DUNCAN MURRAY, alias MACGREGOR.
LAWRENCE MERCER, of Lithendy.
THOS. PARK.
ANDREW PORTEOUS.
JOHN POUSTIE.
SIR ARCHIBALD PRIMROSE, Bart.
ROBERT READ.
ROBERT ROSCOE.
THOS. REILLY.
EDWARD ROPER.
JOHN RADCLIFF.
THOS. RITCHIE.
HUGH ROY.
JOHN ROWBOTHAM.
ROBERT RANDAL.
PAT. RUTTER.
JOHN ROBERTSON.
WM. STEWART, Lieut. in Roy Stuart's.
WM. SHARPE.

JOHN STREETLY.
ALEXR. STEEL.
JOHN SANDERSON, Captain in the Manchester Regiment.
JOHN SMALL.
ANDREW SWAN.
JAS. SMITH, writer.
ALEXR. STEPHENSON.
GEO. STEEL, merchant, Aberdeen.
CHARLES SPALDING, of Whitfield.
PATRICK STEWART.
JAMES SETON.
ROBERT TUESBY.
THOS. TURNER, of Bury.
PETER TAYLOR.
THOS. TURNER, of Walton.
ROBERT TAYLOR, Captain.
JOHN WALLACE.
WM. WYNSTANLEY.
THOS. WILLIAMSON.
GEO WARING.
MATTHEW WARING.
THOS. WARRINGTON.
ROBERT WRIGHT, writer.

These prisoners were then brought to the bar and the Judges desired them to name their Counsel and Solicitors, and ordered subpœnas for their witnesses to be made out, and delivered gratis. The English prisoners chose for Counsel Messrs. PARROT and CLAYTON; the Scotch, Messrs. JAMES GRAHAM and ALEXANDER LOCKHART; and for their Solicitors, Messrs. JAMES FERGUSON and ALEXANDER STEWART. The Court then adjourned till the 9th of September.

The 127 indicted prisoners were immediately separated from the others; and, with the exception of two, heavily ironed and thrust into one room in the keep of the Castle. Two of them Sir *Archibald Primrose* and Captain *Hay*, were "allowed the privilege of the County Jail," a *privilege*, doubtless, it was comparatively with the lot of the others. Those who have seen the room wherein they were confined, which Sir WALTER SCOTT's description of *Fergus Mc.Ivor's* cell may have led not a few to do, will readily form an estimate of the humanity of those who could consign 125 of their countrymen to such a place at such a time. The adjournment of the Court to afford time for preparation of their defence was a merciful and considerate act; but how could they, pent up together in a single room, have the due advantage of it? Their minds, distracted from every thing like calm deliberation, turned in desperation to other schemes. Plots for escape were hatched, and greater strictness ensued upon discovery. How could it be otherwise? So many desperate men cooped up together naturally turned their thoughts upon attempting escape.

The difficulty of getting evidence against the prisoners appears to have been considerable. Hence the admission of *Maddock* as King's Evidence. The Scottish witnesses showed their disinclination by objecting to be sworn in the English form; whereupon the Judges directed that they should be sworn according to the Scottish. And in the interval between indictment and trial, it was found requisite to parade the prisoners before successive detachments of fifteen at a time of the people of Carlisle, to afford the means of identifying such of them as had been in arms in the town. The following letter from Mrs. NICOLSON to Dr. WAUGH details this circumstance:—

"Hawksdale, Sep. 8th.

"Dear Mr. Chanr.

"We had conceived hopes of your speedy return by news that came here before you got to York; and since that have heard the Coll. was to go abroad with Coll. Folliote; but you know better than we what truth there are in such storys. The Bp. talks of you now, drinks your health, and wishes you a safe return; but he it was that told me of the tryal being put off, and his hopes to see you soon return. He is in high good humour with us all now, so much have you mended matters by your good behaviour to him. The weather has been so wett that I have not got to Caldbeck, and when weather is good horses must plough; but I hear, as I hope you do, Peggy's eye is much better, and the rest of your folks well. Mr. Tullie is not yet come. Mr. Webb paid for all charges his horses were at. I know not when Mr. Nicolson goes his Yorkshire journey, the Bp. not being steady as to the time of ordination. We shall be glad to hear you performed as well to London as you did to York. We have no news but that the people of Carlisle are all summoned to the Castle, by fifteen at a time, to see whom of the Rebel prisoners they can swear to; and many of them are challenged that way, tho' they having coats and breeches instead of plads and none, are not so easily known to those who saw them in nothing but dirty pladds. Your maid, Dolly, was accosted by her friend Cappock, tho' he seems very busie in writing and reading when people go in. He merryly came to her and asked her how she did, with a face of assurance as if all was well with him; w'ch made her reply she was much better than when she had his company. I was with the watchmaker, who says he can soder the hook of my watch, so as it shall be stronger than before, so pray don't trouble yourself about it, good sir, but bring it back as it was.

"Mr. Nicolson says he has no news. We long again to hear from you, and are both your truly

"Affectionate and faithful servt.,

"E. NICOLSON."

On the 9th of September the court resumed, and the prisoners were arraigned. A great number of them pleaded guilty,—of whom several afterwards retracted their plea and stood trial. *Charles Douglas* pleaded a Scotch peerage, the Barony of Mordington, and claimed trial by his Peers, which plea, after argument, was allowed. On the 12th and following days the trials proceeded. No report has been kept of any, except that of *Thomas Cappock*, commonly called the Mock Bishop; and that is obviously the work of a fierce partisan, and breathes in every line of it the spirit of hostility to the prisoner. There could be no doubt of his guilt, nor any difficulty in proving it, for he had marched with the insurgents from Derby to Carlisle, quartered himself in Dr. WAUGH's house, and mounted guard on the walls during the siege. But there appears to have been at the time a systematic endeavour to blacken the characters of the prisoners, and to prevent the Royal mercy reaching them. It is stated in a newspaper of that day, "That the news writers, by letters from Carlisle, have given account of the trials, condemnation, and behaviour of the rebel prisoners at Carlisle, both before and after the sentence of death; but such a partial account cannot be sustained, even amongst the most abandoned and profligate writers. Such a multitude of gross calumnies and insidious reflections, without the least foundation, were never inserted in any newspaper by persons indued with the least fear of God, or regard to man; but the poor prisoners see very well their design; and it is obvious to all sober minds that their intent is to deprive them of his Majesty's Royal mercy and known clemency. But let them go on in their execrable designs as much as they please. I assure you that the generality of the prisoners here are so much concerned at their approaching fate, that they behave themselves every way suitable to gentlemen in their misfortunate condition. Though there is no accounting for the behaviour of every single person in such a number of men, so it is hoped that no Christian Reader will give any credit to such a general charge, void of conscience and destitute of humanity."

And of *Cappock* in particular it is stated by a gentleman who visited him:—" I went into the Castle, where I found the young gentleman *(Mr. Cappock)* at his devotions. After he rose from prayers I told him after what manner he was reflected on in the papers. 'Sir,' says he, 'I'm no stranger to such calumnies. I see the views of my adversaries—'tis in order to exclude me from the benefit of the King's royal mercy and clemency. Some, says he, by a gift peculiar to themselves, can discern objects where they are not; and some can see and hear things that were never seen nor heard.' He added, 'Sir, aquaint the world, I've a just sense of my present unhappy circumstances; I'm patient and resigned under my misfortunes; and I thank God I can freely forgive my enemies.'"

No doubt *Cappock* and his fellow prisoners used language in regard to their conduct that sounded provokingly in the ears of the loyal people of Carlisle; and it might be politic, or at least conceived to be so, to talk loudly and violently against them.

Very few were acquitted. *Thomas Barton*, accused of carrying letters to the Magistrates of Carlisle requiring the surrender of the town to the Prince, escaped by the omission of the Crown Solicitor to have the letters in Court for production. *Thos.* and *Patrick Buchanan*, brothers of Francis Buchanan, of Arnprior, were acquitted on account of their youth and having acted under the influence, amounting to force, of their brother. Captain *James Hay* was demanded by the French officer, (who commanded the French troops at Culloden, and there surrendered, and was sent prisoner of war to Carlisle,) as a French subject—he being a Captain in Lord JOHN DRUMMOND's regiment in the French King's service; and on reference to the Judge Advocate this was allowed of. *Mr. James Murray*, surgeon, was acquitted on account of his having diligently assisted the wounded soldiers after the defeat at Preston Pans. Two English lads also, on account of their youth. And eight others claimed and had release on the ground that they surrendered upon the Duke of CUMBERLAND's Proclamation after the Battle of Culloden.

Sir Archibald Primrose, of Dunipace, retracted his plea of Not Guilty and pleaded Guilty, as also *Colonel James Innes*, and *Mr. Clark:* in hopes, no doubt, of obtaining mercy from the Crown. *Major Macdonald*, of Tyendrish, and *Macdonald*, of Kinloch Moidart, stood their trial—for them it was the only chance of escape—of mercy there was no hope in the then state of feeling on the part of the Government.

Donald Macdonald, the Laird of Kinloch Moidart, is described as being a plain honest-hearted gentleman; an exceedingly cool-headed man, fitted for either the cabinet or the field; and attached by hereditary ties of affection to the STUARTS. His brother, ÆNEAS MACDONALD, a banker in Paris, was one of the "Seven men of Moidart" who came over from France with CHARLES EDWARD, in July, 1745; and although KINLOCH MOIDART could not but perceive the extreme degree of peril attending the project, he was unable to resist the persuasions of his brother, and the fascination which the Prince seems to have exercised upon those whom he personally addressed. "*Lord, man! what could I do when the young lad came to my house?*" was the simple but affecting reply which he gave to a friend who visited him afterwards in his prison, and asked how he came to embark in so desperate an undertaking. His accession was valuable. He was immediately made a Colonel and Aid-de-Camp to the Prince; and had they succeeded was to have been created a Peer of Scotland. His services were principally in going amongst and arousing the friends of the cause; and he was not with the Highlanders in England. In one of his expeditions he was seized by some country people at Lesmahago, and committed to Edinburgh Castle, on the 12th November, 1745, from which he was transferred to Carlisle for trial.

Major Donald Macdonald, of Tyendrish, was a man of different character, and it may be presumed that Sir WALTER SCOTT had him in mind when he drew the character of FERGUS MAC IVOR, in his novel of "Waverley." *Major Macdonald* was amongst the first to join Prince CHARLES after his landing, and the first to strike a blow against the government. Two newly-raised companies being sent by the Governor of Fort Augustus, under the command of Capt. SCOTT, in consequence of vague rumours of warlike preparations in the Western Highlands, to march to Fort William, had arrived within eight miles of their destination on the 16th August, 1745, when, in passing the ravine of High Bridge, they were suddenly startled by the sound of the bagpipe, and received a galling fire off the heights above, from a party of the MACDONALDS, of Keppoch, headed by *Macdonald*, of Tyendrish. They fled in return towards Fort Augustus; and at the eastern extremity of Loch Lochy were encountered by a larger body under the command of KEPPOCH, the Chief of the Clan, to whom they were obliged to surrender.

Macdonald, of Tyendrish, immediately had a Major's commission in KEPPOCH's regiment, and with it marched into England. After the retreat he was with his regiment at the battle of Falkirk, and was there taken prisoner by an unlucky mistake. It has before been noticed that at Falkirk there was a want of combination and arrangement on the part of the Highland Chiefs, so that many of the troops kept their ground, not knowing the advantage that was gained; whilst, had they been vigorously carried onwards, a total rout of HAWLEY's army might have been effected. A strong proof of this is afforded by the incident of *Macdonald's* capture. He had rushed on in pursuit when others halted, so that he found himself alone amongst the artillery abandoned by the King's troops. He walked up and down amongst the field pieces for some time without either friend or foe to interrupt him. At length a man came up and asked what he did there? He answered, "I am diverting myself looking at these pieces of cannon." The man replied, "I would have you, sir, to take care of yourself; for the CAMPBELLS and others are rallying at the back of Falkirk to return to the battle."

On this the Major thought proper to return to his own men. In his way, espying a body of men in a hollow, he took them to be Lord John Drummond's regiment and the French picquets; the dusk of the evening caused his mistake. He hastened up to them with his sword still drawn, and exclaimed passionately, "Gentlemen, what do you here? Why don't ye follow after the dogs, and pursue them?"

Scarcely had he uttered the words when he discovered his mistake. It was Barrell's regiment, which had never been engaged, nor seen the Highlanders at all, there being a rising ground between them. Immediately they cried out, "A Rebel! a Rebel!" *Macdonald*, having advanced so far that he could not retreat, endeavoured to screen himself by saying he was one of their own Campbells, his white cockade being so dirty with rain and smoke that there was no discovering the colour of it. But Genl. Husk, who was with Barrell's regiment, swore it was easy to discover what he was by his sword, the blade of which was covered with blood and hair. Husk cried out, "Shoot the dog instantly." Seven or eight muskets were presented at his breast; but Lord Robert Kerr generously interposed and saved his life by beating down the muskets. Being obliged to surrender his arms, he said, "As he was himself an officer, he would choose to deliver up his arms to General Husk, because he appeared to be an officer of dignity." Husk swore he would not do him that honour; upon which Lord Robert Kerr politely stepped forward to receive the Major's arms. Whilst he was pulling off his pistol from the belt, he happened to do it with such an air that Husk swore the dog was going to shoot him. To which the Major replied, "I am more of a gentleman, Sir, than to do any such thing. I am only pulling off my pistol to deliver it up." When he at any time afterwards spoke of delivering up his good claymore and his fine pistol, he used to sigh, and to mention Lord ROBERT KERR with great affection for his generous and singular civilities.

Francis Buchanan, of Arnprior, appears to have joined the Prince at an early period, and to have been a man of some consideration with him, since, in the letters which were issued in August, '45, to the friends of the cause throughout Scotland, intimating that he had set up the royal standard, and expected the assistance of all his friends—and asking money—it is desired to be paid into the hands of Arnprior, or sent by a sure hand to the Prince himself. *Buchanan's* two younger brothers were also out, and were taken and tried at Carlisle. His own trial lasted five hours—there being ten witnesses for the crown, and three on his part. He was found guilty, and his brothers acquitted on the ground of their having been influenced by him.

Amongst others also found guilty was one *John Macnaughten*, against whom it was proved that he shot COLONEL GARDNER, at Preston Pans, and cut him when down with his broadsword twice on the shoulder, and once on the head. The correctness of this charge has been questioned, but certainly the evidence was so given against *Macnaughten* on his trial, and caused his execution. Though it is much to be wished that a report of the trials of the two *Macdonalds* had been preserved, yet, possibly, had it been so, we might have to pronounce the affecting narrative of Mc.IVOR's trial by Sir WALTER SCOTT (which, whilst we peruse it we feel assured he must have drawn from the details of some that heard it) to be merely a fiction. For we learn that the general plea and defence of the prisoners at Carlisle was that they were *forced* into the rebellion—that is, they were put under influences by clanship and such like, morally equivalent to force. We know how *Cappock* was stigmatized for the bold language he made use of when he was convicted; and we may be sure that if *Macdonald* had in Court justified his loyalty to the STUARTS, it would have procured for him a similar malediction. But nothing of the kind appears.

On Monday, the 22nd September, were brought up to the bar for sentence:—

THOMAS CAPPOCK—the Bishop.
JOHN MACNAUGHTEN.
JAMES BRAND.
MAJOR MACDONALD.
JOHN HENDERSON.
COL. JAMES INNES.
JAMES ANCRUM.
HUGH CAMERON.
DAVID HOME.
ROBERT RANDAL.
RONALD MACDONALD.
ALEXANDER ANDERSON.
ROBERT MAXWELL.
PHILIP HUNT.
JAMES CAMPBELL.
EDWARD ROPER.
STEPHEN FITZGERALD.
MICHAEL DELARD.
JAMES FORBES.
RICHARD MORRISON.
ALEX. HUTCHINSON.
ANDREW JOHNSTON.
WILLIAM HOME.

Chief Baron PARKER, after the usual formalities, pronounced their sentence as follows—

"You and every of you, prisoners at the bar, return to the prison from whence you came, and from thence you must be drawn to the place of execution; when you come there you must be hanged by the neck,—but not till you be dead; for you must be cut down alive; then your bowels must be taken out, and burnt before your faces; then your heads must be severed from your bodies, and your bodies divided each into four quarters, and these must be at the King's disposal. And God have mercy on your souls!"

When the sentence was given, *Brand*, one of the prisoners, shed tears, on which *Cappock* exclaimed, "What the Devil are you afraid of? We shan't be tried by a Cumberland jury in the next world."

On the 23rd, the like sentence was pronounced upon :—

THOMAS LAWSON.
WILLIAM LECKEY.
JOHN WALLACE.
JOHN CAMPBELL.
WILLIAM DUNCAN.
ROBERT FORBES.
WILLIAM WYNSTANLEY.
GEORGE HARTLEY.
ROBERT REED.
RICHARD BROWN.
JOHN CAPPOCK.
WILLIAM COOK.
MOLINEUX EATON.
ROGER FULTHORPE.
WILLIAM HARGRAVE.
THOMAS HAYS.
THOMAS HARVEY.
JOHN HARTLEY.
THOMAS KEIGHLEY.
SAMUEL LEE.

And on the 24th upon :—

JOHN MACNEIL.
JOHN RATCLIFF.
DONALD MACKENZIE.
BARNABAS MATTHEW.
HUGH ROY.
THOMAS PARK.
ROBERT FINSLEY.
THOMAS TURNER, of Walton.
PETER TAYLOR.
JOHN ROBOTHAM.
JOHN SANDERSON.
THOS. TURNER, of Bury.
GEORGE WARING.
MATTHEW WARING.
VALENTINE HOLT.
LEWIS BARTON.
JOHN SMALL.
JAMES MELLON.
JAMES CHADWICK.
JOHN DAVIDSON.
JOHN MACKENZIE.
ROBERT TAYLOR.
SIMON LUGTON.
JOHN POUSTIE.
ANDREW SWAN.
JAMES SMITH.
JAMES HARVEY.
WILLIAM GRAY.
ROBERT MURRAY.
FRANCIS BUCHANAN.
SIR ARCHIBALD PRIMROSE.
ROBERT WRIGHT.
ALEX. STEPHENSON.
JAMES MITCHELL.
PATRICK STEWART.
ANDREW PORTEOUS.
PETER LINDSAY.
LAWRENCE MERCER.
WILLIAM SHARP.
CHARLES GORDON.
PATRICK KEIR.
ALEXR. DAVIDSON.
HENRY CLARK.

In all 96 were sentenced to die, of whom 31 were executed, and two died in prison, and the remainder, with the exception of a few pardoned, transported.

At the conclusion of the Assizes the Judges ordered the release of those who had been apprehended by order of the Duke of CUMBERLAND, on the recapture of the town, and since detained in prison. Amongst these was *Mr. Salkeld*, whose case deserves notice as showing how uneasy must have been the position of the Roman Catholic gentry at that juncture. Mr. SALKELD was the last male representative of an ancient Roman Catholic family formerly seated at Corby Castle; which in the reign of James the First they sold to Lord WILLIAM HOWARD, of Naward, and thenceforward settled at Whitehall, about fourteen miles west of Carlisle, where Mr. SALKELD and his wife were residing when the Highlanders came to Carlisle in November, 1745.

It was his intention to remain perfectly quiet at home; being out of the line of their march, and not likely to be disturbed—moreover, he was ill of the gout. Some years before that, Mr. SALKELD had, for his steward, one JOHN SANDERSON; the same it would seem, who joined the insurgents, and held a Captain's commission in Colonel TOWNLEY's regiment. In the latter end of November there arose a great hurry and noise in the country against the Roman Catholics. A rumour got abroad that a letter had been intercepted at Brampton, written by Mr. ALLAN HODGSON of Tone, in Northumberland, to this SANDERSON, containing treasonable matter; and that Mr. SALKELD's name was also implicated in it. HODGSON being apprehended and committed to Newcastle jail it seems to have occurred to some of the gallant yeomanry of Cumberland that it would be feasible to lay hold of the gouty old Squire at Whitehall, and send him off also to Newcastle. One GIBSON, a light horseman for Sir GILFRID LAWSON, was the active instrument in stirring up the country people: no one ever dreaming of the propriety of procuring the sanction of a Magistrate's warrant.

Early in the morning of the 29th November a person came hastily and informed Mr. SALKELD, then in his bed, that GIBSON was about to arrest him, and send him to Newcastle; and advised him immediately to get out of the way. In the greatest perplexity, apprehending that by being carried at that season to Newcastle, and immured in a jail there, his life might be endangered, he hastily resolved to go to Carlisle, and to remain there until he could be better informed, being utterly ignorant of the proceedings of HODGSON of Tone, and not having had anything to do with SANDERSON for some years past. He accordingly set out immediately for Carlisle with his servants and horses, carrying the usual arms of that period.

On his his arrival at Carlisle he gave up his arms to Mr. GOODMAN, a person of known loyalty, and applied to two justices of the peace to take his voluntary affidavit of the facts. They, after making enquiry and being satisfied of the propriety of the step, took his affidavit; in which, after detailing the reasons of his quitting his house and coming into Carlisle, he declared that without any mental reservation or equivocation he neither then nor ever had any correspondence or dealings either with ALLAN HODGSON or JOHN SANDERSON in any ways treasonable, or against His MAJESTY KING GEORGE and his Government, nor had assisted his enemies either with men, money, horses, or arms; and that to answer the trial of that his deposition he was ready, if he could procure, to give bail; or otherwise, upon sufficient assurances to have such treatment as his health required, to deliver himself a prisoner to any of his Majesty's officers, civil or military.

It is difficult to decide what course would have been the best for this unfortunate gentleman. As it was, his house at Whitehall was subjected to the plundering visits of the mob, with threats of burning and destruction, to the great terror of his lady, who remained; and he himself, instead of finding rest in Carlisle, incurred the anger of the Scottish Governor and Garrison, on account of his voluntary affidavit, and had gone to prison but for the intervention of Colonel STRICKLAND, a French officer, whom he discovered to be a distant relative or connection of his family.

Mr. SALKELD remained at the Grapes Inn, at Carlisle. Having in early life practised as a physician, he attended *Colonel Strickland*, who was afflicted with dropsy; for this he asked and had the approbation of two Justices of the Peace, and, with this exception, he avoided all communication with the Garrison.

When the Duke of CUMBERLAND's army came before Carlisle in the latter end of December, the Garrison demanded Mr. SALKELD's coach horses to drag their cannon out of the Scotch gate to the Bridge, to cover the introduction of a party with some sheep. He refused, and ordered his servant rather to stick the animals than part with them for such purpose. A great altercation took place, which ended in the horses being taken by force.

When the town was surrendered to the Duke, one of his first acts was to send *Mr. Salkeld* to jail, by mere parol order, and without any information or charge against him whatever. No intimation of his commitment was laid before the Secretary of State. Sir EDWARD FAULKENER, the Duke's secretary, who was the only person that could have given any particulars of the charges against him, went on into Scotland, carrying with him several letters of Mrs. SALKELD which had been intercepted and opened; it was therefore impossible for *Mr. Salkeld* to apply to be admitted to bail; neither with the Secretary of State nor with any Magistrate was there any specification of a charge against him. The *Habeas Corpus*

Act was suspended. For no other earthly reason than his being a Roman Catholic, and having attracted the notice of Sir GILFRID LAWSON's bullying light horseman, was this gentleman immured for seven months in Carlisle Jail,—a miserable lodging it was for such an invalid,—and at last discharged without even the formality of an acquittal to protect him from future annoyance, much less satisfaction for the damage and distress he had sustained in his property and person. Can it be matter of surprise that he quitted the country where he had suffered such injustice, and died shortly afterwards in France?

On Saturday, the 18th October, ***Thomas Cappock***, ***Major Macdonald***, ***Kinloch Moidart***, ***Francis Buchannan***, ***Brand***, ***Henderson***, ***Roper***, ***Cameron***, and ***Macnaughton***, were taken from Carlisle Castle to Gallows Hill* to suffer the execution of their sentence. The stroke of death is light compared with the preparatory ceremonial. The striking off the fetters, and pinioning the arms—the Sheriff's demand of the bodies, and the formal delivery of the prisoners to his significant requisition — the arrangement of them on those rude black hurdles, with that grim official whose blunted sensibilities almost seem to revive in the prospect of the bloody work he has to do upon them—the slow procession through the town, crowded with people from all parts—those gory wasting heads on the English gate, recognised by the prisoners as they once more, but for the last time, pass through, as the mutilated remains of their comrades in arms,—all these were circumstances calculated to test the courage of the unfortunate men. They remained unshaken. Arrived at the place of execution they one and all

---

* "*Harribee*," a mile south of Carlisle, a place fatal to the Scotch from remote antiquity.

declared they died under the conviction that their cause was just. *Cappock* is said to have read a sermon to the rest, and when finished to have flung it to the crowd; but the Sheriff seized it. If extant, it might now be a curiosity.* The pamphlet published as "The Rebel Bishop's Speech," is obviously the work of some other person. They then engaged briefly in prayer, and gave the signal—the hurdles drew off, and the executioner performed his duty.

William Stout, of Hexham, was the man who undertook this wholesale job of butchery for twenty guineas, and the perquisites of clothes, &c. After the bodies had hung a few minutes he cut them down, ripped them open, burnt their bowels before their faces, and severed the heads from the bodies. The remains of *Cappock* and two others were buried on the spot; the bodies of the rest were interred in the Churchyard at Carlisle. The heads of *Major Macdonald* and *Kinloch Moidart* were placed on the Scotch-gate, where they remained many years.† A Highland regiment, in after times, passing through Carlisle, is said to have been halted on the Sands, without the gate, in order to avoid marching under these revolting mementos; and "*Carlisle Yetts*," though they have disappeared before the advances of modern improvement, survive in song:—

"White was the rose in his gay bonnet,
As he faulded me in his broached plaidie;
His hand which clasped the truth o' luve,
O it was aye in battle readie.

---

* The Sheriff was Christopher Pattinson, Esquire, of Penrith, the Under-sheriff Mr. Thomas Richardson.

† The sister of Major Macdonald was at Warwick Hall whilst the fate of her brother was pending; and his son was kindly sheltered by Mr. Warwick afterwards, and educated for the Church, but died young. The Major's broadsword is said to be at Corby Castle, but how it came there it is difficult to explain, seeing that Major Macdonald was taken prisoner at Falkirk, gave up his sword and pistol to Lord Robert Kerr there.

"His lang, lang hair, in yellow hanks,
Waved o'er his cheeks sae sweet and ruddie;
But now they wave o'er Carlisle yetts,
In dripping ringlets clotting boodie.

"When first I came by merrie Carlisle,
Was ne'er a town sae sweetly seeming;
The white rose flaunted owre the wall,
The thristled banners far were streaming.

"When I came next by merrie Carlisle,
O sad, sad seemed the town eerie,
The auld, auld men came out and wept—
'O maiden, come ye to seek your dearie?'"

A reprieve is said to have arrived for ***Mr. Buchanan*** but two hours after his execution. He is stated to have excited the admiration and pity of the Clergymen who attended the prisoners after condemnation, by the sweetness of temper and undisturbed calmness, firmness, and presence of mind which he displayed: his sentiments about religion and death were just, and the whole of his carriage from his sentence till his last moment uniformly good. After the rope was about his neck he said, "If I have offended any I earnestly beg they will forgive me, for I am sure I forgive all the world."

The following letter of Mr. Goldie on this subject is curious:—

"*Mr. Goldie to Dr. Waugh.*

"Dear Sir,—

"I received your's of the 20th, for which I thank you. Arnprior's behaviour in his last moments is very surprising, if we give credit to many of the bad things that were said of him; such as his having poisoned a gentleman of his own name whose estate he succeeded to: his debauching first one then another sister of his wife, and having several children by the last, whom he kept, notwithstanding, in his own house. The murder of Stuart, of Glenbucky, and his oppressive temper to those in his neighbourhood, and under his authority, and the general bad character he had amongst the greatest part of all ranks, Jacobites included,—I say, if we give credit but to some of these things, and it is difficult to believe that his bad character was purchased for nothing, we cannot think it strange that such an one came to an untimely end. It is often wisely ordered by the divine providence that such are overtaken when they least think of it, as was the case with him; for when he passed thro' here he was under no apprehension of danger, and the officers who commanded the party seemed to be of the same opinion, for he had liberty to walk the streets, lay in a public inn, and I dare say if he had a mind might have escaped. In public company he positively denied his having been in arms; and if I be not misinformed, he was not at Glascow as was proved agst. him; but cd. have proven himself alibi, but in a place where it was as criminal for him to be. But on the other hand there were a few, and among these some persons of great honour and integrity, such as Drummond, of Blair Drummond, (who is a gentleman well affected, married, I think, to the Earl of Stamford's daughter, and Arnprior's neighbour,) whom he kept well with; and they on every occasion spoke extremely well of him, and regarded him much; and upon the whole his character among the generality was excessively bad, and among a few very good. Which of them were in the right we cannot know; but as he has paid his last debt I shod. have been far from saying any harm of him to any but yourself, who I know will make no bad use of it.

"Kinloch Moidart has been represented to me as a plain honest man, and you'll give me leave to relate you a story that moved me somewhat, that I had from an acquaintance of his that went to see him after he was confined in the Castle of Edinr. After the first salutation was over, the gentleman said, 'Dear Kinloch; how came you to engage in so desperate an undertaking, which has never had a probability of success, but when you embarked was ridiculous.' He replyed, 'I, myself, was against it; but, Lord man, what cd. I do when the young lad came to my house?' As to your query anent our nonjuring Episcopal clergy, I am sorry I can give you no better accts. of them; with respect to their religious principles, I bear them not the least grudge, and I think the difference betwixt you and us so small that we might easily agree, were it not for hotheaded and perhaps designing men on both sides. But in this I humbly think all sho'd agree, that it wd. be of the last consequence that a good correspondence sho'd be kept up between the sister churches of England and Scotland; and I am glad to tell you that I hope there is a better disposition in the members of both for this purpose at present than at any time by past. And may I not be allowed to say that as the Protestants at home and abroad have one dangerous and common enemy, it is a reproach that little insignificant differences in opinion sho'd hinder them from uniting so closely as they ought to do. With respect to the sensible part of the clergy, who are happily become most numerous, I can freely say they wd. not be agst. a toleration to Episcopals under proper regulations; but you know the former toleration was established by the Tory Ministry in the end of Queen Ann's reign with views wch. were not at all secret; and it was foretold that these meetings would be so many nurserys of Jacobitism, and they have proven to be so, and have been more successful, at least more open than even the Roman Catholics. Why not allow a toleration to those of different sentiments in religious matters? But was it ever heard of in any other country that a set of men were tolerated to propagate disaffection to the established Government, and in their public meetings to pray, not indeed in express words, but in terms as well understood, for another as King and lawful Governor of these realms than the Prince on the throne, under whose authority they obtained that very liberty they so grossly abused? You ask me how the nonjuring Episcopal clergy take, or how they act under the new law for qualifying them to keep meeting houses, and how many have comply'd with it? I am sorry to answer that only 3 in all Scotland, and one of these in this place, and not one in Edinr., have qualified themselves in terms of that Act. You query further how the rest act, or what they propose to do? To this I cannot so well answer; I have heard that some of them intend to take to other employmts., but I believe the generality are very diligent among their disciples, to keep up the spirit, waiting for the performance of the great promise they say they have from France; and in the meantime have come to no fixed resolution what they themselves are to do, and probably their stipends are yet made good to them. I am told very few of their hearers attend the qualified meeting house in Edinr., and that the generality there and also in the country stay at home and go to no place of public worship: but if matters were once fully settled, I am hopeful that they will be ashamed of this practice. I am extremely glad to find mercy mixed with justice; the executing of too great numbers is shocking. Mrs. Goldie joins me in offering of our best respects to you, your lady, and family; there is nothing I more wish for than an opportunity of seeing you, but we must be deprived of this satisfaction some time, as I must go to Edinr. in the beginning of Novemr., where I shall be glad to execute your commands. I deld. your complimts., and spoke to Provost Bell about your wine. He tells me that dining in your house you presented some mountain wch. you, Brigr. Fleming, and Colonel Howard commended much; and that he having said that he had some such, some of the company desired him to send some of it; and that he expected you would have taken what came among you. However, he is very willing to take it back; I send you the note I got of all the wine. My compliments to the Brigadier, and believe me to be.

"Dear Sir, yours' sincerely,

"JO. GOLDIE.

"D'fries, 24th Oct., 1746.

"I shall mind your snuff."

On the 21st October *Innes*, *Lindsay*, *Ronald Macdonald*, *Park*, *Peter Taylor*, *and Delard* suffered the execution of their sentence at Brampton. *Fitzgerald* escaped by death in prison.

And on the 28th October, *Lyon*, *Hume*, *Swan*, *Harvey*, and *Holt* were executed at Penrith.

With these it might have been expected that the purposes of justice should have been held satisfied. The execution of no less than twenty, with every accompaniment of barbarity, did not however seem sufficiently exemplary in the eyes of the government of the day. The City of Carlisle had received a rebel army within its walls on the 16th November, 1745—the 16th November, 1746, must exhibit a retributive commemoration—and more victims must be selected to figure on the occasion.

Accordingly on that day—

SIR ARCHIBALD PRIMROSE, BART.,
THOMAS HAYS,
MULLINEUX EATON,
PATRICK MURRAY,
JAS. MITCHELL,
PATRICK KEIR,
CHARLES GORDON,
JNO. WALLIS,
ROBERT REED,
BARNABAS MATTHEWS, AND
ALEX. STEPHENSON,

suffered death on the Gallows Hill, at Harraby, with firmness equal to that exhibited by their fellows in misfortune.

Sir Archibald Primrose is said to have had the strongest assurances that he would be spared, and to have indulged the vain hope till his last hour. His faithful wife* remained with him at Carlisle till the morning of his execution, but the trial was beyond her strength. In one short year she witnessed the death of four of her children, and the execution of her husband. Bereft and broken-hearted, she died within a month afterwards.

This was the closing scene of the rebellion of '45 in the City of Carlisle. A garrison was kept there for some years afterwards; and the numerous unexecuted prisoners remained till late in the spring of 1747, when they were sent off to the seaports for expatriation.

Mr. Wardale, in April, 1747, writes in the following irreverent strain of the Secretary of State, whose geographical knowledge, indeed, would seem, from other circumstances, to have been confused and indefinite enough to warrant the sarcasm:

"*Mr. Wardale to Dr. Waugh.*

"Revd. Sir,—

"I will take care of the widows as you direct; I think we have nothing new in Carlisle worth your hearing but the chimes, which began yesterday, (the Duke's birth-day,) and go very well. I hope we shall get rid of the Rebel Prisoners next week, at least those in the Jayl; I am told the Sheriff had an order last week to carry them to Liverpool, from the D—— of N———. I suppose for want of a map they thought Liverpool in Cumberland, but he writ back that he apprehended there must be a mistake in the orders, for he did not see how he could be order'd out of his county;

* She was Lady Mary Primrose, daughter of Archibald, Earl of Roseberry.

so he expects on Monday fresh orders. The merchant (or his clerk) that is to transport them has been here, but will not take the charge of them till delivered at Liverpool.* The condemn'd prisoners in the Castle I am told, are not mentioned in the order; so there must be another escort for them. I thank you for your care about the chest, I am in no hurry about it; I'll speak to Kirkbride. I beg my best respects to all at Caldbeck, and am,

"Revd. Sir,

"Your most obliged humble servant,

"ROBT. WARDALE."

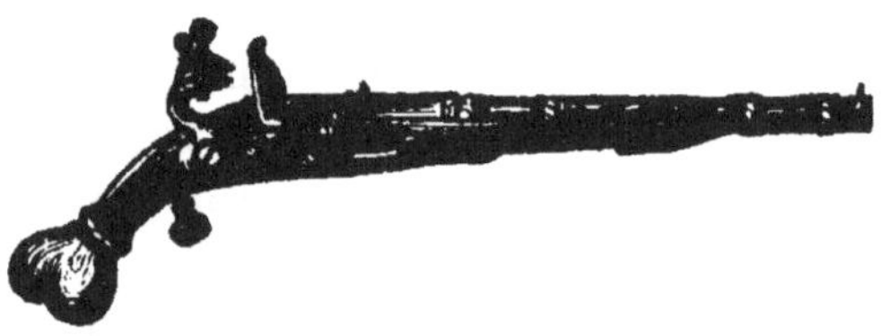

The Pistol, of which a drawing is given above, was left by Gordon, of Glenbucket, at the house of a relative of the late Mr. Norman, of Kirkbampton, at Grinsdale, in November, 1745, when the Highlanders crossed the Eden to approach Carlisle,—(see p. 42)—and is now in the possession of Mrs. Holliday, of Wigton. It is about eighteen inches long, mounted with gold and silver, and the stock is of iron.

---

* The prisoners here spoken of, are those who had accepted transportation by drawing lots. How long afterwards the condemned prisoners remained, it does not appear.

JAMES STEEL, PRINTER, JOURNAL OFFICE, 3, ENGLISH STREET, CARLISLE.

Lightning Source UK Ltd.
Milton Keynes UK
UKOW07f0602281215
265375UK00001B/93/P

9 781179 20